THE LANGUAGE LIBRARY

EDITED BY ERIC PARTRIDGE AND SIMEON POTTER

THE LANGUAGE AND
OF ANTHONY TROL

John W. Clark

🐚🐚🐚🐚🐚🐚🐚🐚🐚🐚🐚🐚🐚🐚🐚🐚🐚🐚🐚🐚🐚🐚🐚🐚🐚🐚🐚🐚

THE LANGUAGE AND STYLE OF ANTHONY TROLLOPE

🐚🐚🐚🐚🐚🐚🐚🐚🐚🐚🐚🐚🐚🐚🐚🐚🐚🐚🐚🐚🐚🐚🐚🐚🐚🐚🐚🐚

Exclusive distributor for U.S.
and Canada:

WESTVIEW PRESS
1898 Flatiron Court
Boulder, Colorado 80301

ANDRE DEUTSCH

First published 1975 by
André Deutsch Limited
105 Great Russell Street London WC1

Copyright © 1975 by John W. Clark

Printed in Great Britain by
W & J Mackay Limited, Chatham

ISBN 0 233 96641 2

TO MY WIFE, LUCILE,
WHO ALSO – EVEN YET –
LOVES TROLLOPE

Contents

꧁꧁꧁꧁꧁꧁

Preface

❧❧❧❧❧❧

I AM indebted to Richard Schmeltzer, for first introducing me to Trollope, over forty years ago; to Professor Samuel Holt Monk, for first luring me outside of Barsetshire, nearly twenty years ago; to Eric Partridge, for bullying me into writing this book; to Professor Simeon Potter, for helpful advice; to Professor John McKiernan, for invaluable assistance with Gaelic and Irish English; to Professor Robert Sonkowski for identifying a number of Latin quotations that I could neither identify myself nor find in any dictionary of quotations; to the Reverend Donald Maclean of Dochgarrogh and his wife for information about the history of the Lordship of the Isles[1] – information that exigencies of space unhappily in the end prevented my making full use of; to the Right Reverend Michael Geoffrey Hare Duke, Lord Bishop of St Andrews, for putting me in touch with the Macleans; to M. Dell, Esq., of the London solicitors' firm of Moon, Beever and Hewlett, for information about the Petty Bag Office; and to my fellow Trollopian Mrs Gertrude S. Battell, for the generous and trusting loan, from her private collection, of six novels of which the library of the University of Minnesota has lost its copies by theft. But my greatest debt is to the person named in the dedication, who for over two years has had Anthony Trollope as an invisible guest at every family meal, and who has several times dreamt that he has been occupying our spare bedroom.

As for books about Trollope, I have at least skimmed most, but

1. I became interested in this subject because, in *The Small House at Allington*, 'Lady Glen's' father, the Marquis of Auldreekie, is said to have had as his second title 'Lord of the Isles', borne, by courtesy, after his death, by his nephew and successor's eldest son (he himself having left no son). But in *The Way We Live Now*, the courtesy title has become 'Lord Nidderdale'. Evidently Trollope learnt, some time between 1863 and 1873, that 'Lord of the Isles' had for over two centuries been a title of the eldest son of the sovereign (and one that, like 'Duke of Cornwall', he is born with).

have (consciously) drawn virtually nothing from any but (1 – far above all others) Michael Sadleir, *Trollope: A Commentary* (Oxford University Press, 3rd edition, 1941), cited simply as 'Sadleir'; (2) T. H. S. Escott, *Anthony Trollope: His Work, Associates and Literary Originals* (London: John Lane, The Bodley Head, 1923), cited simply as 'Escott'; (3) Spencer Van Bokkelen Nichols, *The Significance of Anthony Trollope* (New York: Douglas C. McMurtrie, 1925), cited simply as 'Nichols'; (4) James Pope-Hennessy,[1] *Anthony Trollope* (Boston: Little, Brown and Company, 1971), cited simply as 'Pope-Hennessy'; (5) Trollope's *An Autobiography* (edited with an introduction by Bradford Allen Booth, Berkeley: University of California Press, 1947, cited simply as '*Autobiography*'; written in 1875–76, and first published in 1883). Of the multitude of articles on Trollope in periodicals I plead guilty to have gone to the trouble of hunting down and reading scarcely any. I having constantly and very profitably consulted *The Oxford English Dictionary*, cited simply as '*OED*', and Eric Partridge, *A Dictionary of Slang and Unconventional English* (London: Routledge and Kegan Paul Ltd, 5th edition, 1961 – and the *Supplement*, printed as 'Volume Two', same date), cited simply as 'Partridge'.

After this Preface I give two lists of novels covered in this book. The first is indispensable to the reader's convenience because of my use of short titles; the second will serve as a useful reminder of the order in which the novels were completed.

JOHN W. CLARK

Minneapolis, 24 April 1974, being the one-hundred-and-fifty-ninth anniversary of the birth of Anthony Trollope.

To save space, each novel is referred to throughout not by its complete title, but by a single prominent word from it (sometimes an abbreviation). A numeral following such a short title is a chapter number. The short titles are listed alphabetically below in column 1; the complete titles in column 2; the year of completion (which, rather than that of publication, is, unless another is specified, the one given along with a short title when any is given), in column 3; the year(s) of serial publication if any (sometimes in magazines, sometimes in parts), in column 4; and the year(s) of

---

1. By a melancholy coincidence, I wrote these words just half an hour before reading of the brutal murder of Mr Pope-Hennessy. R.I.P.

first publication in book form in column 5. For all these dates I
am totally – and most gratefully – indebted to Sadleir.[1]

1	2	3	4	5
Anna	*Lady Anna*	1871	1873–74	1874
Ayala	*Ayala's Angel*	1878		1881
Belton	*The Belton Estate*	1865[2]	1865	1865
Bertrams	*The Bertrams*	1858		1859
Caldig	*John Caldigate*	1877	1878	1879
Castle	*Castle Richmond*	1860		1860
Children	*The Duke's Children*	1876	1879–80	1880
Chron	*The Last Chronicle of Barset*	1866	1866–67	1867
Claver	*The Claverings*	1864	1866–67	1867
Clerks	*The Three Clerks*	1857		1857
Dark	*Kept in the Dark*	1880	1880	1882
Eustace	*The Eustace Diamonds*	1870	1871–73	1872
Eye	*An Eye for an Eye*	1870	1878–79	1879
Fay	*Marion Fay*	1879	1881–82	1882
Finn	*Phineas Finn*	1867	1867–69	1869
Forgive	*Can You Forgive Her?*	1864[2]	1864	1864–65
Framley	*Framley Parsonage*	1860[2]	1860–61	1861
Gangoil	*Harry Heathcote of Gangoil*	1873	1873[3]	1874
Henry	*Cousin Henry*	1878	1879	1879

1. Sadleir gives the year of first publication in book form in three places (except for
one novel – see below) in Appendix A: '(*a*) Calendar of the Events in the Life of
Anthony Trollope'; '(*b*) Bibliography of Anthony Trollope'; and '(*c*) Classification of Trollope's Fiction'. In his dates for seven novels, he is at odds with himself
(and with Escott). The dates he gives in '(*a*)' for these differ from those given in
'(*b*)', '(*c*)', and Escott, all of which give for *Clerks* 1858, not 1857; for *Orley*, 1862,
not 1861–62; for *Forgive*, 1864, not 1864–65; for *Belton*, 1866, not 1865; for
Hotspur, 1871, not 1870; and for *Eustace*, 1873, not 1872. For *Redux*, '(*a*)' gives,
through oversight, no date; '(*b*)' and Escott give 1874; and '(*c*)' gives 1876 –
almost certainly a printer's error. I reproduce the years given in '(*a*)' (except for
Redux): I do so (1) because probably some of the novels dated earlier there were
actually on sale late in the earlier year, but dated by the publisher in the later;
(2) because of those in two or three volumes (as most were), one (or two) volumes
may have been on sale in the year before the second (or second and third), but
both (or all three) dated in the later year; and (3) because, in '(*a*)', Sadleir often
gives the precise day and month of actual publication, without regard to the year
on the title page.
2. The six novels with this footnote reference, here and on page 12, are the only ones
that began serial publication before they had been completed.
3. Published complete in the Christmas number of *The Graphic* (and hence not
literally 'serial'), and, not surprisingly, Trollope's shortest novel. It appropriately
ends (happily) on Christmas Day.

Hotspur	Sir Harry Hotspur of Humblethwaite	1869	1870	1870
House	The Small House at Allington	1863[2]	1862–63	1864
Kellys	The Kellys and the O'Kellys	1847		1848
Land	The Land-leaguers	1882[1]		1883
Love	An Old Man's Love	1882		1883
Macd	The Macdermots of Ballycloran	1845		1847
Mack	Miss Mackenzie	1864		1865
Orley	Orley Farm	1861[2]	1861	1861–62
Popenjoy	Is He Popenjoy?	1875	1877–78	1878
Prime	The Prime Minister	1874	1875–76	1876
Ralph	Ralph the Heir	1869	1870–71	1871
Ray	Rachel Ray	1863		1863
Redux	Phineas Redux	1871	1873	1874
Right	He Knew He Was Right	1868	1868–69	1869
Scarb	Mr Scarborough's Family	1881	1882–83	1883
Senator	The American Senator	1875	1876–77	1877
Struggles	The Struggles of Brown, Jones, and Robinson	1861[2]	1861	1870
Thorne	Doctor Thorne	1858		1858
Towers	Barchester Towers	1856		1857
Vicar	The Vicar of Bullhampton	1868	1869	1870
Warden	The Warden	1853		1855
Way	The Way We Live Now	1873	1874–75	1875
Wortle	Dr Wortle's School	1879	1880	1881

Below, the novels are listed (by short titles) in the chronological order of their completion. The Barsetshire series are marked with a single asterisk; the Parliamentary series[3] with two.

1845	Macd	1869	Hotspur
1847	Kellys		Ralph
1853	Warden*	1870	Eustace**
1856	Towers*		Eye
1857	Clerks	1871	Redux**
1858	Thorne*		Anna
	Bertrams	1873	Gangoil

1. Unfinished at Trollope's death.
2. See p. 11, n. 2.
3. Called by Sadleir 'The Political Novels', and by others 'The Palliser series (or novels)'.

1860	*Castle*		*Way*
	*Framley**	1874	*Prime***
1861	*Orley*	1875	*Popenjoy*
	Struggles		*Senator*
1863	*House**1	1876	*Children***
	Ray	1877	*Caldig*
1864	*Forgive***	1878	*Ayala*
	Mack		*Henry*
	Claver	1879	*Wortle*
1865	*Belton*		*Fay*
1866	*Chron**	1880	*Dark*
1867	*Finn***	1881	*Scarb*
1868	*Right*	1882	*Love*
	Vicar		*Land* (unfinished)

1. According to Sadleir (p. 417, n. 2), 'Trollope set so strict an interpretation upon the phrase "Chronicles of Barsetshire" that [when they were republished together under that title in 1879] he was unwilling to reckon even *The Small House at Allington* among their number. When at last he yielded to pressure from friends and publishers, it was against his better judgement.' Posterity agrees, I think, with Trollope's friends and publishers. Trollope was in love with Barset *qua* Barset as no one else has been. It is true that Allington's county town is said to be Hamersham and not Barchester, and that Courcy Castle is said to be in the next county. But some of the action occurs in Barsetshire, and several characters introduced in (earlier) undoubted Barset novels reappear in *House*. (1) In *House*, 16, Adolphus Crosbie, on his way from Allington to Courcy Castle, stops in Barchester to change trains, and, having time to kill, goes to church at the cathedral, hears Mr Harding sing the Litany, and later meets him. (2) The De Courcys, the Dumbellos, and Frank Gresham's father and sister all appear, and at Courcy Castle. (3) The Duke of Omnium and his agent, Mr Fothergill, appear, and at Gatherum Castle. Further, Archdeacon and Mrs Grantly appear (though not in Barset), Sir Omicron Pie is mentioned, and Mrs Proudie is alluded to, though not by name. And the connexion obtains forward as well as backward: Lily Dale, her mother, Johnny Eames (belatedly identified in *Chron*, 31 as first cousin once removed of Mrs Crawley), Adolphus Crosbie, and Lady Julia de Guest, all first introduced in *House*, all appear in *Chron*. Most important, perhaps, the Lily Dale-Johnny Eames plot, begun in *House*, is continued and ended in *Chron*, where, indeed, it is imperfectly intelligible to one who has not read *House*. Trollope's readers have always been rightly more interested in his characters than in his locales. Incidentally, *House* looks beyond the Barset novels to the Parliamentary ones: 'Planty Pall' is first introduced there, and Lady Glencora first mentioned.

Introduction

꩜꩜꩜꩜꩜꩜

THIS book has two limitations (and I do not mean faults, of which it doubtless has many). One is implicit in the title: the book restricts itself to Trollope's language and style, and does not pretend to deal with the structure of his plots or with his narrative method, except now and then when a brief reference to those subjects is incidentally necessary or illuminating to observations about language and style. But there is another limitation, or rather pair of limitations, *not* implicit in the title. (1) The book limits itself to Trollope's novels, excluding everything else, even the short stories, chiefly because it is practically only as a novelist that Trollope is still read, but partly because life is short. (2) It does not even deal with all the forty-seven novels that Trollope wrote; it excludes five: (*a*) His one experiment in science fiction (one wonders what he would have made of that expression), *The Fixed Period*, set in 1980, written between October 1880 and February 1881, and published serially from October 1881 and in book form in March or April 1882, only eight or nine months before the author's death. (*b*) His four romances with Continental settings – *La Vendée* (his third novel), written in 1849 and published in 1850; *Nina Balatka*, written in 1865, and published serially in 1866–67 and in book form in 1867; *Linda Tressel*, written in 1867, and published serially in 1867–68 and in book form in 1868; and *The Golden Lion of Granpère*, written in 1867, and published serially and then in book form in 1872 [*sic*]. All these are excluded as not characteristically Trollopian in style or setting.

Of the remaining forty-two, thirty-six are set wholly or mainly in England, though there are a few brief Continental scenes, and some in Scotland (the longest in *Eustace*), in the United States (*Wortle*), in Australia (*Caldig*), and in Palestine and Egypt (*Bertrams*). All but one of these are Trollopian in style. That one – *Struggles* – I would have omitted if, besides knowing that it was notoriously bad, I had also known how radically un-Trollopian it is stylistically. Five are set wholly or mainly in Ireland. The first of these, *Macd*, is somewhat un-Trollopian (though incomparably less so than *Struggles*), but is of special interest because it is the first novel Trollope wrote – and is by way of being a great book. Finally, one, *Gangoil*, is set entirely in Australia.

Of these forty-two, I had read about half before beginning work on this book, some of them many years ago, many of them twice, and several many times: the whole Barsetshire series, the whole Parliamentary series, and eight or ten more. All these I have re-read for the purposes of this book. I have read the novels in the following order: (1) *Macd* and *Kellys* (1845 and 1847), Trollope's first two novels, both Irish in setting; (2) *Castle* (1860), the eighth novel (excluding those not dealt with in this book), the last to contain much Irish English; (3) the Barsetshire series of six (1853–1866); (4) the five written between 1857 and 1863 (besides *Castle*, already read) outside of both the Barsetshire and the Parliamentary series; (6) the six of the latter series (1864–1876); (6) the thirteen written between 1864 and 1875 outside of both series; (7) the last nine, also outside of both series, written between 1877 and 1882. In themselves these facts are intensely uninteresting; I mention them only because they give me – and, I think I may reasonably believe, the reader – some assurance that I was not gradually lulled – or fatigued – into taking fewer and fewer notes, at least for the first thirty-three written, as I might well have been had I read all forty-two in the order of composition, with the consequence of gaining – and giving – a seriously false impression of progressive changes in Trollope's practice. This does not mean that I have recorded or even observed every instance of the features I was looking for (I think only a computer – or perhaps Alexander Cruden – could do so), and I have tried to avoid such precise and unqualified statements as 'This feature appears twenty-seven times,' but some may have slipped by, in which case I caution the reader to be sceptical, though I feel reasonably confident that they are not significantly far from the facts.

Everyone will agree that it is impossible to draw a sharp line between language and style. Chapters I, II (most of it), III, and IV are almost wholly confined to language; but (verbal) ornaments, the subject of Chapter V, though they are certainly matters of language, are also matters of style. I have entitled the Chapter

'Ornaments – Mostly Bad'. Indeed, I think all but one of them ('Mischievous Language') are on the whole bad. If, throughout Trollope's career, instances of all six of these ornaments, or even of all five 'bad' ones only, appeared with roughly equal frequency, or increased or decreased in number at roughly the same rate, or 'peaked', if at all, for the most part in the same years, I should merely say so. But none of these is a fact; and I therefore think it advisable to give the reader here a preliminary notion, for comparative purposes, of what the facts are.

'Literary' archaisms (Section 1): rare after 1866, virtually non-existent after 1873. Playful language (Section 2): heavily concentrated between 1856 and 1860; very rare after 1868. Mischievous language (Section 3): pretty evenly distributed throughout. Facetious names (Section 4): very unevenly distributed from beginning to end, though with a *slight* tendency to *average* fewer to the novel in the later years, and reaching an incomparably high peak in *Clerks* (1857). Latin (non-legal) tags (the first part of Section 5): roughly even in distribution, except that they – especially the comic or otherwise 'ornamental' ones – peak in *Towers* and *Clerks* (1856 and 1857). Legal tags (the second part of Section 5): used seriously and literally whenever called for by the context; used humorously and metaphorically only before 1869. French words and phrases (Section 7): of those used *comically or otherwise ornamentally in Trollope's own language*, over a half appear in novels written before 1858; over a third in two of these (*Towers* and *Clerks*); and nearly nine-tenths before 1861.

In short, the only 'good' ornament, 'mischievous language', is also the only one that becomes neither more nor less frequent *and* does not peak; the only other ornaments that become neither more nor (much) less frequent are 'Latin (non-legal) tags' (but they do peak – in *Towers* and *Clerks*) and 'facetious names' (and they peak in *Clerks*). The rest become rare after various years from 1861 to 1869. That is, (1) Trollope came, at various times during the sixties, to regard all the 'bad' ornaments except facetious names as cheap, facile, tawdry, and tiresome, and (2) he was decidedly most enchanted by most of them in *Towers* or *Clerks* or both.

Chapters VI, VII, and VIII deal exclusively with style – or at least, they do not deal with language at all so far as that is separable from style. Chapter VI, to be sure, because it is devoted solely to literary allusions, quotations, and echoes, does not concern

Trollope's style in the narrow sense (or, *a fortiori*, language); it concerns rather a conspicuous and lasting *habit* in literary composition – the habit of interspersing literary references, of the three kinds mentioned just above, in his authorial passages, and to a considerably lesser extent in the speeches of his characters. Chapter VII deals (1) with Trollope's firm and lifelong conviction that the revelation of character is much more important in a novel than plot, and (2), mostly by means of extensive quotations, with his three methods of conveying that revelation. Finally, Chapter VIII, again consisting chiefly of extensive quotations, illustrates another conspicuous and ingrained habit of his: the habit of suspending his narrative to write sometimes quite long 'sermons' on a great variety of social questions – political, legal, economic, and ecclesiastical – and on human morality and happiness – 'the human condition', to use a phrase now popular. To fail to treat in this book of the subjects of any of these three chapters, dealing, as they do, with three uses of language strikingly frequent and prominent and often protracted, would have been to adopt too narrow a definition of *style*, or at any rate of *Trollope's* style. A novelist's style is something broader than his tone, his diction, and the length and construction of his sentences and paragraphs.

But some generalizations can and should be made about those stylistic points. First, what may be called Trollope's normal style is remarkably uniform, from beginning to end; uniformly easy, flowing, clear, plain, unlaboured, unaffected, unmannered, and above all businesslike. It is also remarkably 'modern' – or perhaps, rather, remarkably 'timeless', to use Monsignor Ronald Knox's term.[1] Trollope does, indeed, on occasion, deliberately write in a style that does not deserve all these adjectives;[2] *viz.*, when he over indulges himself (1) in the 'bad' ornaments referred to above, and

1. I should add that Monsignor Knox applied this term to what he thought the language of any new English translation of the Bible should be and what he tried to make the language of his own; that he was a notable Trollope devotee and expert is coincidental, and he might conceivably even have disagreed with my application of the term to Trollope's English.

2. The farmhouse where he lived alone with his father for several months in 1830 and 1831 during the absence of the rest of the family in the United States contained no light reading but 'the two first volumes of Cooper's . . . *The Prairie* . . .' I wonder,' says Trollope (*Autobiography*, Chapter 1), 'how many dozen times I read those two first volumes.' Luckily they had no marked effect on his style; I have noted just one (serious) sentence in repulsively high-flown diction: 'No first shadow from Love's wings had been drawn across the pure tablets of [Lily Dale's] bosom.' (*House*, 6).

(2) in (at least elaborate) biblical and classical *allusions* (though not quotations and echoes). But as Chapter V and Sections 3 (the first part) and 5 of Chapter VI show, almost all these departures from what I have called Trollope's normal style become much fewer by 1870 and, even before then, they occupy comparatively little space.

His *tone* varies widely, but always appropriately, from the waggish to the solemn. His vocabulary is copious and precisely used. The structure and the length of his sentences are pleasingly varied, and judiciously adapted to what he has to say. In passages of 'internal debate', balanced sentences, and pairs of sentences balancing each other, the clauses or sentences being joined by adversative conjunctions, are noticeably common, but very properly so. A good example occurs in *Finn*, 39. Phineas visits Lady Laura Kennedy, whom he has previously loved, and who still loves him, to solicit her help in his suit for Violet Effingham. She refuses, emphatically, adding, cynically and contemptuously, that he will soon recover from his passion.

He stood silent before her, thinking over it all. He certainly had believed himself to be violently in love with Lady Laura, and yet when he had just now entered her drawing-room, he had almost forgotten that there had been such a passage in his life. And he had believed that she had forgotten it, – even though she had counselled him not to come to Loughlinter [her husband's Scottish seat] within the last nine months! He had been a boy then, and had not known himself; – but now he was a man, and was proud of the intensity of his love. He had been willing to risk everything – life, prospects, and position, – sooner than abandon the slight hope which was his of possessing Violet Effingham. And now he was told that this wound in his heart would be soon cured, and was told so by a woman to whom he had once sung a song of another passion. It is very hard to answer a woman in such circumstances, because her womanhood gives her so strong a ground of vantage! Lady Laura might venture to throw in his teeth the fickleness of her heart, but he could not in reply tell her that to change a love was better than to marry without love [as she had done], that to be capable of such a change showed no such inferiority of nature as did the capacity for such a marriage. She could hit him with her argument; but he could only remember his, and think how violent might be the blow he could inflict, – if it were not that she were a woman, and therefore guarded.

Longish periodic sentences are not rare, but neither are they involved;[1] the only kind that appears with any noticeable frequency is one beginning with a series of grammatically parallel subordinate phrases or clauses such as this from *Children*, 76 (in one of Trollope's 'sermons'): 'For most of our bishops, for most of our judges, or our statesmen, our orators, our generals, for many even of our doctors and our parsons, even our attorneys, our tax-gatherers, and certainly our butlers and our coachmen, Mr Turveydrop, the great professor of deportment, has done much.' Paragraphs, especially of narrative, but also of psychological analysis and of sermonizing, are on the average longer than is now the fashion (often running to over 700 words), but they are rhetorically unified – and rhetorically complete, as those of the novelists, and, even more, the journalists of our day often are not.

Trollope's vocabulary is so copious, and he seems to have so readily recollected almost always precisely the word he needed, that I have observed very few words or phrases that he uses with conspicuously undue or tiresome frequency. One that is not only used too much, and sometimes in dialogue as well as in Trollope's own language, but also tautological, is *essentially necessary*, which occurs scores of times. Indeed, he seldom uses *necessary* alone. He had too good a sense of the meaning of words to allow many inadvertent tautologies to remain in his final draft, but *essentially necessary* was a blind spot – the only one, I think. A usage that resembles a tautology is really a little worse – it is self-contradictory, when used in such a sentence as 'He knew he must submit to the demand; there was no other alternative.'

Another expression, or rather image, that recurs continually (though not nearly so often as *essentially necessary* or even *no other alternative*) is exemplified in the following quotation from *Wortle*, 20: 'Would it not be wrong to love the young man? Would it not

1. It may be relevant to quote, in this connexion, Trollope's reference (*Autobiography*, Chapter 10) to how easily a writer, forgetting how he has begun a long and involved sentence, falls into, *eg*, tautologies and grammatical discord. 'I need not multiply these causes of error,' he says, 'which must have been stumbling blocks indeed when men wrote in the long sentences of Gibbon, but which Macaulay, with his multiplicity of divisions, has done so much to enable us to avoid'.

be a longing for the top brick of the chimney, which she ought to know was out of her reach?' The top brick of the chimney is most often, as it is here, a young man loved by a young woman of inferior station or fortune – as is hardly surprising, considering the frequency of this situation in Trollope's novels.

In five novels written in various years between 1858 and 1873 I have been struck by a recurrent use of the word *stern*. What is striking about it is not its frequency, and in these novels only, but that it is, in these novels, almost never applied, as I should say it almost always is now, to the manner of a parent to a child, a master to a servant, a teacher to a pupil, a judge to a felon, or even a husband to a wife. In *Bertrams* it almost always applies to the manner of a lover to his fiancée; in *Orley*, to the manner of a son to his mother; in *Ray*, to the manner of a daughter (from the age of nine!) to her mother; in *Vicar*, a lover to his fiancée again; and finally, in *Way*, a girl to her fiancé. In short, sternness in at least these five novels is most commonly attributed in what seems an almost perverse way to what we may call the natural inferior rather than to the natural superior, or at least to the person conventionally regarded as owing deference rather than to the person conventionally regarded as deserving it.

During the writing of *Bertrams*, Trollope had a brief love affair with the adjective *missish*, but never, so far as I have observed, resumed it.

Trollope evidently shared the still-existent superstition that *that* should preferably not be used as a relative pronoun referring to persons. And he went beyond that: he almost always uses *which* instead of *that* when the reference is to a thing. (I do not mean that he avoids *that* in non-restrictive clauses only; everybody does that. I mean that he avoids it in restrictive clauses as well.)

Finally, again and again, throughout his career, Trollope, after describing a challenge to authority certain to disconcert or terrify the hirtherto dominant person, begins a new paragraph with a short sentence introducing a description of the effect on him or her. Up to about 1870 this sentence is almost always 'This was very terrible to X'; but from then on, instead of 'terrible', we almost always get 'dreadful' – but no other change. I cannot but think that Trollope, who made frequent use of this kind of paragraph in this position beginning with this kind of sentence, observed, or had it pointed out to him, that 'terrible' here was getting tiresome, and shifted to 'dreadful' – but could not give up the pattern. He never did give it up; but I have not observed that he ever shifted back to 'terrible', or hit upon a third possibility.

He is almost never guilty of the careless use of a word in two different senses within a short compass; I have, in fact, observed only two instances (not counting a borderline case in the second sentence of the first long quotation below): '. . . on her part, she did not think that her aunt was inclined to take her part in the quarrel with Augusta.' (*Ayala*, 6); and 'He was very particular in regard to the particular drawer. . . .' (*Way*, 75.) I think the extreme rarity of this fault in the novels as published may well be owing to his practice (see *Autobiography*, Chapter X) of reading 'everything four times at least – thrice in manuscript and once in print' (*ie*, presumably, in proof), and 'very much . . . twice in print' (*ie*, probably, the second time, between serial publication and publication in volume form). In this passage, to be sure, he is lamenting chiefly the number of instances of grammatical discord or anacolutha that have, despite the re-reading, escaped his notice; but such slips are more likely to do so than careless repetitions of words, many of which, I should wager, were removed from the original manuscript.

The opposite of careless repetition, 'elegant variation', I have found somewhat oftener, though Trollope's native sturdy preference for plainness and simplicity in (serious) speech has prevented him from falling more than six times into the trap, so far as I have noted. The instances are spread over the years from 1860 to 1878: not only was he not commonly given to this false ornament; he was not given to it, as he is to some tricks, for a single brief period. The instances I have noted (I may of course have missed a few) follow: '. . . she consented to receive the child – on condition that the bairn should not come to her empty-handed.' (*Castle*, 5); '. . . she thought of her cousin George's face when he left her room a few days since, and remembered Mr Gray's countenance when last he held her hand at Cheltenham. . . .' (*Forgive*, 36); 'If once the Earl's friends could be brought to be eager for the match on his account, as was she on her daughter's behalf. . . .' (*Anna*, 11); '[When the swimmer] begins to feel . . . that there is peril where before he had contemplated no danger . . .' (*Way*, 95); 'The Colonel was in truth well pleased that Larry Twentyman had taken his place, though he probably would not have been gratified had he seen

Captain Batsby assume his duties.' (*Ayala*, 24); 'She never asked herself whether he were or were not a gentleman. She had never even inquired of herself whether she herself were or were not a lady.' (Note of source lost.) It will be observed that all these are authorial language – a natural consequence of the fact that 'elegant variation' is a vice of writing, not of conversation.

Trollope is not much given to the (at least elaborate) description of landscapes, buildings, rooms, or settings of any kind after about 1860. I think this may be partly owing, somewhat paradoxically, to his evident habit of visualizing his settings (and his characters) so vividly that it seldom occurred to him that many people do not share that habit, at any rate when reading the writing of others. That it *was his* habit, at least in the Barsetshire novels, he makes very clear in the unforgettable touching and almost pathetic last paragraph of *Chron*, and I cannot but believe that it was equally his habit in all his novels.

And now, if the reader will allow me to seize him affectionately by the arm, we will together take our last farewell of Barset and of the towers of Barchester. I may not venture to say to him that, in this country, he and I together have wandered often through the country lanes, and ridden together over the too well-wooded fields, or have stood together in the cathedral nave listening to the peals of the organ, or have together sat at good men's tables . . . I may not boast that any beside myself have so realized the place, and the people, and the facts, as to make such reminiscences possible as those which I should attempt to evoke by an appeal to perfect fellowship. But to me Barset has been a real county, and its city a real city, and the spires and towers have been before my eyes, and the voices of the people are known to my ears, and the pavement of the city ways familiar to my footsteps. To them all I now say farewell.

There is, indeed, one long and notable description of a room and its appointments – Archdeacon Grantly's breakfast-parlour in *Warden*, 8. But this exception almost proves the rule: it is written not to enable the reader to visualize the room as Trollope did (though it does so), but to reinforce the impression of the archdeacon's manner of life, taste, and even character, as reflected by the room and its contents.

And now let us observe the well-furnished breakfast-parlour at Plumstead Episcopi, and the comfortable air of all the belongings of the rectory. Comfortable they certainly were, but neither gorgeous nor even grand; indeed, considering the money that had been spent there, the eye and taste might have been better served; there was an air of heaviness about the rooms which might have been avoided without any sacrifice of propriety; colours might have been better chosen and lights more perfectly diffused; but perhaps in doing so the thorough clerical aspect of the whole place might have been somewhat marred; at any rate, it was not without ample consideration that those thick, dark, costly carpets were put down; those embossed, but sombre papers hung up; those heavy curtains draped so as to half-exclude the light of the sun: nor were these old-fashioned chairs, bought at a price far exceeding that now given for more modern goods, without a purpose. The breakfast-service on the table was equally costly and equally plain; the apparent object had been to spend money without obtaining brilliancy or splendour. The urn was of thick and solid silver, as were also the tea-pot, coffee-pot, cream ewer, and sugar bowl; the cups were old, dim dragon china, worth about a pound a piece, but very despicable in the eyes of the uninitiated. The silver forks were so heavy as to be disagreeable to the hand, and the bread-basket was of a weight really formidable to any but robust persons. The tea consumed was of the very best, the coffee the very blackest, the cream the very thickest; there was dry toast and buttered toast, muffins and crumpets; hot bread and cold bread, white bread and brown bread, home-made bread and bakers' bread, wheaten bread and oaten bread, and if there be other breads than these, they were there; there were eggs in napkins, and crispy bits of bacon under silver covers; and there were little fishes in a little box, and devilled kidneys frizzling on a hot-water dish; – which, by the by, were placed closely contiguous to the plate of the worthy archdeacon himself. Over and above this, on a snow-white napkin, spread upon the sideboard, was a huge ham and a large sirloin; . . . Such was the ordinary fare at Plumstead Episcopi.

In transcribing passages from the novels, I have been at pains to reproduce exactly Trollope's capitalization, punctuation (with exceptions noted below), and spelling, including inconsistencies. He always writes, *eg*, 'Archdeacon Grantly', but 'the archdeacon'; so do I, and not only in transcription (contrarily to my usual practice). He vacillates between 'de Courcy' and 'De Courcy'; I follow him. He usually puts commas or semicolons before dashes instead of letting the dashes stand alone; so do I (contrarily to virtually everyone's practice now, and to that of most of Trollope's contemporaries). When he leaves a sentence incomplete, he uses a dash without a following period and, in a quoted one, sometimes without the final quotation mark; so do I. He usually but not always follows the now peculiarly American practice of placing a comma or a full stop (period) – and even a semicolon, where he goes beyond the American practice – before quotation marks instead of after them when only the last word or words, and not the whole sentence or clause, are logically quoted; so do I. (Incidentally, I ordinarily follow the American – and Trollope's – practice, but have adopted the undoubtedly more logical present British one in my own writing in this book.) In only three ways do I depart from Trollope's typographical practice: (1) In writing French and Latin, Trollope follows no principle whatever; sometimes he italicizes, sometimes he quotes, sometimes he does both, and sometimes he does neither. I have adopted the advice of the Messrs Deutsch, which I think sensible, of always italicizing, but in addition quoting if Trollope does. (2) Trollope always writes 'Mr.', 'Mrs.', 'Dr.', and 'St.'; again at the publishers' suggestion, I omit the periods. (3) Trollope (to judge from editions earlier than *c.* 1900) follows the almost universal American practice of using double quotation marks for primary quotations and single for quotations within quotations; I follow the now commonest British practice of reversing this order.

As for spelling, I have reproduced Trollope's inconsistencies – *judgment* (surprisingly frequent) and *judgement*, *jail* and *gaol*, *marquis* and *marquess*, *civilized* and *civilised*, *practice* and *practise* (verb). 'Lady Glen's' maiden name he contrives to spell in four ways – *MacCluskie*, *M'Cluskie*, *M'Closkie*, and *McCloskie* – and I have faithfully followed him.

In my own writing I have done my best to use British spellings when they differ from American (which I ordinarily use); not that I think the former always or even usually better (or worse), but to preserve the British compositor's peace of mind. And the reader's;

more Britons than Americans are likely to read this book, and Britons, if they will pardon me for saying so, seem to be much more commonly upset by *honor* than Americans are by *honour*. Indeed, to do my countrymen justice, scarcely any of them are upset at all.

I am not so conceited as to fancy that any reader will be much interested in, or attach any importance to, knowing what novels are my favourites;[1] I will say what they are only because at least some of my choices may puzzle or amuse, or even enrage, other Trollopians, and perhaps enliven their discussion of our favourite English novelist. For better or worse, then (and for various reasons), my favourites are as follows: (1) The whole Barsetshire series, especially *Towers*, *House*, and *Chron*; (2) the whole Parliamentary series, especially *Redux* and *Children*; (3) *Macd*; (4) *Castle* (my liking for this, and perhaps for *Macd* as well, is a heresy); (5) *Orley*; (6) *Ray* (another heresy); (7) *Mack* (yet another); (8) *Vicar*; (9) *Way*; (10) *Caldig*; and (11) *Scarb*. And I would give them all for *Towers* (despite its excessive number of bad ornaments) – the first I ever read, the one I have re-read oftenest, and the one I hope most to live to read often again.

I have now contrived to write the most irrelevant and anticlimactic and generally uninteresting ending an Introduction ever had.

1. My favourites, not the only ones I like; the only ones I dislike, and would never think of reading again, are *Struggles* and *Land*.

CHAPTER I

Grammar[1]

🐚🐚🐚🐚🐚🐚

I T *is very important to note and remember that this chapter is limited to Trollope's own language* and that of his *educated* characters; regional dialects and the language of the uneducated are dealt with in Chapter IV. It includes (1) a good many usages distinguishing the at least occasional colloquial practice of the educated of Trollope's time (and often of ours too) from the literary standard; some of these Trollope never uses when writing *in propria persona*, and others seldom, and then probably by oversight. It includes (2) a number of usages that I think were not literary standard but that Trollope thought were and accordingly employs commonly, and that are, at least in my opinion, not so now (though they are often heard and seen). It includes (3) some literary standard usages still occasionally found, but less often than in Trollope's day. It includes (4) some constructions that are anacolutha in everyone's view, including Trollope's, and a few other that are not (though they are in mine). It includes (5) a few odds and ends hard or at least inconvenient to classify. It does *not* include expressions that were standard literary usage in Trollope's time but that are no longer so; these are dealt with in Chapter III.

The preceding paragraph might very naturally lead the reader to expect that what follows in this chapter would be organized into treatments of the five subjects mentioned above, and in the order given. But because a considerable number of words and constructions figure (in different ways) in two or more of these subjects, it has proved more practical to organize most of the chapter under headings of certain of the parts of speech, with sub-divisions when necessary. The last two of the five subjects, which do not lend themselves best to that treatment, are dealt with by themselves at the end of the chapter.

1. I use this word here, for practical reasons, in a limited – and the commonest popular – sense; many things that are parts of grammar in the earlier and broader and scholarly sense are dealt with in other chapters.

A. PRONOUNS

1. Case.

a) Objective for nominative (personal) after *be*, etc. Type, 'It's me.'

This construction, long almost universal in uneducated speech (and writing), once not altogether absent from educated writing, now never found in educated writing (except when that deliberately follows the use of (informal) speech, as in a familiar letter), has been common in the familiar speech of the educated for a good three hundred years at least. Trollope's characters of all social classes and all degrees of education not only use it much of the time or most of the time; they use it virtually always. So, I feel sure, did Trollope, in familiar conversation; but in his novels, not once, so far as I have observed, does he use it when writing *in propria persona*. In all the many instances I have recorded, the pronoun is *me*, *him*, or *her*, but I am certain that *us* and *them* are missing only by accident. The verb may be in any tense or mood.

b) Nominative for objective (personal). This, the converse of the foregoing, I have observed only three times – and two of them in *let you and I:* Lady Lufton (*Framley*, 41) says, ' ". . . let you and I say a few words about this . . . affair," ' and in *Bertrams*, 1, one Oxford undergraduate says to another, ' ". . . let you and I be seen walking together. . . ." ' This logically ungrammatical usage comes about, clearly, from losing sight of the fact that *let* here is a verb, and treating it as what I will venture to call a modal signal.[1] It does not give the impression of illiteracy or even of carelessness; in fact, it *sounds* 'elegant'. Of illiteracy in this connexion, indeed, I have noted no examples, and only one of carelessness: in *Land*, 24 a young lady (unquestionably a lady, and unquestionably educated) writes in a letter, ' "Only think of Ada and I at a ball. . . ." ' This usage has never had anything like this status of its converse. It has become, since Trollope's time, regrettably much commoner; the half-educated have been (misguidedly) so thoroughly taught that they must *never* say 'me' for 'I' that they often say – and write – 'I' for 'me'.

1. I have invented this expression as a shorthand way of saying that, in normal present-day English prose, spoken or written, the universal translation (and semantic equivalent) of the Latin hortative subjunctive is *let us* (informally, *let's*) followed by the (signless) infinitive: 'Let us pray' = '*Oremus*'.

c) Objective for nominative after *such* (*a one* or the like) *as*. A good example is in a speech of Mr Arabin's in *Towers*, 21: ' ". . . you would not be inclined to say that I should do battle with such as him." ' In the speech of characters, the objective here is incomparably commoner than the nominative, of which I have observed only two examples: ' "I wonder whether you think that it is a pleasant thing for such a one as I to . . . live in such a place. . . ?" ' (*Right*, 78), and ' "I cannot imagine that you should be jealous of such a one as she." ' (*Caldig*, 22.) Somewhat surprisingly, of the seven instances I have observed of the construction in Trollope's own language, five have the objective and only two the nominative; he would seem to have been much less alert to the non-literary character of *such as him* than to that of *it is him*. The error is a natural one; when *such* is the object of a verb or a preposition (and that is the only situation I am concerned with here), so that, if *such as* were omitted, the objective form of the following personal pronoun would be used, it also gets used, by attraction, when *such as* is present. Another influence may be that of the fact that *a man such as he* means the same thing as *a man like him*, and the objective pronoun of the latter gets carried over by analogy to the former, which thus becomes *a man such as him*.

d) Objective for nominative after *as good* (or the like) *as*; *eg*, 'There are others just as bad as me' ('Lady Glen', *Prime*, 51). The construction with either case of the pronoun is surprisingly rare; I have recorded only four in dialogue (always objective) and none in Trollope's own language, though I feel almost certain it does occur there (but pretty certainly with the nominative).

e) Objective for nominative after *than*; *eg*, ' "You speak . . . of yourself as one . . . lower than me" ' (a Trinity (Oxon) double-first, *Bertrams*, 9). This is at least virtually universal in dialogue; I have recorded eighteen instances, and *none* of the nominative. Trollope himself falls into it at least four times, though he much oftener uses the nominative. As everyone knows, both this usage and the one immediately preceding have long been common in the (familiar) speech of all classes.

f) *Who for whom*. As the first word of a sentence, this is virtually universal in dialogue; *eg*, ' "Who does Miss Todd love?" ' (a clergyman – and a gentleman – *Mack*, 11), and ' "Who is the letter from?" ' (Isabella Dale, *House*, 30). After a verb or a preposition it is much rarer, but occurs at least twice – ' "Seen who?" ', and

' "Saying to who, sir?" ' Trollope himself uses *who* for *whom* just once, I think, and then as the first word of a clause – 'who should he meet with but his old friend Mrs Robarts. . . ?' (*Chron*, 17.) I have noticed only one strictly comparable instance of the exact converse (but see *g* below) – ' "Whom is it then you love?" ' (*Castle*, 38.) *Who* for *whom* in the initial position, as we all know, is almost universal in the familiar speech of all levels of society; so was it in Trollope's time, and long before. The usage is explained, of course, by the fact that the great majority of all Modern English sentences begin with the subject (nominative), just as the frequency of *it is him* is explained by the fact that almost all verbs except *be*, if they are followed by anything, are followed by an object (objective). In other words, we tend, and our ancestors tended, to think (so far as we think or they thought at all), not 'What case form is syntactically logical?', but 'What case form comes at the beginning of a sentence?' or 'What case form comes after a verb?'

g) *Whom* for *who*. Besides the uniquely freakish and perverse 'Whom is it then you love?' quoted above, I have noted four other instances of *whom* for *who*, all of them in Trollope's own language, and all of them of another (and the same) kind – a kind extremely common today in at least the writing of the educated (and of the half-educated, who seldom use *whom* in speech), though not among the uneducated, who never use *whom* at all. An example (from *Vicar*, 23) is, 'Were there not other women whom the world would say were as good?' The error is a very natural one; a relative pronoun followed by a subject and a transitive verb is so much oftener the object of that verb than (as in the example above) the subject of a later verb that *whom* gets automatically used for *who* in the latter situation as well as in the former and much commoner one. But the usage certainly has nothing like the social standing of, *eg*, 'Who do you want to see?' (or 'It's me'). It is, alas, much commoner in the language of the average novelist of our day (British and American alike) than of Trollope's, and in (at least American) newspapers it is pervasive.

2. *Number*.

Type, 'Give everyone their due.' Trollope himself uses this only once, I think; he writes (*Towers*, 50) that the archdeacon 'forgave every one [*sic*] in Barchester their sins. . . .' But his characters use it virtually always, and in every possible variety – *everybody*, *every one* (usually *sic*), *anyone* (sometimes *any one*) *nobody*, *no one*, and even *a person* followed by *they*, *them*, *their(s)*, and even *themselves*. The usage is still, as we all know, extremely common. Its frequency is explained, I think, not so much by the genderlessness of *everybody* and the rest as by the plural implication of most of them despite their singular form.

B. ADJECTIVES

1. Degree.

Superlative instead of comparative with two; *eg*, '. . . the major was the most cross-grained of the two.' (*Chron*, 68.) Somewhat surprisingly, I have recorded only one instance of this in dialogue – ' "It is the least of two evils." ' (The (younger) Duke of Omnium, *Prime*, 42.) But even more surprisingly, perhaps, the comparative also, I think, appears in dialogue only once – ' ". . . you are so much the cleverer of the two." ' (*Land*, 24.) Comparisons of two things (using this pattern), that is, are by chance extremely rare in the speech of Trollope's characters. In his own language, they are fairly frequent (I have recorded eleven); and nine times out of the eleven he uses the superlative. The two comparatives, further, occur in the same paragraph (*House*, 6) – 'Lily was the shorter of the two . . . And when I said that Bell was the prettier. . . .' And yet further, these occur almost immediately after '. . . they were two pretty, fair-haired girls, of whom Bell was the tallest and prettiest.' Trollope knew the 'rule', that is, but almost never remembered it. And I put quotation marks round *rule* advisedly: it is pretty certainly an invention of eighteenth- (or possibly late-seventeenth-) century grammarians. For better or worse I am inclined to think that it is observed today in both the writing and the speech of the educated somewhat more commonly than it was in Trollope's time, or at least by Trollope. I always follow it (I think), but never without a subliminal feeling that I am perhaps being priggish or pedantic. The 'rule' can be defended logically, but so can the contrary, with an only slightly subtler logic.

2. Number.

Type, 'these (those) kind (sort) of things'. Extremely common in dialogue, though not elsewhere; and yet Trollope slips at least four times. My impression is that the illogical construction is not quite so common in educated speech today as it apparently was in Trollope's time. The error is a very natural one. The speaker starts with the idea of things (not a thing) of a kind (not kinds); and ends by anticipating the plurality of *things* in *these*, but saying *kind* instead of *kinds* because he is thinking of only one kind.

C. VERBS

1. One verb for another.

a) Can for *may*. I have not observed this in Trollope's own language, but it appears now and then in dialogue, though it is not universal there. One amusing example occurs (*Popenjoy*, 46) in a conversation between Lady Sarah Germain, who is stiff and formal, and the Dean of Brotherton, who is decidedly not. She says, ' "May I see her?". He replies, ' "Of course you can see her." ' I suspect the Dean of malice. As everyone knows, the usage is still very common in the familiar speech of all classes.

b) I (we) will (would) instead of *I (we) shall (should)*.

i. With *like, wish, prefer,* and the like. I have recorded nine instances of this in dialogue (though *shall (should)* is much commoner); none in Trollope's own language. He was clearly alert to the non-literary (or provincial) standing of the usage.

ii. With other verbs (where no determination of promise or threat is involved). Perhaps at first thought surprisingly, the usage is very much less common than the one just discussed; I have recorded only two instances: ' "Would that I could have looked forward to a life in which I would be regarded as his friend." ' (*Love*, 22.) ' "Then I would not have failed. Had you remained here, I should [!] certainly not have failed then." ' (*Love*, 23.) That the usage is rare with other verbs than *like*, etc., demonstrates the firmness with which the 'rule' was established, and in speech as well as in writing. The fact, odd at first thought, that it is fairly common with *like*, etc., can be explained only by the assumption of the tendency to an unconscious anticipation of the expression of the volition or the like signified by the following verb.

These distinctions, as most Englishmen know, are far less common in the United States than in England – less common even in the formal writing of the educated; and in the speech of the un-educated they are virtually never made. Most Americans go through life without ever saying 'shall' (except in certain kinds of first- and third-person questions). In my limited experience, it is otherwise in England, or at least in London; I have heard more than one uneducated Cockney, incapable of 'putting it on', handle their *shalls* and *shoulds* with a discrimination that would excite the admiration of Lindley Murray. It is often said that the 'rules' are the invention of late-seventeenth-century grammarians, but this is decidedly an exaggeration; the principal and fundamental one, at least, is rooted in the speech of late-seventeenth-century Londoners, educated and uneducated alike, and has been inherited by their descendants through unbroken oral tradition; then, (educated) London English being the basis of modern Standard English, the 'rules' came to be observed nationally by educated writers – who extended them to their speech. But I have observed in recent years that many English writers are adopting the common American usage.

c) *Shall* (*should*) instead of *will* (*would*) in indirect discourse in the third person; *eg*, ' "Don't go in for it." Lady George had declared it to be very improbable that she should go in for it. . . . She called in Green Street, fearing that she should see Grace Mildmay.' (*Popenjoy*, 17.) The first *should* above exemplifies this use in literal discourse (*ie*, with verbs of utterance); the second, its extension to use with verbs of thinking. Unlike the 'rule' that I have just above called the 'principal and fundamental' one, this 'rule', though it was long regarded as standard, was never so commonly followed, even in the formal writing of the educated, and still less commonly, I am pretty sure, by descending degrees, in their formal speech, their familiar speech, and the speech of the uneducated. I have virtually never heard it from an American; it probably occurs in American writers of the past writing in the 'genteel tradition', but I have *never* seen it in recent ones, however 'genteel' in other ways; it was common in English writers of Trollope's time, and long before (*eg*, Defoe), and *perhaps* in educated speech; but it seems now to have become nearly as uncommon in England, both in writing and in speech, as it always has been in American speech. I have recorded over seventy clear examples (most of them in the preterite) – almost all that occur, I think – of the disregard of the rule, but Trollope still follows it much oftener than not, and now and then even extends it. It might well be expected to be disregarded oftener in characters' language than in Trollope's own, but the reverse is true – or rather, there are far fewer examples of its being either regarded or disregarded by the characters than by the author because people conversing have fewer occasions for indirect discourse in the third person than the writer of a narrative. At least that is true of Trollope's people and of Trollope himself. It is particularly true of Trollope, perhaps, because he gives such an extraordinary amount of space to reporting, in indirect discourse, the unspoken thoughts of his characters (though this involves, of course, not literal discourse – with verbs like *said* – but the extension to sentences with verbs like *thought*). Three typical examples of this variety of *would* instead of *should* are found within the confines of two consecutive short sentences: '. . . she felt that she would have more courage for persistency down at Allington than she would be able to summon to her assistance up in London. She knew she would be weak. . . .' (*Chron*, 52.) Instances of *would* instead of *should* in literal indirect discourse are much rarer, but only, I think, because literal indirect discourse is itself rarer (in Trollope's novels); and yet I have recorded three occurrences: '. . . [he] remarked that he would be rejoiced. . . .' (*Mack*, 6); 'He could hardly dare to tell his chief . . . that he would certainly be beaten. . . .' (*Prime*, 72); and '. . . [he] asked where he would find the ladies. . . .' (*Right*, 9).

All this may leave the impression that Trollope less often followed the 'rule' than not. The fact is the contrary: he thought the 'rule' was 'right', he followed it when he remembered to do so, and he remembered much oftener than he forgot. Here are four specimens, the first three in literal indirect discourse and the last in a report of thought rather than speech: '. . . he told her that he should only just have time to wait for her reply.' (*Dark*, 5); 'She declared . . . that she should die if he were . . . dragged to that . . . place.' (*Macd*, 25); '[He] had sent a letter . . . explaining that for reasons with which the chairman was unacquainted he should absent himself. . . .' (*Way*, 45); and '. . . he thought it very improbable that he should accept any counsel. . . .' (*Ayala*, 33.) And Trollope not only follows the 'rule' much oftener than not; he sometimes extends it to situations in which the clause containing *should* is not the object either of a preceding verb like *said* or of one like *thought*; *eg*, 'He felt that he was taking no steps to approach the subject which he should have to discuss before he left her. . . .' (*Way*, 42); '[The bishop's] mind . . . slightly inclined itself to the appointment of Mr Harding, seeing that by such a step he should have the assistance of Mr Slope in opposing Mrs Proudie.' (*Towers*, 16); '[He] had . . . sent up notice that he should probably be at home that night, but in such a case would [!] be compelled to return to . . . Birmingham on the following afternoon.' (*Orley*, 10.) 'For himself, he should resolve what steps to take.' (*Wortle*, 3. Here we go one step further: even the preceding sentence contains nothing like 'had sent up notice'. Trollope thought, so to speak, that it did.) '. . . it might be that he should have the opportunity of seeing Mary Laurie. . . .' (*Love*, 12. One step further still; nothing like *said* or even *thought* anywhere in the neighbourhood.)

The example from *Orley*, 10, incidentally, also contains a completely pointless shift from *should* to *would* in consecutive sentences. I have recorded one other instance of the same shift in nearly adjacent sentences. 'He said that he hoped he should meet him soon somewhere . . . The sum . . . which he so much feared that he would be called upon to pay . . .' (*Framley*, 9.) And there are two examples of the converse shift from *would* to *should*, one in nearly adjacent sentences and the other actually within a single sentence: '. . . he was quite sure that . . . he would be called on for a declaration of his sentiments . . . He did not believe that he should ever be reduced to marrying Miss De Molines . . .' (*Chron*, 80); and '[He] had begun to . . . be afraid that he would lose all share in the great prize . . . and that he should himself be the means of excluding his own finger from the pie.' (*Kellys*, 4.) Within a single page, that is, or even within a single sentence, Trollope can forget the 'rule' and then remember it, or remember it and then forget it.

I will leave this subject with an example of this use of *should* that to most Americans at any time, and probably to most Englishmen today, would be ambiguous – until the following sentence is read (and then an American or even an Englishman might think it merely restated the preceding one). Perhaps the passage illustrates at least one reason why this use of *should* established itself in America at no time, and in England only for a while (and very imperfectly even then). 'He knew that he should never win the game. In his sadder moments he felt that he ought not to win it.' (*Way*, 87.)

2. *Ain't; an't; don't* for *doesn't*.

a) Ain't. It is perfectly clear from Trollope's novels that *ain't* was common and entirely acceptable (with one limitation) in the familiar speech of the educated and upper classes (which are almost identical) – but *not* in their formal, especially public, speech or in their writing – including Trollope's writing (in his novels), in which it never appears. This is not to say that it is usual in such speech; it is very much less common than the correct forms. I have, however, recorded thirty-nine instances (very nearly all there are, I think). All but three occur in the order exemplified by 'I ain't', not 'ain't I', but that is doubtless because statements are so much commoner in language generally than questions. I have recorded fourteen instances in the first-person singular, fourteen in the second-person singular, seven in the third-person plural, one in the second-person plural, and one with a compound subject in different persons ('I and he'). In the third-person singular, however, I have observed it only twice; it is clear that though *ain't* for *am not* or *are not* (or *aren't*) was very generally acceptable, *ain't* for *is not* (or *isn't*) was certainly not. The Duchess of Omnium and Martha Dunstable use it several times, but that is hardly surprising considering their exceptionally free-and-easy habits of speech. Its most surprising occurrence is perhaps the (single) one from the (younger) Duke of Omnium, who is a grammatical purist, just as he never uses slang, and dislikes its use even by other gentlemen. My impression is that the usage was beginning to be frowned on something like a decade before Trollope's death, as were a good many others, including such features of pronunciation as substituting [in] for [iŋ] or what is commonly called 'dropping the *g*' in the inflection *-ing*. This movement is certainly to be attributed to the spread of primary education; children of all classes formerly learnt their English from their parents, but when lower-class children began to attend primary schools in great numbers, they sought, or at least were more or less successfully driven, to acquire and not only to write but to speak the language of literature – along with spelling pronunciations, chiefly because their masters and mistresses were themselves of lower-class background, and supposed that, because the upper classes used more (apparently) spelling pronunciations than the lower, all spelling pronunciations were preferable. The lower classes increasingly tended to drop not only exclusively lower-class usages, but also certain usages that may be called in one or another sense or degree irregular once shared by all classes. As a result, the upper classes, which had never used and certainly did not begin to use the former, and which heard the latter along with the former from the unreformed part of the lower classes, gradually came to confound the two, and to avoid certain once universal usages as they had always avoided exclusively lower-class usages. The triumph of 'correctness' has been almost total in the United States, except in certain particulars in the 'Old South'; my impression is that it is a little less than total, again in some particulars, in England.

It will be well to end this section with a reminder that it does not touch on the usage of the lower-class and lower-middle-class characters in Trollope's novels, who use, and almost invariably use, *ain't* for *all* forms – including notably *isn't*. They also use it often for *haven't* and only less often for *hasn't* (as their betters *never* do). The practice continues, as we all know, all over the English-speaking world, though probably a greater fraction of the number that ordinarily follow it can, and occasionally do, use the standard forms.[1]

b) An't I have observed four times only. It is impossible to say which pronunciation was intended – 'ant', or 'ahnt' – or whether the same pronunciation was intended all four times. Both were and perhaps still are current; 'ahnt' must be older (in those dialects that now pronounce *can't* 'cahnt', as 'Received Standard' does), and certainly supplies the explanation of *aren't I*? This

1. *Ain't*, taking all its uses together, has two quite distinct sources. (1) As a form of *be*, it began with *am not (I)*, of which it was a perfectly natural and regular ultimate phonological development (shown also in 'cain't' for *can't*, at least in the United States in some 'Old South' dialects); indeed, if it had been restricted to that person and number, in that order, it would fill a real gap in the standard language. (2) As a form of *have*, it began with 'I *(we, you, they) have not*, of which it is an equally natural and regular ultimate phonological development (cf. the old-fashioned pronunciation of *Daventry*) – *but* at first in the form *hain't*, and in dialects that preserved the *h*; then, in dialects that didn't, it of course became homonymous with *ain't* from *am not*. Finally, there are some dialects, or at least were not long ago, in which *hain't* is preserved as distinct from *ain't*. My eastern New England great-grandmother (born 1837) always said, 'Ain't I going?', but never 'Ain't I been there before?' – *always* 'Hain't I been there before?'

spelling must, obviously, have originated in 'r-less' dialects, but it has extended itself (through reading, not through hearing) to others, where it is not only so spelt, but *pronounced* with the 'retained r'.

c) Don't for *doesn't*. The distribution is essentially the same as for *ain't*: of the twenty-one instances (absolutely many, but by no means relatively so) that I have recorded (again, at least virtually all there are), all are in dialogue, and none in Trollope's own language. The expression is used by persons of both sexes and all ages, with no significant variation in frequency. Among its users are one peer, four ladies of title, and two clergymen. Only three times does the verb occur before the subject, and then, of course, in questions. Trollope probably sometimes said 'don't' for 'doesn't' in familiar conversation, and was clearly aware of its acceptability there in the mouth of any lady or gentleman, but he was quite as clearly aware that it was strictly non-literary. Like *ain't* (at least with *I*), it has not yet completely vanished from the speech of educated people in the 'Old South' in the United States, or in England. Indeed, it is commonest in both places among people of gentle birth and breeding and certain, not so much that they speak Standard English as that Standard English is what they speak. (Here, as with *ain't*, I am not dealing with the language of the lower classes, with whom *don't* for *doesn't* is almost universal, both in Trollope and in the real world of today.)

3. Number – plural verb with singular subject (either and neither).

a) (N)either (singular) *are* and the like.

Strictly speaking, this never occurs; but its inversion does occur at least once: ' "Have either of them told you that I made an offer to your sister?" '

b) (N)either (singular) *of them are* and the like.

This, unlike the foregoing, is not only common, and equally in characters' language and in Trollope's own, but almost universal. Of the 'correct' alternative, I have observed just one instance – '. . . neither of Lady Laura's counsellors was able to give her advice . . .' (*Finn*, 55.)

c) (N)either he (n)or she are and the like.

Like the foregoing this is normal in both characters' language and Trollope's, though a trifle less nearly universal: I have observed only three instances, but still three, of the 'correct' alternative: '. . . it was Thursday evening before either Mrs

Stanbury or Priscilla was told of his coming.' (*Right*, 21); '. . . neither the attorney nor Larry . . . was in the room.' (*Senator*, 19); and ' "Neither the place nor the occupation is fit for me," ' (*Redux*, 77.) It is perhaps significant that the first two are Trollope's own, and the third is in a lady's letter – a very formal one – to a stranger, not in conversation.

It appears that Trollope had indeed heard at some time that in all three of these constructions the plural verb is 'wrong' and the singular 'right', but that he very seldom remembered it. They (or at least the second and third) have long been, and, as we all know, still are virtually universal among the uneducated, and extremely common among all classes, at least in speech. The educated today probably tend oftener than in Trollope's time to use the singular in formal writing or even in formal, public speech, though, when they don't, we hardly get the impression of illiteracy. According to precisely logical grammatical analysis, the plural is certainly wrong; but, as usually with *everybody* . . . *they* and the like (A. 2 above), the fact that more persons or things than one are involved is so prominent to the mind that the tongue or the pen easily slips naturally into the plural verb.

Appendix. (N)*either* of more than two. I deal with this here, despite the fact that it is not a logical division of c. 3, because (1) there is no really logical place for it anywhere, and (2) it involves (*n*)*either* as c. 3 *a*, *b*, and *c* do and as nothing else does. There are seven (and I think only seven) instances of this oddity in Trollope's novels, four in his own language and three in that of his characters. Four samples will be quite enough. '. . . neither of the three spoke.' (*Way*, 75); ' "I can't conceive it possible to find a worse Prime Minister than either of the three . . ." ' (*Finn*, 7); '. . . either of the four might have made the speech of any of the others.' (*Redux*, 8); and ' "She'll have £5,000 at once . . . which does make her equal to either of the [four] Miss Halls." ' (*Love*, 13.) However common the usage may have been in Trollope's time, I doubt whether any native speaker of English today would follow it in either speech or writing.

4. Tense.
   a) In conditional and temporal clauses.
   Today, almost always except in the language of statutes, contracts, and the like, in *certain kinds* of conditional and temporal

clauses, speakers and writers of all classes and all places use simpler – and strictly speaking less precisely logical – tense forms than either Trollope or his characters do much the greatest part of the time. Though at first thought it may seem wrong-headed to begin the discussion of this subject with instances of Trollope's now and then departing from his usual practice and adopting ours, I am sure that it will prove to be more conducive to clarity then the alternative. I have recorded just eleven such instances, and I think that is all there are (as against *hundreds* of the other kind). The eleven are found in nine novels written in various years from 1861 to 1880. I transcribe only four. (1) 'If he wrote to her, should he simply ask her for money . . . ?' (*Forgive*, 38; Trollope would ordinarily write 'should write'.) (2) '. . . now had come a time in which she must be plain, unless she made up her mind to abandon her plan altogether.' (*Ayala*, 37; ordinarily 'should make'.) (3) '. . . he did this in a tone which . . . signified that not a man would be sent . . . till this request had been conceded.' (*Forgive*, 44; ordinarily 'should have been conceded'.) (4) 'As soon as the Marquis *should have settled* [italics mine] himself in the house, of course [the Dean] would call; and when the Marquis *had settled* [italics mine] himself . . . the Dean would bestir himself.' (*Popenjoy*, 21.) This is striking and unique – both usages in one sentence.

It is clear from these (1) that today's usage already existed, though it was (in Trollope's novels) decidedly uncommon, and (2) that its growth is a gain (by making sentences shorter) because, though such clauses would be ambiguous in isolation, they never in practice appear in isolation, and the context always prevents ambiguity. There is a loss in explicitness, that is, but the old and longer form is superfluously explicit: the difference in meaning is real and the distinction in form logical, but the context always makes the meaning clear.

b) Perfect infinitive after verb in past tense. This is a favourite construction with Trollope – indeed, he very seldom uses the present infinitive in that position – and with many of his contemporaries. It is very much less common today; and it never was, and never is, necessary, or even preferable. Sir Ernest Gowers, in his revision (1965) of Fowler's *Modern English Usage*, p. 444, writes: 'After past tenses of *hope, fear, expect*, and the like, the perfect infinitive is used, incorrectly perhaps, but so often and with so useful an implication that it has become idiomatic. That implication is that the thing hoped etc. did not in fact come to pass, and the economy of conveying this without a separate sentence justifies the usage.' I give seven examples (out of hundreds) of the construction, including three in sentences in which another infinitive is in the present, for no better reason than the first might have been. In none is the perfect infinitive necessary, and in only the first does it perhaps – not certainly – meet Gowers's test. Finally, I give two examples of Trollope's very rare avoidance, throughout a sentence, of the construction. (1) (Perhaps 'right'.) '[Eleanor] had intended to have gone with her sister. Now her plans had altered, and she was going with the Stanhopes.' (2) ('Wrong', as, in my opinion, are examples 3 and 4.) ' "I had not intended to have told you at present . . ." Then she communicated her good news.' (3) '. . . instead of going, as he had at first thought to have done . . . he listened to Brady's traitorous advice . . .' (4) 'Lady Arabella resolved to open her mind to the Doctor . . . She would have given much, however, to have escaped this business.' (5) (Both uses in one sentence, without reason; illustrated also in examples 6 and 7.) ' "I meant to have told you . . . : but I did not mean to tell it tonight." ' (6) 'It would have been . . . opposed to the whole principle of her life to endeavour . . . to persuade her daughter to the match, or to have used her maternal influence in Norman's favour.' (7) 'His intention was to see the judge . . . and then once more to have thrown himself at [the judge's daughter's] feet.' (8) (Construction entirely avoided, as it is in example 9.) 'Had he done so, it would have been impossible for him to recover the respect of the House.' (9) ' "I was too young . . . when you had that trial . . . to have anything to do with the matter.'

The frequency of the construction, 'right' or 'wrong', in Trollope and his contemporaries, is, I think, owing to a natural (though illogical) attraction of the infinitive into the tense of the preceding verb. It is equally natural today, but I think its present infrequency is owing to an increased perception of its redundancy rather than of its illogicality.

5. *Mood*
   a) Present subjunctive instead of indicative. This usage, in sentences of the kind quoted below, was never and is not now

incorrect, nor is it altogether obsolete, at least in very formal writing. It is, however, very infrequent even there, whereas in Trollope's day it was normal, at least in *if it be*, where it was his almost invariable usage. A representative specimen (out of hundreds) is 'A seat in Parliament, if it be for five or six years, is a blessing . . .' With other verbs than *be*, it is rather uncommon (least so with *have* – '. . . the blessing becomes very questionable if it have to be sought every other Session.'); ' "I will not have his money, unless he come also himself." ' It also occurs rather often with *whether*: ' "The question is," she said, "whether it be fitting." ' ' "Then, of course, there is the doubt whether this man be aware of it." ' Doubtless the reason for the obsolescence of the usage is that, unlike *if it was* and *if it were*, *if (whether) it is* and *if (whether) it be* mean precisely the same thing.

b) Were for *was*, *was* for *were*, and kindred subjects. This is chiefly – but not wholly – a matter of conditional clauses. If we are to take Fowler for a guide, the standard, or at least preferable, literary usage of the late nineteenth and early twentieth centuries – and, in my opinion, of the present time – is as follows:

(1) 'If he was here, he left no sign.' *Preterite indicative* form, referring to the *past*. (I *don't* know whether he *was* here or not.) 'Simple condition.'

(2) 'If he were here, he would give some sign.' *Preterite subjunctive* form, referring to the *present*. (I *know* he *is not* here.) 'Contrary-to-fact condition.'

It will save a great deal of space if, for the purposes of this section, I call this distribution 'right', and departures from it 'wrong', though it is arguable that, taken literally, these appellations are too sweeping and even dogmatic, and in certain particulars perhaps more or less factitious, more or less recent, and too regardful of logic and too little regardful of (cultivated) usage. But I will omit quotation marks round *right(ly)* and *wrong(ly)* throughout the section; if their absence makes the reader nervous, he should go back and re-read this paragraph.

i) Were wrongly used for *was*. This occurs with much the greatest frequency in conditional (and, secondarily, concessive) clauses, though a little less often in dialogue than in Trollope's own language, where it is the almost invariable form. A typical example out of hundreds is 'If this were true, he had already committed an oversight.'[1] I have recorded only five instances of the right *was* in Trollope's own language. Three of them follow. '. . . if her mouth was defective, the symmetry of her chin . . . was perfect.' 'If the thing was done, it was done.' '. . . if there was ground for hope, then the desirability of putting off the ball was very much reduced.' *Were* is also wrongly used with *whether*: 'She never asked herself whether he were or were not a gentleman. She had never even inquired of herself whether she herself were or were not a lady.'[2] Sometimes one wrong *were* leads to another and *unquestionably* wrong one: 'If she were innocent, let him know that she were innocent . . .' 'If it were the case this were an unfitting match, it was clearly her duty to decide that there should be no marriage.' Even a right *were* can bring an unquestionably wrong one in its wake. I have recorded five instances, of which two follow: ' ". . . if I were to say that she were engaged to . . . Colonel Snubs, then he would go." ' ' "If I were to write to you against your will, it would seem that I were persecuting you." '

ii) *Was* wrongly used for *were*. Though Trollope, and almost as often his characters, habitually use *were* for *was* as above, they part company in using *was* for *were* – though only after *if* (and *whether*) alone, not after *as if* (and *as though*). I have observed only one instance in Trollope's own language: 'If a prince of our own was found, for the good of the country, to go among far-distant outlandish people, and there to be poked in the ribs, and slapped on the back all round, the change to him could hardly be so great.' Trollope's characters, on the contrary, much more often say 'was' than 'were'. A few examples out of many follow. ' "If I was to lose Fanny now . . . I think I should give it up altogether." ' ' "I wouldn't have him now, if he was to ask me ever so . . ." ' ' "What . . . would Marian do if aught but good was to befall

1. This kind of wrong subjunctive, as common today, especially in newspapers and popular fiction, as in Trollope, classified by Fowler as an 'Arrival' (as against 'Alives', 'Revivals', and 'Survivals'), should perhaps be classified rather as a 'Survival'; in Old and Middle English, it is almost universal; *eg*, Chaucer says of the Knight in the General Prologue to *The Canterbury Tales*, 'Thogh that he were worthy [*ie*, valiant], he was wys [*ie*, prudent].' But though it may have been at least in part a 'Survival' in Trollope's time, I should say that it is at least mainly an 'Arrival' now. And there can be no doubt of the reasonableness and usefulness of Fowler's 'rules'.
2. This might be defended as the proper preterite of 'She never even inquires [*or* has inquired] of herself whether she herself be or be not a lady,' which Fowler would call a 'Survival' (or perhaps a 'Revival') rather than an 'Arrival'. See c. 5 *a* above.

you?" ' ' "I shouldn't trouble you now . . . if it was only about myself." ' ' "I could do it so much better if I was not a clergyman". . .'

In short, Trollope uses *were* for *was* too much, and his characters use *was* for *were* too much.

Oddly enough, when it comes to *as if* and *as though*, Trollope uses *was* for *were* (five recorded instances) at least as frequently as his characters do (three recorded instances). I give two examples of each (though in the first two, strictly speaking, *was* is used for *had been*, not for *were*). 'He wrote to the Vicar as though the Vicar's coming to Salisbury . . . was a matter of course . . .' '. . . he was as constant to their long hours as though the venture was his own . . .' ' "She speaks of [her coming marriage] as if she was going to be hung,". . .' ' "Bid you indeed! As if it was for me to bid you." ' (It is a mere accident that the examples from Trollope have *as though* and those from his characters *as if*.)

Though Trollope himself, then, as well as his characters, once in a while uses *as if* (*though*) *it was* for *as if* (*though*) *it were*, he *never* takes the next step of writing 'as if (though) it is' – *ie*, of altering the tense as well as the mood. Neither do his characters – with *be*; but they do it with other verbs (as Trollope never does, any more than with *be*) at least five times. Two examples follow: ' "As if a girl ever knows what a man says to her!" ' ' "I feel . . . as though I wish he had had his head blown off in battle." ' This usage has since become extremely common, in both Britain and America, among the educated as well as the uneducated, and in writing as well as in speech. It is probably commonest after *seems* and *looks* – 'It looks as if he is guilty.' I take this sort of thing to be what one might call a syntactic euphemism; the speaker means 'It is pretty – or even quite – clear that he is guilty,' but is reluctant to say so bluntly, and compromises by retaining the *as if* of the contrary-to-fact condition, but abandoning the preterite – even the indicative preterite – form of the verb.

It *still* sounds illiterate to me.

c) *Were* for *would be*. This is fairly common in Trollope's own language, and appears now and then in dialogue. A good example is from *Fay*, 51: 'What were any other love or any other sadness as compared to his love or to his sadness?' I do not place this under ' "Literary" Archaisms' because it does sometimes occur in passages not generally stilted in tone, and I do not place it under

'Out-of-mode Usage' because, like *if it be* and *till he shall have come*
and the like, it still has a limited formal usage.

ANACOLUTHA (AND SOME ODDS AND ENDS)

Trollope wrote rapidly, and consequently now and then falls into,
and, despite re-reading, passes over without notice, anacolutha
(his wife, who, poor soul, copied most of his manuscripts for the
printer, probably removed a good many). By far the commonest
are disagreements in number between subject and verb. These fall
into three main classes (apart from those treated in c. 3 above):
(1) *There is* or the like followed by a plural subject. (2) Verb
attracted into the number of a preceding noun *not* its subject. (3)
One of the few that is and the like for *one of the few that are*. Somewhat surprisingly, all the instances of class 1 and all but one of
class 2 that I have observed are in Trollope's own language, not
in his characters'. Of class 1 – *eg*, '. . . there was great demonstra-
tions of joy . . .' (*Caldig*, 23) – I have recorded six instances, from
as many novels. Examples of class 2 are more than twice as
numerous; there are at least fourteen from eleven novels. Examples
are (singular for plural) '. . . over each . . . bookcase was
printed . . . the names of those great divines whose works were
ranged beneath . . .' (*Warden*, 12), and (plural for singular)
'. . . with these were mingled an idea that Carry and Sam were
in league together.' (*Vicar*, 47.) Of instances of class 3, unlike
classes 1 and 2, I have recorded more (five) in dialogue than in
Trollope's own language (three). Examples: ' "The whole thing
is one of the most ridiculous that ever was made." ' (*Vicar*, 55.)
'Mr Robarts had been selected to be one of the clergymen who
was to sit in . . . judgement upon Mr Crawley.' (*Chron*, 55.)
(This construction – now extremely common – is often defended
as logical by people who can't think.)

A somewhat different kind of lack of agreement in number
between subject and verb comes about from what is in effect the
use of *with* for *and*. I have recorded eleven instances from as many
novels. Examples: '. . . the nearest apothecary with his assistant
were in the room . . .' (*Chron*, 66) and 'Lord Alfred with his son
were already on the stairs.' (*Way*, 37.)

The unattached (or dangling) participle or gerund is, perhaps a little surprisingly, very rare: I have observed only four instances, three of them in Trollope's language. Example: 'After being kept waiting in the hall for about ten minutes, the Italian courier came down to him.' (*Popenjoy*, 31.) The quasi-double negative *not hardly* appears at least eight times; five times in dialogue, but three in Trollope's own language. Example (from Trollope himself): '. . . she had not spoken hardly above a word . . .' (*Love*, 9.)

Everyone who cares about grammatical propriety at all will agree in condemning both these usages; there are four others found in Trollope's novels that some such people do not object to: *different*(*ly*) *than*, the *and which* construction, *like* for *as*, and *than* without a comparative adjective or adverb. *Different*(*ly*) *than* I have observed nine times in eight novels – and all but one of them in Trollope's own language! Of the use of *and which* that many people (more than in Trollope's time or before) object to I have observed six instances – again, all but one in Trollope's own language. Examples: 'The cheque given by Lord Lufton, and which had been lost, had been a private matter . . .' (*Chron*, 1); and 'An old clergyman, attached to the cathedral, and who had been chaplain to Bishop Plunkett . . .' (*Land*, 1.) *Like* for *as*, so common now even in the formal writing of more or less educated people, is strikingly rare in Trollope, and never, I am pretty sure, appears in his own language, and only three times in dialogue – *ie*, the dialogue, as I cannot too often remind the reader, of educated characters. *Than* without a comparative adjective or adverb, very common today on quite high levels, I have observed four times, and always in Trollope's own language. I reproduce all four. '. . . Mr Crawley would almost have preferred that [his son] should work in the fields, than that he should be educated [at the expense of his godfather].' (*Chron*, 1); '. . . her feelings would have made her much prefer to beg her bread . . . than accept her late lover's generosity.' (*Belton*, 12); 'She would have infinitely preferred to see Mary an old maid, than to hear that she was going to give herself to any suitor contaminated by trade.' (*Vicar*, 9); and 'Whom should they meet, standing on the path, armed with a gun . . . than the Marquis himself?' (The last example is a mere slip, and would certainly have been corrected by Trollope if he had noticed it; but the first three, I suspect, he would have left unaltered. It must be admitted that they do make sense (as the last one does not), and that changing them would be troublesome.)

Of one syntactic oddity there is only one example. I mention it only because it is now – and may have been for a long time – extremely common in the speech of the uneducated (at least in the United States), who seem incapable of forming a sentence to express grammatically the kind of idea here expressed. In *Thorne*, 14, Lady De Courcy (of all people!) says to her daughter, ' "A girl that nobody knows where she came from!" ' The uneducated perpetrate this kind of thing oftenest in such sentences as 'That's the man that I knew his father,' being somehow leery of *whose* as a relative pronoun.

One point that is perhaps not a matter of 'grammar' at all as I have for the most part used the word in this chapter but that fits here better than anywhere else is the confusion of *lie* and *lay*. The confusion is ancient, and almost universal among the uneducated, who almost never say 'lie' (and still less often 'lain'). But among the educated the distinction is, and I think long has been, a familiar shibboleth; and it is accordingly nothing less than astonishing to find Trollope guilty of the crime no fewer than nine times – six of them in his own language. Examples: ' "I have done more than sleep upon it," said the Warden [!]; "I have laid awake on it." ' (*Warden*, 17); and ' "Go up to your room at once, dearest, and lay down." ' (*Senator*, 39; the speaker is a nobleman.) These show the familiar *lay* for *lie*; but twice Trollope manages to say (once in his own language) *lie* for *lay* (or rather *lain* for *laid*), as the half-educated not infrequently do: '. . . his handkerchief [was] smoothly lain upon his knees . . .' (*Warden*, 3); and ' "He's not only forgotten the opinions and notions of a gentleman, but he has lain down the manners of one, too." ' (*Macd*, 26; the speaker is an *Irish* gentleman to be sure, but he *is* a *gentleman*.)

These solecisms occur so often that one is driven to suppose that the distinction was one that somehow never became quite second nature to Trollope. Another, however, which also occurs several times, is certainly (all but in the last example) a mere slip. (The contexts seem to me to make it pretty clear that it is not a printer's error.) This is using *Sir* with a surname. In *Way*, 4 Trollope makes fun of a foreign woman for doing it; but alas! in the line immediately after one in which he has spoken of Lady Carbury, he calls her husband, Sir Patrick Carbury, 'Sir Carbury'. Again, in *Ayala*, 18, he makes a decidedly highbred lady say that ' "one sister became Tringlish after Sir Tringlish . . ." ' (The omitted Christian name is Thomas.) The final case is not a slip, and certainly not a printer's error, but clearly the result of Trollope's having changed his mind in mid-course about the name of a character, and forgotten to go back and make the adjustment consistently. On the opening page of *Right*, 'Sir Marmaduke Rowley' is introduced as governor of the 'Mandarin Islands'. But a few lines further on, Trollope writes, '. . . the gentlemen who ate Sir Rowley's dinners were not exactly the men whom he or Lady Rowley [!] desired . . . as their son-in-law.' Then after a second 'Sir Marmaduke Rowley' on p. 2 (*World's Classics* edition), we get, on the same page, three 'Sir Rowleys', and two more on p. 3. Thereafter Trollope gets it right – except in Chapter 6, and two or three times much further on in the book. Clearly what happened was that he at first meant Rowley to be the knight's Christian name, and then decided to make it his surname (and Marmaduke his Christian name). He altered the first occurrence (and probably others), but by no means all. (The latest occurrences may have been due not to his careless neglect to make the alteration, but to his forgetting that he had changed his mind.)

About a dozen more incorrect or inelegant expressions I have found once each, and about half a dozen more twice, but they are not worth the reader's time; some are the merest slips, some may be Mrs Trollope's or the compositor's errors, the incorrectness or inelegance of others is perhaps disputable, and none are psychologically or historically interesting, and their rarity is proof of their not being typical of Trollope's usage.

CHAPTER II

Slang, Profanity, Euphemisms, and Terms of Address and Reference

쎄쎄쎄쎄쎄쎄

I. SLANG

THE novels are full of slang (some of it now regarded as merely familiar or informal, or even, in a few cases, Standard English). It is now and then used by Trollope himself, but almost always with an (only half-serious) apology; it is (not surprisingly) used hardly at all by the rustic uneducated; it is used (rather surprisingly) comparatively little by the urban uneducated; it is used mostly by – and among – young gentlemen; and above all, it is man's language,[1] almost as much as is profanity. Young ladies now and

---

1. That a woman's, or at least a lady's, language was expected to differ recognizably from a man's in other ways than the avoidance of slang is evident from the following letter (*Dark*, 17) – or perhaps more evident from Trollope's comments than from the letter itself. ' "Lady Grant is here at this moment," Miss Altifiorla said in one of her letters [to a man]. She had by this time fallen into that familiar style of writing which hardly declared whether it belonged to a man's letter or a woman's. "I suppose you know who Lady Grant is. She is your fortunate rival's sister, and has come here I presume to endeavour to set matters right [between the 'fortunate rival', Mr Western, and his wife, from whom he has separated himself]. She is the exact ditto of her brother, who of all human beings gives himself the finest airs. But Cecilia since her separation has given herself airs too, and now leads her lonely life with her nose high among the stars. Poor dear Cecilia! her misfortunes do not become her, and I think they have hardly been deserved. They are all the result of your bitter vengeance, and though I must say that she in sort [*sic*] deserves it, I think that you might have spared her. After all she has done you no harm. Consider where you would be with Cecilia Holt [her maiden name] for your wife and guardian. Hard though you are, I do not think you would have been hard enough to treat her as he has done. Indeed there is an audacity about his conduct to which I know no parallel. Fancy a man marrying a wife and then instantly bidding her go home to her mother because he finds that she once liked another man better than himself! I wonder whether the law couldn't touch him! But you have escaped from all that, and I really can't understand why you should be so awfully cruel to the poor girl." Then she signed herself "Yours always, F. A.," as though she had not been a woman at all.'

then use it, but seldom without rebuke by older ladies. They, indeed, do not like it even in men, whom they sometimes rebuke for it, and who sometimes apologize to them for using it.

Let us take first Trollope's apologetic uses. (1) 'Had there not been something crooked,[1] a screw loose as people say, she would never have been within his reach.' (*Eustace*, 63.) (2) 'Of course he must see his wife. Of course he must – if I may use a slang phrase – "have it out with her". . . .' (*Popenjoy*, 32.) (3) '[Mrs Proudie] had never, – if on such an occasion I may be allowed to use a school-boy's slang, – taken a licking from anyone . . .' (*Chron*, 34.) (4) 'If I were to use the word "flabbergasted" as expressing Miss Baker's state of mind, I should draw down on myself the just anger of critics, in that I had condescended to the use of slang; but what other word will express so well what is meant?' (*Bertrams*, 31.) (5) 'John Eustace [Lady Eustace's brother-in-law] had told his friend . . . that . . . the lawyer intended to "jump upon" that lady. Making such an allowance and deduction from the force of these words as the slang expression will allow, we may say that John Eustace was right.' (*Eustace*, 4.) '. . . he shut up, as the slang phrase goes . . .' (*Thorne*, 5.) (6) '. . . a good deal of light-spirited sarcasm – or chaff, as it is called in the slang phraseology of the day.' (*House*, 36.) (7) 'She was less disposed to attack him with what the world of yesterday calls [*sic*] "chaff," or with what the world of to-day calls "cheek." ' (*Prime*, 51.)[2]

When ladies use slang, they are usually rebuked for it, but once in a while not – though in the first example, Trollope himself does so. In *Thorne*, 47, Martha Dunstable writes, with reference to Mary Thorne's wedding, ' "I shall certainly come and see you turned off". . . Miss Dunstable, it must be acknowledged, was a little too fond of slang; but then, a lady with her fortune, and of her age, may be fond of almost whatever she pleases.' Bishop Proudie seems to agree; in *Framley*, 17 he does not wince when she says to him, ' "I certainly think that I shall have some of these conversaziones. I wonder whether Mrs Proudie will come and put me up to a wrinkle or two." ' A few other bits of slang from ladies pass without comment: *eg*, ' "He's such a duck of an Apollo." ' (*House*,

---

1. It is worthy of remark (1) that *crooked* (in the metaphorical sense) itself was once slang; and (2) that *a screw loose* here means 'dishonest', not, as now, 'mentally unbalanced'.
2. *House* written 1863; *Prime*, 1874. *Tempora mutantur*.

3); ' "If he don't like it, he may lump it." ' (*Eustace*, 9); and ' "The deuce is in it if we can't have our way with her among us." ' (*Scarb*, 11.) This last is perhaps rather what might be called euphemistic profanity than slang, but it is man's language. As a rule, however, old ladies (for Trollope, anyone over fifty is old), and some young ones, dislike slang, even in the speech of men. Thus in *Eye*, 4, a young army officer says to his aunt, of his brother, ' "I think Master Jack is making it all square with Sophia Mellerby." If there was anything that Lady Scrope hated as much as improper marriages it was slang. She professed that she did not understand it; and in carrying out her profession always stopped the conversation to have any word explained to her which she thought to have been used in an improper sense.' But commonly old ladies are far from professing not to understand slang, and, though they do not always voice their dislike of its use by men, seldom fail to do so of its use by women; *eg*, from *Finn*, 42:

> '. . . I did not know that he was an especial friend.'
> 'Most especial, aunt. A 1 I may say; among young men, I mean.'
> . . . Miss Effingham was certainly wrong to speak of any young man as being A 1. Fond as I am of Miss Effingham, I cannot justify her, and must acknowledge that she used the most offensive phrase she could find, on purpose to annoy her aunt.
> 'Violet,' said Lady Baldrick, bridling up, 'I never heard such a word before from the lips of a young lady.'

Again, in *Popenjoy*, 25, Trollope remarks:

> Perhaps there was a little innocent slang in their conversation. Ladies do sometimes talk slang, and perhaps the slang was encouraged for the special edification of Lady Susanna. When Lady George declared that some offending old lady ought to be 'jumped upon,' Lady Susanna winced visibly. When Jack told Lady George that 'she was the woman to do it,' Lady Susanna shivered almost audibly. 'Is there anything the matter?' asked Lady George, perhaps not quite innocently.

From *Chron*, 31: ' "Mamma, Major Grantly has – skedaddled." "Oh, Lily, what a word!" ' Earlier in Lily Dale's life (*House*, 2) she is rebuked for slang, and by her somewhat strait-laced sister, not by her mother:

'I don't like those slang words, Lily.'

'What slang words?'

'You know what you called Bernard's friend.'

'Oh; a swell. I fancy I do like slang. I think it's awfully jolly to talk about things being jolly. Only that I was afraid of your nerves I should have called him stunning. It's so slow, you know, to use nothing but words out of a dictionary.'

'I don't think it's nice in talking of gentlemen.'

In *Dark*, 20 it is again a young lady that rebukes another. Francesca Altifiorla tells her friend Mrs Green that she is to be married:

'And who is it to be?'

'. . . Can you make a guess?'

'Not in the least. I don't know of anybody who has been spooning you.'

'Oh, what a term to use! No one can say that anyone ever – spooned me. It is a horrible word. And I cannot bear to hear it fall from my own lips.'

The (younger) Duke of Omnium is the only male character in the novels who reveals a distaste for slang. He does it once in a conversation with his wife (*Prime*, 21):

'I don't remember . . . that I have ever quarrelled with any one [*sic*] to your knowledge. But I may perhaps be permitted to –'

'Snub a man, you mean.'

'I wish you wouldn't put slang phrases into my mouth, Cora.'[1]

He does it again while he is reading a letter from his son, who has been helping a friend canvassing for election to Parliament. (*Children*, 56.)

'It was beastly work.' The duke made a . . . memorandum in his own mind to instruct his son that no gentleman above the age of a schoolboy should allow himself to use such a word in such a sense . . . 'And of course all we said was bosh.' Another memorandum . . . as to the slang . . . 'Our only comfort was that [the opposing candidate's] people were quite

1. Trollope often uses *snub* himself, and makes his characters use it, without any implication that it is slang. The Duke's standards of decorous language seem uniquely high.

as badly off as us.' Another memorandum as to the grammar.

Now and then men refrain from using slang to a lady or ward off rebuke by apologizing. (1) ' "When you are talking you are as bad as your brother," said the Marquis as he left [his daughter]. Only that the expression was considered to be unfit for female ears, he would have accused her of "talking the hind legs off a dog." ' (*Fay*, 4.) (2) ' "He has been very much shaken [by a footpad's assault] and altogether 'knocked out of time,' as people say. Excuse the phrase, because I think it will best explain what I want you to understand." ' (*Prime*, 22.)

The most extensive collocation of slang (and near-slang), used by its most typical kind of user, a young gentleman (a *very* young gentleman – he is in his first year at Oxford), is a letter (*Children*, 65) from Lord George Palliser, the Duke of Omnium's younger son (writer also of the letter just quoted), to his elder brother, Lord Silverbridge. I feel driven to include it not only because of the slang, but because of the skilful and vivid and delightful way in which Trollope makes it reveal the personality of the writer.

'Dear Silver, – I was awfully obliged to you for sending me the I.O.U. for that brute Percival. He only sneered when he took it, and would have said something disagreeable, but that he saw I was in earnest. I know he did say something to Nid, only I can't find out what. Nid is an easygoing fellow, and, as I saw, didn't want to have a rumpus.

'But now what do you think I've done? Directly I got home I told the governor all about [having lost £3400 at cards to Percival]! As I was in the train I made up my mind that I would. I went slap at it. If there is anything that never does any good, it is craning. I did it all at one rush, just as though I was swallowing a dose of physic. I wish I could tell you all that the governor said, because it was really tip-top. What is a fellow to get by playing high, – a fellow like you and me? I didn't want any of that beast's money. I don't suppose he had any. But one's dander gets up, and one doesn't like to be done, and so it goes on. I shall cut that kind of thing altogether. You should have heard the governor spouting Latin! And then the way he sat upon Percival, without mentioning the fellow's name! I do think it mean to set yourself to work to win money at cards, – and it is awfully mean to lose more than you have got to pay.

'Then at the end the governor said he'd send the beast a cheque for the amount. You know his way of finishing up, just like two fellows fighting; – when one has awfully punished the other he goes up and shakes hands with him. He did pitch it into me, – not abusing me, not even saying a word about the money, which he at once promised to pay, but laying it on to gambling with a regular cat-o'-nine-tails. And then there was an end of it. He just asked the fellow's address and said that he would send him the money. I will say this; – I don't think there's a greater brick than the governor out anywhere.

'I am awfully sorry about Treager [whom Lord Silverbridge has accidentally injured in a fox-hunt]. I can't quite make out how it happened. I suppose you were too near him, and Melrose [Silverbridge's horse] always does rush at his fences. One fellow shouldn't be too near another fellow, – only it so often happens that it can't be helped. It's just like anything else, if nothing comes of it then it's all right. But if anybody comes to grief then he has got to be pitched into. Do you remember when I nearly cut over old Sir Simon Slobody? Didn't I hear about it!

'I am awfully glad you didn't smash up Treager altogether because of Mary [their sister, in love with Treager]. I am quite sure it is no good anybody setting up his back against that [*ie*, Mary's marriage to Treager, opposed by her father]. It's one of those things that have got to be. You always have said that he's a good fellow. If so, what's the harm? At any rate it has got to be.

'Your affectionate brother,
'Gerald.'

How many 'memoranda as to the slang' would the Duke have made had he read *this* letter? But his eyes might have misted as he made one on ' "I don't think there's a greater brick than the governor out anywhere" '.

I conclude with an alphabetical list of nearly all the other slang expressions that occur in the novels, most of them in dialogue. I explain only those that I think might now need explaining (and add notes when the word is a standard one used in a slang sense).

all U-P; *blue* – unfortunate (fact); *boss; cheek*;[1] *cut* (in the sense

---

1. In the following passage (*Clerks*, 44) this means 'impudent self-assurance', as indeed it does now, not 'banter', as in the second paragraph of this Section: 'Undy

'pass without sign of recognition'); *cut up* (in the sense 'distressed'); *cut up rough* (equals the preceding phrase); *give leg bail* – run away; *go the whole hog; go tick* – buy on credit; *kick the bucket; lad of wax* – fine fellow; *muff* – fool (n.); *no small beer* – fine fellow; *pony* – £25; *punch* (in the sense 'strike'); *quodded* – jailed; *like bricks* – hard, industriously (as in 'read like bricks'); *rhino* – money; *take a rise out of* – attack (with words); *tight* (in the sense 'drunk'); *tin* (in the sense 'money'); *trump* (in the sense 'fine fellow'); *whitewash* (in the sense 'a glass of sherry after port or claret').

2. PROFANITY

Profanity in the novels is limited to *damn(ed)* (with two or three instances of *damnation*), *devil, hell* (only two or three instances), and *God*. Only about a dozen times are the words (*ie*, when used profanely) written out; and these, I think, are oversights by Trollope, who most commonly substitutes dashes, except for the initial letter, and now and then the final one as well.[1] The profanity always occurs in speeches, never in Trollope's own language; the only apparent exception to this is only apparently one, where he is quoting a proverb: ' "Better the d—— you know than the d—— you don't know," is an old saying, and perhaps a true one . . .'

Profanity is man's language. Just once does a woman – and a lady, at that – use it (in *Caldig*, 8): ' ". . . you would tell Mr Shand to go to – the devil . . ." ' But ladies not only do not use it: they are (at least conventionally) shocked or even insulted by it, and often say so, even when it is used, and in private conversation,

---

Scott . . . possessed an enormous quantity of that which schoolboys in these days call "cheek". . . He must perform some exploit uncommonly cheeky in order to cover his late discomfiture . . . he lived but on the cheekiness of his gait and habits; he had become a Member of Parliament, Government official, railway director, and club aristocrat, merely by dint of cheek . . . Undy, Undy, more cheek still, still more cheek, or you are surely lost . . . Oh, Undy, Undy, thy supply of cheek is not bad; . . . but yet it suffices thee not. "Can there be positions in this modern West End world of mine," thought Undy to himself, "in which cheek, unbounded cheek, will not suffice?" '

1. Cf. *H.M.S. Pinafore* (1878), where Captain Corcoran proclaims, ' "Though 'Bother it' I may/Occasionally say,/I never use a big, big D——." ' (Well – ' "hardly ever." ')

by their husbands. Of this there are eight or ten examples. The most elaborate is in *Fay*, 18. Lord and Lady Kingsbury are quarrelling because, he asserts, and correctly, she has driven his daughter (her step-daughter) out of the house. Lady Kingsbury denies the charge:

'I haven't made it impossible for her to live here. I have only done my duty by her. Ask Mr Greenwood [their chaplain].'

'D—— Mr Greenwood!' said the Marquis. He certainly did say the word at full length, as far as it can be said to have length, and with all the emphasis of which it is capable . . . Her lady-ship heard the word very plainly, and at once stalked out of the room, thereby showing that her feminine feelings had received a wrench which made it impossible for her any longer to endure the presence of such a foul-mouthed monster.[1]

Often the 'foul-mouthed monster' apologizes, as in *Ayala*, 31: ' "And who the d—— is he?" said Tom . . . "Tom!" exclaimed Mrs Dosett [his aunt]. "I beg your pardon; but you see this is very important?" '

Ladies carried so far their objection to words commonly used profanely that they sometimes felt a wicked joy in using them un-profanely; eg, *Belton*, 17: ' "These are the damning proofs." There are certain words usually confined to the vocabularies of men, which women such as Lady Arthur delight to use on special occasions.' Some ladies, to be on the safe side, widened the bounds of the profane, eg, in *Ayala*, 60: ' "I call that an infernal nuisance,"

1. *Pinafore* again. When Ralph Rackstraw reveals to Captain Corcoran that he loves the Captain's daughter Josephine, the Captain says (or rather sings), ' "I'm very sorry to disparage/A humble foremast lad,/But to seek your captain's child in marriage,/Why damme, it's too bad!" ' Automatically Hebe, the leading figure among Sir Joseph Porter's 'sisters and his cousins and his aunts', exclaims to them, ' "Did you hear him – did you hear him?/Oh, the monster overbearing!/ Don't go near him – don't go near him – /He is swearing – he is swearing." ' Trollope and Gilbert clearly saw eye to eye on the subject. It is rather striking that both should use *monster* with precisely the same application. *Pinafore* had its first performance on 25 May 1878 and ran for almost two years. Trollope began *Fay* on 23 December of that year, worked on it intermittently, and finished it on 21 November 1879. It is hard to believe that he did not hear the opera – apparently everyone did – and tempting to think that he unconsciously picked up *monster* from Gilbert in an exactly similar context; there is nothing inevitable or peculiarly appropriate about the use of the word by a lady reprimanding a gentleman for swearing.

he said to his aunt. "My dear Frank, you need not curse and swear," said the old lady. "Infernal [said Frank] is not cursing nor yet swearing." ' And ignorant men might make the same mistake: Captain Cuttwater, in *Clerks*, has such frequent occasions for apologizing to his female relatives for real profanity that he automatically apologizes to them also for *infernal* and *deuce*.

Profanity is almost as offensive to clergymen as to ladies; *eg*, in *Macd*, 8 Captain Ussher says in Father Cullen's presence, ' "Well, may I be d——d – begging your reverence's pardon – if this isn't as cold a night as I'd wish to be out in . . ." ' Just once – in *Popenjoy*, 28 – does a clergyman himself use profanity – and with the usual effect on 'feminine feelings': ' "The d—— she did," said the Dean. Mary almost jumped in her chair, she was so much startled by such a word from her father's mouth.'

3. EUPHEMISMS

Euphemisms are few, and limited to the expression of a very few ideas. That they are so is no doubt owing to the considerable number of ideas that Trollope, like virtually all his contemporaries, squeamishly avoided referring to in any language, plain and literal or euphemistic. Once (*Forgive*, 53) he expresses a dislike of euphemisms for death: ' "If anything should happen," – people when writing such letters are always afraid to speak of death by its proper name, – "I will send you a message . . ." ' But within the following three pages he himself twice uses *pass away*, as he does once in *Fay* and twice in *Eustace*. *Kill oneself* never, I think, occurs; instead we have *destroy oneself* and the still lamentably common *commit suicide* at least three times each – half the time in Trollope's own language. To pass from death to life, he once (*Eustace*, 9) descends to saying, 'She had never sacrificed her beauty to a lover,' meaning she had been a virgin when she married.[1] *In*

1. I have observed only three plainer allusions than this to coitus, and then always between husband and wife. One will be found in the long dialogue from *Bertrams*, 36 in Chapter VII; the two others follow. (1) In *Dark*, 16, Mr Western, who suspects his wife not, indeed, of adultery, but of what can hardly even be called a flirtation, writes, in a letter to his sister (to a brother or other man it would be less surprising), ' "How could I live with a wife of whom I knew so much as I had then learned of mine – but had known so little before? Had I been a man of the world, careless as to my own home except for the excellence of my dinner and the comfort of my bed, it might have been possible." ' (2) In *Caldig*, 46, after John

the family way occurs three times, but twice in the language of characters, and the third time in a passage of narrative in which Trollope uses several expressions natural not to him, but to the character, an Irish peasant, whose thoughts he is relating. The others are rather special, in different ways. The first is comic, and in an Irish-bullish – or cowish! – sort of way: Father John, in *Macd*, says to a peasant, ' "And is her cow really in the family way?" ' The second, in *Popenjoy*, occurs in a letter from a duke's son to his brother: ' "I ought perhaps to have told you sooner that [my wife] is in the family way." ' The expression is still current, of course, but hardly in the (serious) language of the upper classes: I am not at all sure that it was so even in Trollope's time; in fact, the last example may have been meant as a jocose vulgarism.

4. TERMS OF ADDRESS AND REFERENCE

a) Parents and Children

Young ladies virtually always speak both to and of their fathers and mothers as 'papa' and 'mamma'. (Young gentlemen *never* do.) Only Dorothea Ray (*Ray*, 4) calls her mother by that name – a sign of the unusual 'sternness' (see Introduction) of her disposition. Young gentlemen address their fathers almost always as 'father' (or 'sir') and their mothers as 'mother'. In reference, it is always 'my mother', but perhaps as often 'the (or 'my') governor' as 'my father', at least among male contemporaries. The only young lady to use the term is Charlotte Stanhope, whose awareness of her position as the only practical and responsible member of the family once in a while leads her into masculine language. She says to her brother Bertie (*Towers*, 15), ' "I look forward with dread to the time when the governor [on the income of whose ecclesiastical

---

Caldigate has been found guilty (on perjured testimony) of bigamy, his second wife, now not his wife in the eyes of the law, insists that she *is* his wife, and will regard herself as such, except that, until she is proved right, she ' "will never again lie with my head upon his bosom unless all that be altered. But I will serve him as his wife, and obey him; and if I can I will comfort him. I will never desert him. And not all the laws that were ever made, nor all the judges that ever sat in judgment, shall make me call myself by another name than his." '

preferments the family are completely dependent] must go." ' The word is so common among young gentlemen (though usually in the absence of their fathers and of ladies, but still with no necessary or even probable disrespectful intent) that it seems odd that Trollope once (*Castle*, 8) puts the word between quotation marks as if it were vulgar. Since the speaker happens not to be a gentleman, perhaps Trollope unconsciously and rather unfairly thought it vulgar only when used by vulgar persons.

Children-in-law and stepchildren were less familiar; *eg*, in *Popenjoy*, Lady George Germain calls her mother-in-law, the Dowager Marchioness of Brotherton, 'mother', but only at the latter's express request – and note, not 'mamma'. In *Fay*, 22, Lord Hampstead and his stepmother quarrel. ' "I beg your pardon, Lady Kingsbury," – he had never called her Lady Kingsbury before.' He is nowhere else quoted as calling her anything, and I am inclined to believe that that is what he always *would* have called her, and that Trollope was simply not thinking.

Masterful children can frighten their timid parents by un accustomed formality. Thus Archdeacon Grantly in *Warden*, 9: ' "Why, my lord," he said speaking to his father: and when he called his father "my lord," the good old bishop shook in his shoes, for he knew that an evil time was coming.' And almost conversely, Mr Harding once (*Chron*, 22) addresses the archdeacon, his son-in-law, as 'my dear', over their wine, in the presence of the archdeacon's son; and later (*Chron*, 81), on his deathbed, he says – and they are his last audible words – to the archdeacon and to his other son-in-law, Dean Arabin, ' "There is nothing left for me to wish, my dears; – nothing." ' These are the only instances of the expression's being used man to man, and are consonant with the feminine softness of Mr Harding's nature.

b) Husband and Wife

Lady De Courcy, in *House*, regularly addresses her husband as 'De Courcy'; Lady Kingsbury, in *Fay*, 11, being angry with her husband, addresses him as 'Lord Kingsbury', as Trollope clearly implies she does not usually, but what she usually does, he does not say. In *Thorne*, 27, throughout a long conversation, Lady Arabella consistently calls her husband 'Mr Gresham', to which he as consistently responds with 'my dear'. (They are not quarrelling.) This deferential formality from wives (and Lady Arabella is less given to deference than most), responded to by a (perhaps patronizing and quasi-paternal) endearment from husbands, is common: Mrs Grantly says to her husband (*Warden*, 2), ' "As to his vulgarity, archdeacon," (Mrs Grantly had never assumed a more familiar turn of speech than this in addressing her husband), "I don't agree with you." ' (They are in the connubial bed!) He ordinarily calls her Susan; but once (*Towers*, 50), when he has heard that his sister-in-law is to marry his bosom friend Mr Arabin, ' "So we're sold after all, Sue," he said to his wife, accosting her with a kiss as soon as he entered his house. He did not call his wife Sue above twice or thrice in a year, and these occasions were great high days.' On a somewhat lower social plane, wives seem often to have addressed their husbands, and sometimes referred to them, by their surnames alone: so, *eg*, Mrs Walker, an attorney's wife (*Chron*, 71). But when angry, they could be as formal as Lady Kingsbury: in *Senator*, 18, Mrs Masters 'appeared at dinner, and called her husband Mr Masters when she helped him to stew.' On a lower plane yet, a wife may substitute the initial letter of her husband's surname: in *Ray*, 3, Mrs Tappitt, a country brewer's wife, says, ' "Laws, T., don't be so foolish," . . . She always called her husband T., unless when the solemnity of some special occasion justified her in addressing him as Mr Tappitt. To have called him Tom or Thomas, would, in her estimation, have been vulgar.' Husbands sometimes reciprocated: in *Orley*, Mr Moulder (a lower-middle-class and ungrammatical commercial traveller) and his wife regularly address and refer to each other as 'Mr M.' and 'Mrs M.'. And in *Towers*, the disastrously prolific Mrs Quiverful, who is a lady, but whose poverty has pardonably almost made her forget the fact, regularly addresses – though she never refers to – her reverend husband as 'Q.'. This usage Trollope clearly regards as merely vulgar in vulgar mouths, but as worse than that when used mockingly by the educated: thus in *Caldig*, 19, ' "But Mrs B. ?" said William [a gentleman], who would thus sometimes disrespectfully allude to his stepmother.' Finally, in the great chapter (*Chron*, 66) at the end of which Mrs Proudie dies, she addresses her husband in a single conversation sometimes as 'bishop' (as she always, I think, does elsewhere), sometimes rises to 'my lord', but now and then descends to 'my dear' – and once – pathetically – goes so far as 'Tom'.

c) Outside the Family

In *Warden*, the bedesmen of Hiram's Hospital never (except Mr Bunce sometimes) call Mr Harding by either his name or his title, but 'your reverence'. This seems to have been common among the lower classes not only in Ireland (where it was apparently in almost universal use – even, with charitable ecumenicity, by Roman Catholic peasants to Protestant clergy), but in England as well. In England, to judge from Trollope's novels, neither the educated classes nor others addressed, at least customarily, (beneficed) parochial clergy as 'Vicar' or 'Rector' (without a surname), as people of all classes so commonly do today, but as 'Mr So-and-so'. This form was evidently used also in Ireland in addressing Roman Catholic clergy, instead of the the now universal 'Father (So-and-so)'; chiefly by the educated classes, but not exclusively: *eg*, in *Kellys*, members of a crowd of demonstrators (all of them Roman Catholics) in Dublin acclaim a popular hero, personally unacquainted with them, with ' "Well, yer reverence, Mr Tierney!" ' – thus very pleasantly combining two kinds of courtesy. Evidently the demonstrators felt that 'Well, yer reverence!' would have been too impersonal, 'Well, Father Tierney!' too familiar, and 'Well, yer reverence, Father Tierney!' tautological. That *Mr* is sometimes used in Trollope's Irish novels by Roman Catholics as well as by Protestants shows that it was then regarded as anything but disrespectful; that *Father* is sometimes used there, and used respectfully, by Protestants (*always*, I think, by Trollope himself) shows that many of them, at least, had no sectarian objections to using it to (and of) Roman Catholic clergy. In England, *Father* for Roman Catholic clergy (other than friars, and one's own confessor) did not begin to replace *Mr* in the use of (at least English) Roman Catholics as well as of others till some time after 1850. Some priests there didn't like it – Newman, for one, at least as late as 1864 (perhaps partly because Manning *did* like it, and promoted its use). The now frequent extension to the Anglican clergy began later still, grew more slowly, and is of course the mark of the Beast to some Anglicans, both lay and clerical.

Ladies and gentlemen in Trollope's novels are a good deal more given to addressing lords as 'my lord' than nowadays. But sometimes lords disliked it if they thought familiarity justified something less distant and, so to speak, servile: Lord De Guest in a letter (*House*, 36) to Johnny Eames, who has addressed him in a letter as 'My Lord' (as he has also done in conversation), writes, ' "When you write to me again . . . begin your letter 'My dear Lord De Guest' – that is the proper way." '

I believe bishops today get 'my-lorded' (not only by servants and tradesmen) much more than peers or lords by courtesy do,[1] but the practice was far from universal even in Trollope's time. In *Warden*, 19, Mr Harding, in resigning his wardenship, writes two letters to Bishop Grantly, one official and one not. The first begins 'My Lord Bishop' and ends 'Your Lordship's most obedient servant'; the second begins 'My dear Bishop' and ends 'Yours most sincerely'. But of course the Bishop and the Warden were old and dear friends. And Bishop Grantly, as we have seen, is called 'my lord' by his son, and Bishop Proudie by his wife, only exceptionally, and *in terrorem*.

1. Nothing makes an American bishop – Anglican and Roman Catholic equally – so happy as a stay in England.

CHAPTER III

Out-of-Mode[1] Usage

𑁍𑁍𑁍𑁍𑁍

ALL the subjects dealt with in this chapter are parts of grammar in the broad sense; but I believe the reader will readily see both the *rationale* and the practical utility of restricting the application of that term as I have done in Chapter I, and of keeping for the present one the subjects treated of in it.

It should be noted that hardly any of the usages listed are peculiar to Trollope.

A. SYNTAX

1. *object* (and the like) *to do* for *object to doing*. Example: 'He did ... very strongly object to discuss any such subject . . .' (*Warden*, 3.)

This is Trollope's (and his characters') all but invariable use, whereas I think virtually everyone today, all over the world, says 'object to discussing'. The infinitive for the gerund is much commoner (at least fourteen instances) with *object* and with the equivalent *have an (no, any) objection* (at least ten instances) than with any other verb, but it is also Trollope's customary usage with *be averse*, *be given*, *be used*, *reconcile oneself*, *look forward*, *see one's way*, and *have taken*, of which, all together, I have observed twenty instances. The only explanation of the shift from *to do* to *to doing* that occurs to me is that all the verbs and verb phrases listed above (and many others) are regularly followed by the preposition *to* governing a noun (*object to a plan* and the like), and when the noun is an infinitive, *to* must do double duty – as a preposition and as the 'sign of the infinitive'. People have come to feel, I take it, that this is

---

1. I use this somewhat vague term deliberately because I do not want to give the impression that *none* of the usages listed *ever* occur today; a fair number of them do, though not with great frequency.

awkward and absurd.[1] Some people must have begun to feel that way in Trollope's time: at least four times he uses today's idiom, eg, ' "I have no objection to living in Devonshire . . ." ' (*Right*, 14.)

2. *must have done* (and the like) in the sense 'would certainly or necessarily have done'.

In today's usage, *you must have done* almost always means 'it is necessary to suppose that you have done'. It was otherwise in Trollope's time and before. His (and his predecessors') usual sense can be nicely illustrated from *The Beggar's Opera*:

> MRS PEACHUM: O Polly, you might have toy'd and kist,
>   By keeping Men off, you keep them on.
> POLLY: But he so teaz'd me,
>   And he so pleas'd me,
>   What I did, you must have done.

Polly is not saying to her mother, as many modern readers probably fancy, 'You *have surely done* the same thing' (though she probably had), but, 'You *would surely have done* the same thing.' I have observed nine instances (four of them Trollope's own) from eight novels. Here are three specimens (two in one sentence): 'To return from London to Exeter without seeing her dear friend would be so unfeeling and unnatural! She must have come from Durton Lodge or must have returned to Exeter,' (*Dark*, 7); and ' "If he intended anything of the kind I must have been the first person to hear of it." ' (*Orley*, 15.) To give *must have* in these sentences the now almost invariable meaning makes nonsense of them. The built-in ambiguity probably led to the virtual disappearance of the sense illustrated above, for which there was probably rarer occasion.

3. Verbs now normally intransitive used transitively.
There are at least three of these. (1) *refrain*: '. . . he refrained himself for a little while.' (*Clerks*, 5); '. . . she could hardly refrain herself . . .' (*Right*, 28); '. . . he refrained his hand [from striking a blow].' (*Ray*, 13); (2) *domineer*: '. . . Aunt Ju was weak

---

1. It must be admitted, however, that there are mysterious exceptions – mysterious to me, at least; eg, one never says, 'He is entitled to voting,' but always, 'He is entitled to vote.'

enough to be domineered by Lady Selina.' (*Popenjoy*, 28); ' "... the feminine influences of the house have almost domineered him." ' (*Popenjoy*, 9); (3) *deteriorate*: 'Every great man, who gains a great end by dishonest means, does more to deteriorate his country . . . than legions of vulgar thieves . . .' (*Clerks*, 29.)

B. IDIOM

1. *yourself* (and the like) for *you* or *you yourself*.
This usage, though I believe it is still common in Ireland, certainly is not in either Britain or the United States. It is rather common in Trollope, and not always in dialogue. Five examples follow: ' "I ask yourself whether it is not true?" ' (*Love*, 10); ' "Think of his words when he has spoken to yourself!" ' (*Ayala*, 52); ' "Why do you ask me?" said she. "Why don't you ask himself?" ' (*Towers*, 16); 'It was not till Hamel was near to her that she understood that the man was to join herself . . .' (and note preceding simple 'her') (*Ayala*, 19); 'She was sure that he would never fall in love with herself.' (*Ayala*, 23.) The locution perhaps arose out of a confusion between the reflexive and the emphatic uses of the *-self* forms.

2. *Like* for *likely* (adjective).
This unexpected archaism or provincialism, now heard only in uneducated speech, occurs at least twice, both times in Trollope's own language and both times in *Anna* (26 and 44): '. . . he had hurried [thither] on receipt of news . . . that his father was like to die.' 'He was not dead, nor did he believe that he was like to die . . .'

3. *this* meaning *this house*.
Very common. I have recorded nine instances from eight novels, but there are a good many others. Not unnaturally, they are all in dialogue. I give only two examples (from a conversation in *Orley*, 26) – the best because the context makes the meaning quite unmistakable:

'. . . Sir Peregrine, I will leave this – '
'Leave this! go away from The Cleeve!'

'Yes; I will not destroy the comfort of your home by the wretchedness of my position . . .'

'Lady Mason, my house is altogether at your service.'

4. Both Trollope and his characters almost always say *whence* (though, also almost always, with the redundant *from*) for *from where*, *hence* for *from here*, *thence* for *from there*, and (with verbs of motion) *whither* for *where*, *hither* for *here*, and *thither* for *there*. The only exceptions of any kind I have noted are one[1] instance of *from where* for *whence* – 'It was natural that her mother should believe the story . . ., let it come from where it might.' (*Scarb*, 15) – and two of *where* for *whither*, both, oddly, immediately after sentences using *whither* (the idiom of today was obviously also coming into use – beginning, I suspect, in uneducated speech): 'He was gone, but she did not know whither. The servants, no doubt, knew where, but she could not bring herself to ask them.' (*Dark*, 13); ' "I should like to consult with you as to whither I had better go. Where shall I first take her?" ' (*Wortle*, 10.) Since Trollope's time, as everyone knows, *whither* and *thither* have completely disappeared from normal serious use, *hither* survives only in *hitherto* (and then in a temporal sense), and all three of the *-ence* forms are hardly used (*hence* most frequently) but in the metaphorical sense 'for which (this, that) reason', or the like (though *henceforth* and *henceforward* survive in a temporal sense).[2]

5. *do you go* (and the like) for *go* (imperative).
A usage now completely obsolete in ordinary language spoken or written, but fairly common in Trollope (naturally almost exclusively in dialogue). Example: ' "Do you go and manage it with her." ' (*Ayala*, 12.)

1. Lady De Courcy's ' "A girl that nobody knows where she came from!" ', quoted in Chapter I, is rather a special case, hardly relevant here.
2. An interesting little sidelight on the displacement, already beginning, of *hither* by *here*, and of people's awareness of it, is to be found in *Vanity Fair* (1847–48), Chapter 25, where Becky Sharp (or rather Crawley) is dictating to her husband a letter to be sent (in his name) to his aunt. ' "Which very possibly may be fatal. I have come hither – "
    ' "Why not say come here, Becky? come here's grammar," the dragoon interposed.
    ' "I have come hither," Becky insisted with a stamp of her foot . . .' Rawdon, of all people, would seem to have heard and remembered a dispute about the matter, and takes the liberal side; but Becky remains staunchly conservative.

6. *notify to* for *notify*.

'The Duke of Omnium had notified to Mr Fothergill his wish that some arrangement should be made . . .'

C. VERB FORMS (MOSTLY PAST PARTICIPLES)

1. *gotten*.

Though before undertaking this book I had read about a dozen of Trollope's novels at least twice, and half of those several more times, and though I had observed that he sometimes uses, and makes his characters use, *gotten* for *got* (past participle) in what is now the notoriously American way,[1] I had certainly not observed that it is much his commonest form. I have recorded twenty-four instances of the now American[2] *gotten*, as against only seven of the now British *got* (this does *not* count the international *got* mentioned in n. 1 above). Trollope was capable, that is, of using *got*, but twice out of the seven recorded seven times he also uses *gotten* within a few pages – once, indeed, in the same sentence. I have noted *got* for the first time in 1863 (*Ray*, 23): '. . . each Liberal there would have got a better dinner at home . . .'; then in 1866 (*Chron*, 70 – but with *gotten* a few pages earlier); in 1873 (*Way*, 40); and again in *Way*, 4 – but with *gotten* in the same sentence: 'There was an idea abroad that Melmotte had got his money with his first wife, and had gotten it not very long ago.' The only three other *gots* that I have noted appear in 1874 (*Prime*, 54 – two instances in one sentence) and 1878 (*Ayala*, 49) – seven *gots* over the sixteen years from 1863 to 1878 inclusive, and twice in the near vicinity of *gotten*. The twenty-four instances of *gotten*, on the other hand (twice in the close neighbourhood of *got*) extend from 1845 (*Macd*, 10) through 1877 (*Caldig*, 38). As early as 1863, that is, Trollope

1. Some Englishmen still fancy that Americans *always* use *gotten* for *got* (past participle). They do not. In the first place, many (including me, which may account for my earlier oversight) follow the British practice. In the second place, even those (admittedly the considerable majority) who do not, and who say, *eg*, 'I've gotten over it' instead of 'I've got over it', *never* say, any more than an Englishman does, 'I've gotten two brothers', meaning 'I have two brothers', but always, as much as any Englishman, 'I've got two brothers.'

2. Not *quite* exclusively, I was much surprised to find on recently rereading Aldous Huxley's *Point Counter Point* (1928); Chapter 9 has 'He was shocked because he had always gotten up early himself . . .', and Chapter 11, 'Beatrice had never really gotten over the shock she received as a young girl . . .'

observed that some people were using *got*, and now and then used it himself, but *gotten* remained his normal usage throughout his career. I have noted no later occurrences than 1877, but then, from 1878 to 1882, the date of his last novel, though I have noted, indeed, no *gottens*, I have also noted also no *gots*. I have less confidence in the completeness or near-completeness of my observation of this point than of most,[1] but it seems to me unmistakably clear that, if *gotten* had become as uncommon in Britain in Trollope's day as it is now, Trollope himself was behind the times.

2. Other past participles.

(a) Trollope's almost invariable past participle for *drink* is *drank*, not *drunk*; I have recorded seven instances. (b) Three times, all of them in *Fay*, I find *bade* for *bid(den)*. This, unlike *drank*, is not recorded in *OED* as a participle in use at any time, but must have had some currency in speech; and Thackeray uses it at least twice in *Vanity Fair* ('had bade good-bye'). (c) Also in *Fay* there is one *shrank* for *shrunk*, but this may be a printer's error. (d) In *Chron*, 26, a gentleman says, ' "It seems to me that I . . . have clomb as high as I know how." ' *This* can *not* be a printer's error; but (e) '. . . she was woke with the news that his spirit had fled' (*Bertrams*, 25) may be. (f) '. . . they had throven as honest men . . .' (*Senator*, 2) would appear to be Trollope's invention. (g) The only instance of *eat* for *eaten* that I have observed is 'He had not slept, eat, and worked with them . . .' (*Macd*, 15.)

3. (a) The spelling *eat* for *ate* occurs at least twice, in *Chron*, 13. (b) Every now and then Trollope writes *sate* for *sat*. This is his friend Thackeray's usual if not indeed invariable form at least in *Vanity Fair*; perhaps Trollope caught it from him.

D. VOCABULARY

1. Meanings now obsolete or obsolescent or rare or 'historical only' because of changes mainly in fashion or technology.

1. For the reason that, as I have remarked in n. 1 on p. 67, I myself happen so regularly to use *got* that it would be easy for me to overlook some instances, and correspondingly hard to overlook instances of *gotten*. The important fact remains that, even if Trollope uses *got* oftener than I think, he certainly uses *gotten* very often, whereas hardly any Briton would today. (But cf. n. 2 on p. 67.)

I have placed these in alphabetical order and italicized them. The first, to be sure, *attorney*, happens to have changed its meaning (in England) – or rather all but disappeared there – because of a change neither in fashion nor in technology, and yet because of an external change, not spontaneously, so to speak, like the words dealt with under D. 2 below, and hence seems more logically placed here.

Though *power of attorney* and *attorney in fact* are still in use, the only attorney (at law) officially so called in England since the Reform of the Judicature Act of 1873 is the Attorney-General (and in modern times, at least, he has always been required to be a barrister!). Originally, attorneys practised in the Common Law courts and solicitors in the Court of Chancery (and proctors in the ecclesiastical and Admiralty courts). Originally, too, and up into the late seventeenth century, attorneys had in some ways wider powers and more business and hence higher prestige than solicitors[1] (as had, to some extent and in some respects, the Common Law courts than the Court of Chancery), but for a number of reasons, too many and too various to be detailed here, the situation had reversed itself at the latest by 1800, and, chiefly because of that, the Act of 1873 decreed that henceforth all lawyers not barristers should be entitled Solicitors (to the High Court of Justice). Long before then most attorneys, for good practical reasons, qualified also as solicitors,[2] and acted as such in Equity matters; but the ancient prestige of attorneys continued to be reflected in the popular use of that term, and even after 1873. With a single exception, very surprising because it is so early (*Orley*, 9, 1861), it is Trollope's invariable word (except when he says 'lawyer') up to 1875, when *solicitor* first appears (*Popenjoy*, 26), though in the immediately preceding sentence the same man is called an attorney. Further, Trollope says 'solicitor' just once more – in 1880 (*Dark*, 13) – and here again he calls the same man

1. In the popular mind, this notion of the superiority of attorneys lasted even up into the early eighteenth century; cf. Defoe, *Moll Flanders* (1722): ' "... I was obliged to begin a prosecution in form, and accordingly my governess found me a very creditable sort of man to manage it, being an attorney of very good business, and of a good reputation ... ; ... had she employed a pettifogging hedge solicitor ... I should have brought it to but little." '
2. Cf. Dickens, *Pickwick Papers* (1836–37), Chapter 20: '... Messrs Dodson and Fogg, two of his Majesty's Attorneys of the Courts of King's Bench and Common Pleas ... and solicitors [*sic*] of the High Court of Chancery ...' But never elsewhere are they spoken of as solicitors (though Mr Perker is once or twice).

an attorney a page earlier. Thereafter he returns to *attorney* exclusively. (Cf. Gilbert in *Pinafore*, 1878 – ' "When I was a lad I served a term/As office boy to an attorney's firm" ' – and in *Patience*, 1881 – ' "By the advice of my solicitor/ . . . I've put myself up to be raffled for." ') The ancient precedence of attorneys over solicitors is still reflected in the superiority of the Attorney-General to the Solicitor-General.[1]

'That romance was over . . . "It has taken a good bit out of me," he said . . . "A man doesn't go through that kind of thing without losing some of the *caloric*." ' (*Chron*, 80.) *OED*, 'Lavoisier's name [1792] for a supposed elastic fluid, to which the phenomena of heat were formerly attributed. (Now abandoned.)'

'. . . Augusta was *crossing* a note to her bosom friend . . .' (*Towers*, 17.) When postage and writing paper were dearer than they are now, letter writers – especially, to judge from Trollope's novels, ladies – commonly first filled a page, then turned it ninety degrees, and filled it again, over and at right angles to the first 'go'. What began as an economy became a fashion that outlasted the need for economy, and I can remember having seen 'crossed' letters from old ladies in the United States in my childhood (*c.* 1915).

Among the fittings of Tom Towers's room (*Warden*, 14) is 'a *despatcher* for the preparation of lobsters and coffee.' In neither *OED* nor Partridge. Obviously a kitchen utensil, but whether a small stove or a small range or a pot I do not know.

'. . . now [Undy Scott] poked his "*Honourable*" card in everyone's way, and lugged Lord Gaberlunzie [his father] into all conversations . . .' (*Clerks*, 44); 'She had seen from his card that he was an *Honourable* Mr Glascock.' (*Right*, 17.) These quotations are from 1857 and 1868 respectively. Things had changed in half a century: the *Encyclopædia Britannica*, 11th edition, 1910–11, speaks,

1. For a complex of historical reasons, the nomenclature in the United States differs in almost every possible way. To detail the reasons here would be completely irrelevant to the subject of this book, but the ways will be of interest to Englishmen. In the United States, *all* lawyers (when they are not called that) are *always* called attorneys, *never* solicitors (except Solicitors General and certain law officers of government departments and some municipalities); and even they are not expressly admitted to practice as solicitors, but, like everyone else, as 'attorneys and counselors [*sic*] at law'. The latter term means 'barristers', but that term is *never* used, nor is *counselor at law* in full, though judges sometimes address counsel during a trial as 'Counselor'. To an American, a solicitor is one who *solicits* charitable or political contributions – or magazine subscriptions.

s. v. *Honourable*, of '. . . the conventions by which an "honour-able" does not use the title on his visiting cards and is not announced as such.'

'*Roquelaure.*' (*Towers.*) *OED*, '[1716] now hist.; a man's half-length cloak.' But in *Towers* it is worn by a lady.

'. . . a *surtout* that should be absolutely free from the tailor's hands . . .' (*Bertrams*, 31.) Almost all educated people today probably know what this means, but it is certainly now never used except 'historically'.

Among the furniture kept by Mr Harding on leaving the Hospital (*Towers*, 20) is 'Eleanor's *teapoy*'. *OED*, '*India*. . . . 1828. [f. Hindi . . . *tir*- three + Persian *pāē, pāī* foot.] A small three-legged table or stand, or any tripod; (by erroneous association with *tea*), such a table with a receptacle for tea.' Teapoys are doubtless still to be found at antique dealers'.

The widow 'had not altogether divested herself of [her pretti-ness], even when her *weepers* were of the broadest.' (*Ray*, 1.) *OED*, 'Broad white cuffs worn by widows. 1755.' Evidently they grew narrower as the bereavement grew more distant and the tears appropriately fewer.

2. Other meanings now obsolete, etc.

'He did not wish to *acerbate* the member for Mile End . . .' (*Clerks*, 31.) *Exacerbate* is certainly now the almost invariable word. It is also, according to *OED*, older (1660) than *acerbate* (1731), and has probably always been commoner.

' "Having *Anglican* tendencies, I have been wont to contradict my [fellow Americans] when they have told me of the narrow exclusiveness of your nobles." ' (*Children*, 70.) I have never seen this word used for *Anglophile* anywhere else. Its use here may be either an idiosyncrasy of Trollope's or a solecism put intentionally by him into the American speaker's mouth.

'. . . the boys were *astonished* by the feeling of their loss [of their mother].' (*Children*, 4.) It is clear from the context that this means 'stunned mentally', a meaning that *OED* calls obsolete by 1600 (!).

' ". . . nothing can be nicer and fresher than you are; – especially since you took to *bathing*." ' (*Forgive*, 7.) This – in isolation – would make a very strange impression today, at least on an American. Trollope means, of course, specifically bathing in the sea, as I think he always does, and as his contemporaries usually did. Indeed, I believe it still has a limited currency in Britain.

'So much in this world depends upon *character* that attention has to be paid to bad character even when it is not deserved.' (*Wortle*, 19.) The sense 'reputation' is now virtually obsolete (at any rate in the United States) – probably because in many sentences (though not in this one) it is misleading. (Cf. *complicated* below.)

'Her complexion was not *clear*, though it would be wrong to call her a brunette.' The disappearance of *clear* in the sense 'fair' may be explained as the preceding item is; without the second clause the first would now be taken to mean that the lady had acne.

'. . . should his wife become *complicated* with a sister damaged in character [cf. *character* above], there might come of it trouble and annoyance.' (*Claver*, 38.) *OED* dates this sense ('mixed up *with* in an involved way') from 1673, and does not call it obsolete, but it is certainly nowadays at least very seldom heard. *OED* dates the usual modern (participial) sense, 'ma[d]e complex or intricate', only from 1832; the now regrettably common use as an adjective meaning merely 'complex' it does not mention at all (though all American dictionaries and some British ones now allow it).

'. . . the length of the trial is proportioned not only to the *complicity* but to the importance, or rather to the public interest of the case . . .' (*Redux*, 61.) This sense certainly now never appears, but oddly enough it seems to have been a neologism in Trollope's time; *OED* dates it only from 1847, and the now universal one from 1650. *Complexity* it dates from 1721. The former word is correctly formed, and the latter is not; but the early association of *complicity* with *accomplice* and its dissociation from *complex* gave the new sense a short life.

'He . . . was . . . a *courteous* man, one who paid compliments to ladies.' (*Eustace*, 43.) The word would not be used today in this limited sense ('gallant') even in a sentence that, like this one, makes the limitation clear.

'She had . . . fallen into that familiar style of writing which hardly *declared* whether it belonged to a man's letter or a woman's.' (*Dark*, 17.) *OED* lists this meaning – 'to make clear or plain' – as obsolete after 1691. It still belongs here, not under ' "Literary" Archaisms' (Chapter V, Section 1); there is nothing affected or jocular about its use in the context.

' "You have done yourself neither good nor harm. Nor was I *desirable* [*ie*, desirous] that you should." ' *OED* does not give quite this meaning. It may be a mere slip.

' "I *doubt* it is not so easy to turn her head . . ." ' (*Framley*, 11.) The sense 'suspect' is dated by *OED* from 1509 and labelled '*arch*.'. I should say that it was now obsolete. Coincidentally, *OED* illustrates the usage from Trollope: ' "I doubt that Thackeray did not write the epitaph" ' – which today would be interpreted contrarily to the intention. I suspect [!] that the use was always chiefly colloquial.

' "If I can ever assist you to be happy, and prosperous, and *elate* before the world, I will try my best to do so . . .", (*Bertrams*, 19); '. . . Harcourt was also sufficiently *elate*.' (*Bertrams*, 15.) I am pretty sure that Trollope uses this form, always rare, nowhere else.

' "The squire has unfortunately *embarrassed* the property, and Frank must look forward to inherit [cf. A. 1. above] it with very heavy encumbrances . . ." ' (*Thorne*, 14.) A sense still in legal, but certainly not in ordinary, use. (Cf. next item.)

'Mr Gresham was now an *embarrassed* man, and though the world did not know it, or, at any rate, did not know that he was deeply *embarrassed*, he had not the heart to throw open his mansion and park and receive the county with a free hand as though all things were going well with him.' (*Thorne*, 1.) Any reader today would be misled by the first clause if it stood alone. *OED* dates the now usual meaning only from 1875. (Cf. preceding item.)

' "You are so full of scruple, so green, so young," said Undy, almost in an *enthusiasm* of remonstrance.' (*Clerks*, 24.) The apparent sense here is not precisely noted by *OED* and may be a Trollopian idiosyncrasy; it is somewhere between the sense illustrated in the next item and that which is now virtually the only one – or perhaps rather an extension in a different direction.

'[Dr Gwynne] regarded the *enthusiasm* of such as Newman as a state of mind more allied to madness than to religion . . .' (*Towers*, 20.) The usual sense in the eighteenth century (cf. the famous 'lapidary inscription', 'She was pious but not enthusiastic'); a little surprising, I think, as late as *Towers* (1856), and now 'historical only'. (Cf. next item.)

'[The Proudies' daughters] have . . . not distressed their parents . . . by any *enthusiastic* wish to devote themselves to the seclusion of a protestant nunnery.' (*Towers*, 3); '. . . he had been endeavouring to comfort himself with the idea that the man . . . was merely an ignorant, half-crazed, *enthusiastic* tailor, from whom decent conduct could hardly be expected.' (*Anna*, 34.) (The tailor is a religious fanatic.) (Cf. preceding item. Even more surprising as late as 1871. And for both, cf. *import* below.)

' "I cannot *find* you a carriage . . ." ' (*House*, 56) Husband to wife. It is clear from the context that *find* here means '(afford to) provide (with)'; a very old and perfectly reputable use, but seldom heard nowadays except in the phrase *all found*, 'with all necessaries provided' referring to servants' wages.

'Then there came a faint sound as of an hysterical sob, and then a *gurgle* in the throat . . .' (*Right*, 24.) 'Mrs Masters every now and then *gurgled* in her throat, and three or four times wiped her eyes.' (*Senator*, 18.) This noun and verb, I should say, are today all but always used (of human beings) jocularly. By Trollope they are always used seriously and indeed pathetically. And they are used often; at least nine times in seven novels from 1863 to 1877. I will hazard the guess that what drove them out of serious use was the 'Titwillow' song in *The Mikado* (1885), where Gilbert makes Ko-Ko sing

> He [the 'little tom-tit'] sobbed and he sighed, and a
> > gurgle he gave,
> Then he plunged himself into the billowy wave,
> And an echo arose from the suicide's grave –
> > 'Oh, willow, titwillow, titwillow!'

'. . . a *hardware dealer* . . .' (*Ray*, 27.) No American needs to be told what this means, but a good many Englishmen may not know that it means 'ironmonger' (which in turn many, perhaps most, Americans do not at least readily understand) – as Trollope invariably says elsewhere. It may be American in origin; but in *Ray*, 27 it occurs not in an American character's mouth, or any character's, but in Trollope's own language, and it is not used in a (kindly) humorous context, in which alone Trollope ordinarily (himself) uses an Americanism. (Cf. *mad* below.)

'To play a game of *hockey* in accordance with the times you must have a specially trained pony . . .' (*Fay*, 13.) This is clearly polo. *OED* dates that word from 1872, and describes the game as like hockey but played on horseback. It does *not* give it as a meaning

of *hockey*, but evidently it was called so, and continued to be sometimes called so till at least 1879.

' "I'll tell you what it is, my lord; if you are *imbecile*, I must be
active." ' (Mrs Proudie to her husband in *Chron*, 66.) *Imbecile* has
here the old meaning 'weak-charactered' (and hence 'inactive'); it
now virtually always means 'feeble-minded'. (In this sense, *ie*, it
was originally a euphemism and has suffered the usual – and
condign – fate of most euphemisms.) It would be not only un-
charitable but unjust to suppose that that is what Mrs Proudie
means, angry as she is with the poor bishop.

'He had told all . . . that it will *import* that the reader should
hear.' (*Anna*, 28.) Never today, I should say, used, as it is here, in
the sense 'be important' – a sense first recorded in *OED* from
1588 – later than most other senses, but marked there '*arch.*'. I
place it here rather than under ' "Literary" Archaisms' because
nothing in the context suggests that Trollope is using it affectedly
or facetiously.

'. . . money was *indifferent* to him.' (*Bertrams*, 41); ' ". . . I am
the last man to boast of a woman's regard, but I had learned to
think that I was not *indifferent* to Grace." ' (*Chron*, 28.) This use
(which is Trollope's ordinary but not quite invariable one) would
perplex or mislead most readers today; we should virtually always
turn the thing round, and say, 'Grace was not indifferent to me.'
According to *OED* our meaning is earlier (1519) than Trollope's
(1611).

'He had told Mrs Carbunkle [*sic*] that her *inmate* . . . was
suspected by the police . . .' (*Eustace*, 50.) The word is here (and
also in *Framley*, 14) used in the original and literal sense – 'one
who lives in the same dwelling [*inn* in the old sense] as someone
else'. (Even a dog! Cf. Keats, *The Eve of St Agnes* (1819): 'The
wakeful bloodhound rose, and shook his hide,/But his sagacious
eye an inmate [Madeline] owns.') Today, at least in the United
States, it *never* means anything but one confined in a prison or jail
(or perhaps a madhouse); a prisoner will speak of another not as
'an inmate of mine', but as 'another inmate', and a warder
(*Americanice*, 'guard') living in the prison will not speak of his
charges as *his* inmates, but as *the* inmates.

Dean Trefoil has been stricken with apoplexy, and Mr Slope
says to Bishop Proudie that ' "his *intellects* cannot possibly survive
it." ' (*Towers*, 32.) *OED*: 'Intellectual powers . . . Now *arch.* or

vulgar.' Considering the speaker and Trollope's feelings about him, I suspect that it was already vulgar in 1856.

' "Miss Laurie, pray let me make you known to my *intended.*" ' (A gentleman in *Love*, 15.) Hardly so used seriously now by well-bred people.

'It is not to be supposed that during this time he had no *intercourse* with Marion.' (*Fay*, 55); 'The man had come to her, and had asked her to be his wife, – and yet at that very moment was living in habits of daily *intercourse* with another woman whom he had promised to marry!' (*Way*, 68.) A naïve reader of our time will seriously misunderstand Trollope. *Sexual intercourse* as a euphemism for *coitus* probably existed in Trollope's day, but it was clearly only later that the euphemism itself became too explicit for the squeamish – who, in turn, by leaving out the *sexual*, succeeded in giving *intercourse* by itself (in such contexts as the quotations above) the sexual meaning.[1] (Cf. *lovers* below.)

'The battle was to be fought on the *internecine* principle, no quarter being given or taken on either side . . .' (*Thorne*, 15.) This, a favourite word with Trollope, he always uses in its earlier sense, as exemplified above. Today, at least in the United States, it is so widely understood to mean 'civil, intestine, fratricidal', that it is unwise for a writer or speaker who knows better to use the word at all. Just possibly it began with the American Civil War (1861–1865), which was internecine in both senses.

Just now, which I think today means only either 'at this moment' or 'a short time ago', is several times used in the sense 'shortly': '. . . there was his wife's brother, of whom we will say a word *just now* . . .' (*Orley*, 24); ' "I'll explain it all to you *just now.*" ' (*Framley*, 31.)

'At Hendon Hall . . . the Post Office clerk was made acquainted with Lady Frances Trafford, and they became *lovers.*' (*Fay*, 1.) All Trollope means, it is perfectly clear from the context, is that they fell in love and became engaged to be married. That is hardly what – or at least all – anyone nowadays would mean. (Cf. *intercourse* above.)

A dinner guest, late in dressing, says that his host 'would be *mad* if he delayed.' (*Orley*, 65.) ' "I was so *mad* with myself for having made you jump it." ' (*Anna*, 16.) Cf. *hardware dealer* above, though that may be American in origin, whereas this use of *mad*

1. *Precisely* the same things – both of them – had happened much earlier to *coitus*!

certainly is not; it is an American survival of a use once inter-national, like *guess* for *believe* and the like; see Chapter IV, Section 8. Trollope uses *mad* in this sense two or three more times, and, like *hardware dealer* (but unlike *guess* for *believe*) never in contexts that suggest he is thinking of it as an Americanism.

'But neither [Bishop Proudie nor Mr Slope] had the *magna-nimity* of [Mrs Proudie].' (*Towers*, 17.) The older sense 'fortitude' is hardly ever heard today, 'generosity' being the almost in-variable meaning.

'. . . all her funeral *millinery* had been displayed . . .' (*Forgive*, 7.) Trollope never uses *millinery*, 'goods from Milan', in the now restricted sense of 'women's *hats*'.

Chron, 28 has the following dialogue:

> 'Lady Jane,' she said, 'I don't think we'll *mind* stopping for lunch to-day.'
> 'Nonsense, my dear; you promised.'
> 'I think we must break our promise.'

The first speaker, obviously, means that she thinks she will not fulfil her intention of stopping, not that she will not object to stopping, as one always[1] would now. Two other examples are from *Ray*, 11 and 17: ' "I don't think I will *mind* walking to-day: you are all going so early [*ie*, too early for me to accompany you]." ' ' "We needn't *mind* discussing Miss Ray." ' (The context makes Trollope's meaning clear.)

'As these words repeated themselves . . . within Mark Robarts's mind, his mind added to them *notes of surprise* without end.' (*Framley*, 31.) Never used now, in the United States at least, for *exclamation points*, the invariable expression there.

'. . . there were some there who would have turned a very cold shoulder to Arabella had not her aunt *noticed* her . . . As long as her aunt countenanced her it was not likely that anyone at Mistletoe would be unkind to her.' (*Senator*, 40.) The meaning, which I should say is now obsolete, is clearly 'maintain social intercourse with'.

'Had Lord Lufton *offered* to her, she would have accepted at once . . .' (*Framley*, 29.) We *might* today say 'offered marriage' or 'offered his hand', but hardly 'offered' alone. On the other hand,

1. Not quite; the meaning exemplified above is preserved in certain idioms, notably *never mind*.

we do say, and say almost always, 'proposed' (without 'marriage'), which is precisely as elliptical.

'. . . there had grown up in [his] mind a feeling that his father . . . was displaying too *ostensibly* to the world . . . the things which he had effected.' (*Ralph*, 31.) *OED* calls *ostensible* for *ostentatious* obsolete by 1828. *Ralph* was finished in 1869.

'Crocker in Cumberland?'
'Certainly he was in Cumberland – unless someone *personated* him.'

(*Fay* 16.) *Impersonate* is now, I should say, almost universal in this sense.

Personification in the sense 'visualization of a person'. (*Love*, 3.) The closest meaning to this mentioned by *OED* is 'a dramatic representation, or literary description, of a person or character' – *ie*, 'a "picture" *presented*', not, as here, 'a "picture" *conceived*'.

'I . . . think . . . that . . . his having beaten Crosbie was the most *potential* cause of this affection for our hero on the part of Lady Julia.' (*House*, 52.) In the sense 'potent, powerful', according to *OED*, 'now rare'. That is an understatement. But it is a favourite word of Trollope's (I have recorded four other instances, in three novels, from 1865 to 1876) and one that he seldom if ever uses in its now current sense.

'. . . the outgoing *premier* [of Great Britain] . . .' (*Towers*, 1 – 1856.) Trollope may use this word for *Prime Minister* a few times later than this, but not often, and not, I am sure, much later. I believe it has long been positively frowned on (when the reference is to Britain or the Commonwealth – *except* of Premiers of Canadian Provinces and Australian States), even before 'the first formal mention [of *Prime Minister*]', which was, according to the *Encyclopædia Britannica*, 11th edition, apparently in 1878, and *a fortiori* long before the first strictly legal use of the term, in 1905.

'. . . the judge . . . rode every day on *sanitary* considerations . . .' (*Orley*, 29.) Now virtually restricted to cleanliness, as distinguished from other aspects of health.

'The *seminary* at Bowick had for some time enjoyed a reputation under [Dr Wortle, its founder and headmaster]; – not that he had ever himself used so new-fangled and unpalatable a word in speaking of his school.' (*Wortle*, 1). No more would most people today. It was not really 'new-fangled' – it was so used, according to *OED*, as early as 1485, without the now familiar restriction to theological seminaries; but *school* was certainly the ordinary expression, and I suspect that *seminary* was coming into commoner use for (*preparatory*) *school* – perhaps especially new ones – in the 1870s, and that Trollope thought it pretentious (as indeed it is – 'unpalatable', in fact). I have the impression that it became common earlier with reference to girls' schools than to boys', and lasted longer. Cf. *The Mikado* (1885), 'Three little maids who all unwary/Come from a ladies' seminary . . .'

'. . . young Tudor had produced a very smart paper on the merits – or demerits – of the *strike bushel*.' (*Clerks,* 1.) *OED*: 'A denomination of dry measure (not now officially recognized); usu. identified with the bushel, but in some districts equal to a half bushel, and in others to two or four bushels.' 'Demerits' indeed!

'. . . there were precious *toys* lying here and there about the [drawing] room, – very precious, but placed there not because of their price, but because of their beauty.' (*Finn,* 72.) And in *Chron,* 24, a triple portrait of a lady as all three Graces is called a toy. Now restricted, except in quasi-metaphorical senses, to children's playthings. We should probably say 'ornaments'. In *Chron,* 32, Mr Crawley uses the word in the old sense, but bitterly and sarcastically: ' "He [Dean Arabin] asked me to look at his toys [*ie,* newbound books]." '

' ". . . say the word 'Yes,' or 'No,' by *the wires*." ' (*Framley,* 18.) This expression for (*electric*) *telegraph*, which now seems quaint and rustic, is Trollope's all but universal expression from 1860 to 1877 (at least nine instances in as many novels). Oddly enough, in his earliest reference to the invention, in *Warden,* 16 (1853), he calls it the 'electric telegraph'. Once (*Claver,* 31 – 1864) we get 'by the wires' and 'by a telegram' in consecutive speeches in a dialogue, and once 'by the wires' and 'by the telegraph wires' in a single chapter (*Caldig,* 25 – 1877). In the United States, *a wire* and *to wire* are fairly common, though not so common as fifty years ago; but *the wires* I have never heard.

3. Obsolete spellings.

a. *burthen.* I have recorded this spelling six times in three novels written between 1858 and 1871. There are probably more instances, but Trollope's usual spelling is *burden.*

b. *curaçoa* for *curaçao.* I have noted the former just once (and the latter never). My impression is that it was the Englishman's usual spelling up to about 1880.

c. *landskip* for *landscape* occurs just once. I have not observed whether Trollope ever uses the latter spelling, but I am almost sure he must. The former spelling is the earlier (and etymologically sounder) one, but was certainly rare in Trollope's time.

CHAPTER IV

Non-Standard Dialects

🀫🀫🀫🀫🀫🀫

I. DEFINITION

FOR the purposes of this chapter I mean, by 'Standard English',
the normal language of educated Englishmen in Trollope's day –
and, in all essentials, since that time. It includes not only the
written language of professional writers, but also that of other
educated Englishmen, and not only their written language, but
also their usual speech (so far as that is presumably reflected with
a high degree of faithfulness in the dialogues of Trollope's
educated characters), including their familiar and colloquial speech
as well as the more studied and deliberately formal – which of
course reciprocally reflects and is reflected by written usage, both
professional and non-professional. I find the term 'Standard
English' necessary, and the definition I have given of it the only
practical one, for my present purposes; and I hope that the Scots,
the Irish, Australians, my countrymen, and members of the
Society of Friends will forgive me for dealing with Trollope's
occasional exemplification of their forms of English (including,
in some ways, my own) under the heading of this chapter.

2. THE SPEECH OF THE QUAKERS

I take this first because it is not, as all the rest are, the dialect of a
region or a class, but of a sect, and because it is 'non-standard'
only in being archaic – and archaic only in the use of the second-
person singular. It occurs in only one novel, *Fay*, and in the speech
of only one character, old Mr Fay. Mr Fay consistently uses the
second-person singular of the pronoun and the verb in the
historically correct way. He says always, *eg*, 'thou art', and never
'thee is', as Quakers, at least in America, commonly did (when

they did not altogether abandon the singular), certainly by the 1870s (when *Fay* was written). Perhaps that was not true in England; or just possibly Trollope never heard Quakers speak, but knew that they clung to the singular and supposed that they used it correctly. And Mr Fay does not go so far as William Penn did: though he addresses Lord Hampstead in the singular, he also calls him 'my lord', and not by his Christian name. And he makes no objection to his daughter's saying 'you' to himself and to everyone. She goes to the weekly Quaker meetings with him on Thursdays; but she also goes to church on Sundays with her Anglican friends.

3. ENGLISH PROVINCIAL DIALECTS

Three prefatory generalizations are to be made about these. (1) Most, but not quite all, the speakers are countrymen; a few are provincial townsmen. (2) Each dialect shares with uneducated London English one or more of a number of grammatical and phonological features: *eg, ain't* in all persons and numbers, *don't* for *doesn't*, the third-person singular verb in all persons and numbers, the double negative, *them* (adjective) for *those, as* and *as how* for the conjunction *that, as* as a relative pronoun (without *such*), the treatment of the initial *h, w* for *v*. (3) I doubt whether Trollope was nearly so well acquainted with at least some of these dialects as he was with Irish English, and consequently suspect that he was less accurate and discriminating in representing them: all the southern (especially south-western) dialects are represented as a little more similar than I think they are likely to be (or to have been), and there are some inconsistencies – even within a single speech – in the southern initial *v* and *ʒ* for *f* and *s*, and in a few other features. A geographical order of counties might be more interesting, but an alphabetical order will be more convenient for the reader.

a) 'Barsetshire'[1]

The longest specimen of 'Barsetshire' dialect is to be found in *Towers*, 39. The scene is Miss Thorne's *fête champêtre*; the inter-

1. Sadleir, p. 160, quotes from E. A. Freeman writing in *Macmillan's Magazine* for January 1883, who says there that Trollope, on a visit to the West Country in

locutors are two farmers' wives, and later the husband of one. They are complaining about the social ambitions of a third farmer's family. I transcribe only the *ipsissima verba*.

'I do tell 'ee plainly, – face to face, – she be there in madam's drawing room; herself and Gussy, and them two walloping gals, dressed up to their very eyeses [*sic*].'. . .

'But did 'ee zee 'em there, dame, did 'ee zee 'em there with your very eyes?'. . .

'And how could I do that, unless so I was there myself?'. . . 'I didn't set eyes on none of them this blessed morning, but I zee'd them as did. You know our John; well, he will be for keeping company with Betsey Rusk, madam's own maid, you know. And Betsey isn't none of your common kitchen wenches. So Betsey, she came out to our John, you know, and she's always vastly polite to me, is Betsey Rusk, I must say. So before she took so much as one turn with John, she told me every ha'porth that was going on up in the house.'

'Did she now?'. . .

'Indeed she did.'. . .

'And she told you them people was up there in the drawing room?'

'She told me she zee'd them come in, – that they was dressed finer nor any of the family, with all their nechses [*sic*] and buzoms stark naked as a born baby.'

'The minxes!'. . .

'Yes, indeed,'. . . 'as naked as you please, while all the quality was dressed just as you and I be.'. . .

'Drat their impudence,'. . .

'So says I,'. . . 'and so says my good man,'. . . ' "Molly," says he to me, "if ever you takes to going about o' mornings with yourself all naked in them ways, I begs you won't come back no more to the old house." So says I, "Thomas, no more I will." "But," says he to me, "drat it, how the deuce does she

October 1882, less than two months before his death, stated definitely that *Barsetshire was Somersetshire* – and incidentally insisted that Barchester (city and cathedral) was Winchester, transferred from Hampshire, not Wells (where the cathedral is conspicuous for its towers, as Winchester is not), nor yet Salisbury, where, Trollope says in his *Autobiography*, Chapter 5, he conceived the plot of *Warden* in the purlieus of the cathedral in May or June 1851. (Pope-Hennessy does say, p. 29, that Barchester *close* was a combination of those of Winchester and Salisbury. He does not give his evidence, but I dare say he had some.)

manage with her rheumatiz, and she not a rag on her?" ' . . .

'But to liken herself that way to folk that ha' blood in their veins,' . . .

'Well, but that warn't all neither that Betsey told. There they all swelled into madam's drawing room, like so many turkey cocks, as much as to say, "and who dare say no to us?" and Gregory [the butler] was thinking of telling of 'em to come down here, only his heart failed him 'cause of the grand way they was dressed. So in they went; but madam looked at them as glum as death.'

'Well, now,' . . . 'so they wasn't asked different from us at all then?'

'Betsey says that madam wasn't a bit too well pleased to see them where they was, and that, to his believing, they was expected to come here just like the rest of us.' . . .

'Well, with all her grandeur, I do wonder that she could be so mean,' . . . 'Did you hear, goodman?' . . . 'There's Dame Lookaloft and Bob and Gussy and the lot of 'em all sitting as grand as fivepence in madam's drawing room, and they not axed no more nor you nor me. Did you ever hear the like o' that?'

'Well, and what for shouldn't they?' . . .

'Likening themselves to the quality, as though they was estated folk, or the like o' that!' . . .

'Well, if they likes it and madam likes it, they's welcome for me,' . . . 'Now I likes this place better, 'cause I be more at home like, and don't have to pay for them fine clothes for the missus. Everyone to his taste, . . . and if Neighbour Lookaloft thinks that he has the best of it, he's welcome.' . . .

'And I'll tell 'ee what, dames,' . . . 'if so be that we cannot enjoy the dinner that madam gives us because Mother Lookaloft is sitting up there on a grand sofa, I think we ought all to go home. If we greet [see 'Scots', Section 5 below] at that, what'll we do when true sorrow comes across us? How would you be now, dame, if the boy there had broke his neck when he got his tumble?'

Two other fairly extensive examples are somewhat broader; perhaps women, especially substantial farmers' wives, tended to speak less broadly than men. The first is from *Thorne*, 1:

'I minds well,' said Farmer Oaklerath . . . 'when the squoire hisself comed of age. Lord love 'ee! there was fun going that day. There was more yale drank then than's been brewed at the big house these two years. T'old squoier was a one-er.'

'And I minds when squoire was borned; minds it well,' said an old farmer sitting opposite. 'Them was the days! it an't that long ago neither. Squoire a'nt [*sic*] come o' fifty yet; no, nor an't nigh it, though he looks it. Things be altered at Greemsbury' – such was the rural pronunciation [of *Greshamsbury*] – 'altered sadly, neebor Oaklerath. Well, well, I'll soon be gone, I will, and so it an't no use talking; but arter paying one pound fifteen for them acres for more nor fifty year, I didn't think I'd ever be axed for forty shilling.'

The second is the imaginary reply of an ostler, in *Thorne*, 15, to a question of Trollope's,[1] addressed to him, as to how he feels about the coming of the railway:

'Time was I've zee'd vifteen pair o' 'osses go out of this 'ere yard in vour-and-twenty hour; and now there be'ant vifteen, no, not ten, in vour-and-twenty days! There was the duik – not this 'un; he be-ant no gude; but this 'un's vather – why, when he'd come down the road, the cattle did be a-going, vour days on eend [*sic*]. Here'd be the tooter and the young gen'lemen, and the governess and the young leddies, and then the servants – they'd be al'ays the grandest folk of all – and than the duik and the doochess – Lord love 'ee, zur; the money did fly in them days! . . . Why, luke at this 'ere town . . . the grass be a-growing in the very streets; – that can't be no gude. Why, luke 'ee here, zur; I do be a-standing at this 'ere gateway, just this way, hour arter hour, and my heyes is hopen, mostly; – I zees who's a-coming and who's a-going. Nobody's a-coming and nobody's a-going; that can't be no gude. Luke at that there homnibus; . . . why, darn me, if maister harns enough with that there bus to put hiron on them there osses' feet, I'll – be – blowed!'

All the Barsetshire novels contain brief snatches of dialect, which would add little to what is exemplified above; but there is one that must not be omitted because it is probably the most widely known

---

1. *Sic*; Trollope here pretends that a character in a novel is a real person, whom he has met, as he now and then does, chiefly in his early novels. Cf. p. 196, n. 1.

– perhaps almost proverbial – speech in Trollope – the old brick-maker, Giles Hoggett's, to Mr Crawley in *Chron*, 61: ' "Tell 'ee what, Master Crawley; – and yer reverence mustn't think as I mean to be preaching; there ain't nought a man can't bear if he'll only be dogged. You go whome, Master Crawley, and think o' that, and maybe it'll do ye a good yet. It's dogged as does it. It ain't thinking about it." '

b) *Cambridgeshire*

The only examples of this are from the speech of only one person in one novel, *Caldig*, 3 and 23.[1]

'And so thou be-est going away from us, Mr John,' said the farmer [a tenant of John Caldigate's father] . . .

'Yes, indeed, Holt, I want to travel and see the world at a distance from here.'

'If it was no more than that, Mr John, there would be nothing about it. Zeeing the world! You young collegers allays does that. But be-est thou to come back and be Squoire o' Folking?'

'I think not, Holt; I think not. My father, I hope, will be Squire for many a year.'

'Like enough. And we all hope that, for there aren't nowhere a juster man nor the Squoire, and he's hale and hearty. But in course of things his time'll run out. And it be so, Mr John, that thou be-est going for ever and allays?.'

'I rather think I am.'

'It's wrong, Mr John. Though maybe I'm making over-free to talk of what don't concern me. Yet I say it's wrong. Sons should come arter fathers, specially where there's land. We don't none of us like it; – none of us! It's worse nor going, any one of ourselves. For what's a lease? But when a man has a freehold he should stick to it for ever and aye. It's just as though the old place was a-tumbling about our ears.'

'In course she [the Squire's wife, who has just borne a son] 'll

---

1. I regret to say that this statement, and several like it further on in this section of this chapter, may not be perfectly accurate. I may have neglected now and then to record some few short speeches in this or that provincial dialect, but certainly nothing of any considerable length or independent importance.

do well. Why not? A healthy lass, like she, if I may make so free? There ain't nothing like having them strong and young, with no town-bred airs about 'em. I never doubted as she would do well. I can tell from their very walk what sort of mothers they'll be.' Mr Holt had long been known as the most judicious breeder of stock in that neighbourhood. 'But it ain't only that, squoire.'

'The young 'un[1] will do well too, I hope.'

'In course he will. Why not? The foals take after their dams for a time, pretty much always. But what I mean is; – we all be glad you've come back from them out-o'-way parts.'

c) Cornwall

Of this there is but one and very brief specimen, in *Clerks*, 19: ' "Maybe thee be afeared? . . . and if so be thou bee'st, thee'd better bide . . . Thee bee'st for sartan too thick and weazy like for them stairs" . . .'

d) Cumberland

There are only three examples, all from the same speaker, an old lady who has recently immigrated to Australia, in *Gangoil*, 3, 11, and 12. The ellipses include no dialect.

'This is gay kind of you to run so far to see an auld woman,' . . . 'You're two bright lassies, and you're hearty,' she said. 'I'm auld, and just out of Cumberland, and I find it's hot enough, – and I'm no gude at horseback at all. I didna know how I'm to get aboot.' . . . 'Giles is ae telling me that I'm to gang aboot in a bouggey, but I do na feel sure of thae bouggeys.' . . . 'Did ye ever see rain like that?' she said . . . 'The leddies from Gangoil, Giles, have been guid enough to ride over and see me.'

'Eh me.' . . . 'There's nae Christmas games or ony games here at all, except just worrying and harrying, like sae many dogs at each other's throats.'

'We'll give one toast, Mrs Medlicot,' [Harry] said . . . 'Our

---

1. The squire with delicate courtesy here conforms his speech to his tenant's.

friends at home!' The poor lady drank the toast with a sob – 'That's vera weel for you, Mr Heathcote. You're young and will win your way hame, and see auld freends again, nae doubt; but I'll never see ane of them mair . . .'

e) Devonshire

This is found only in *Ray* (seven times) and *Right* (twice). I print only the longest from each (*Ray*, 19 and *Right*, 24).

'Mr Comfort [the vicar] has been with mamma, – about business [*ie*, whether Rachel Ray, the speaker, should encourage a suitor]; and as I didn't want to be in the way I just came over to you [a farmer's wife].'

'Thou art welcome as flowers in May, morning or evening; but thee knowest that, girl. As for Mr Comfort, – it's cold comfort he is, I always say. It's little I think of what clergymen says, unless it be out of the pulpit or the like of that. What does they know about lads and lasses?'

'He's a very old friend of mamma's.'

'Old friends is always the best, I'll not deny that. But, look thee here, my girl; my man's an old friend too. He's knowed thee since he lifted thee to pull the plums off that bough yonder; and he's seen thee these ten years a deal oftener than Mr Comfort. If they say anything wrong of thy joe there, tell me, and Sturt [her husband] 'll find out whether it be true or no. Don't let e'er a parson in Devonshire rob thee of thy sweetheart. It's passing sweet, when true hearts meet. But it breaks the heart, when true friends part.'

'If there bain't another for Nuncombe,' said Mrs Clegg's Ostler to Mrs Clegg's Boots, as Stanbury was driven off in a gig.

'That'll be young Stanbury, a-going of whome.'

'They be all for a-going to the Clock House. Since the old 'ooman took to thick there house, there be folk a-comin' and a-goin' every day loike.'

'It's along of the madam that they keeps there, Dick,' said the Boots.

'I didn't [*ie*, wouldn't] care if there'd be madam allays. They're the best as is going for trade anyhow,' said the ostler.

f) *Hampshire*

Love is set in a village in Hampshire, and contains many long speeches by Mrs Baggett, born in Portsmouth, and for many years housekeeper to a country gentleman. Her language has all the common features of uneducated grammar, but no dialectal words or indications of dialectal pronunciation. Perhaps we may imagine that her long service in a comparatively elevated situation, and constant, habitual intimate conversation with the gentleman who is her master, have removed from her speech the features peculiar to her region, though not to her class.

g) *Somersetshire*

See 'Barsetshire' above.

h) *Suffolk (specifically Bungay and its vicinity)*

This occurs only in *Way*, and occurs often, but one specimen, from Chapter 33, is so long that it will amply suffice.

One afternoon her grandfather returned from Bungay and told her that her country lover was coming to see her. 'John Crumb be a coming over by-and-by,' said the old man. 'See and have a bit o' supper ready for him.'

'John Crumb coming here, grandfather? He's welcome to stay away then, for me.'

'That be dommed.' . . . 'Why not welcome, and he all one as your husband? Look ye here, Ruby, I'm going to have an eend o' this. John Crumb is to marry you next month, and the banns is to be said.'

'The parson may say what he pleases, grandfather. I can't stop his saying of 'em. It isn't likely I shall try, neither. But no parson among 'em all can marry me without I'm willing.'

'And why should you not be willing, you contrairy young jade, you?'

'You've been a-drinking, grandfather.' . . .

'Look ye here, Ruby,' he said, 'out o' this place you go. If you go as John Crumb's wife you'll go with five hun'erd pound, and we'll have a dinner here, and a dance, and all Bungay.'

'Who cares for all Bungay, – a set of beery chaps as knows

nothing but swilling and smoking; – and John Crumb the main of 'em all? There never was a chap for beer like John Crumb.'

'Never saw him the worse o' liquor in all my life.' . . .

'It ony just makes him stoopider and stoopider the more he swills. You can't tell me, grandfather, about John Crumb. I knows him.'

'Didn't ye say as how ye'd have him? Didn't ye give him a promise?'

'If I did, I ain't the first girl as has gone back of her word, – and I shan't be the last.'

'You means you won't have him?'

'That's about it, grandfather.'

'Then you'll have to have somebody to fend for ye, and that pretty sharp, – for you won't have me.'

'There ain't no difficulty about that, grandfather.'

'Very well. He's a coming here to-night, and ye may settle it along wi' him. Out o' this ye shall go. I know of your doings.'

'What doings! You don't know of no doings. There ain't no doings. You don't know nothing ag'in me.'

'He's a coming here to-night, and if ye can make it up wi' him, well and good. There's five hun'erd pounds, and ye shall have the dinner and dance and all Bungay. He ain't a going to be put off no longer; – he ain't.'

'Whoever wanted him to be put on? Let him go his own gait.'

'If you can't make it up wi' him – '

'Well, grandfather, I shan't anyways.'

'Let me have my say, will ye, yer jade, you? There's five hun'erd pound! and there ain't ere [*sic*] a farmer in Suffolk or Norfolk paying rent for a bit of land like this can do as well for his darter as that, – let alone only a granddarter. You never thinks o' that; – you don't. If you don't like to take it, – leave it. But you'll leave Sheep's Acre too.'

'Bother Sheep's Acre. Who wants to stop at Sheep's Acre? It's the stoopidest place in all England.'

'Then find another. Then find another. That's all aboot it. John Crumb's a coming up for a bit o' supper. You tell him your own mind. I'm dommed if I trouble aboot it. Sheep's Acre ain't good enough for you, and you'd best find another home. Stoopid, is it? You'll have to put up wi' places stoopider nor Sheep's Acre, afore you're done.'

i) Surrey

Of this there is but one example, an old farmer's wife's speech in *Claver*, 3: ' "A puir feckless thing, tottering along like, – not half the makings of a man. A stout lass like she could almost blow him away wi' a puff of her mouth." '

j) Westmorland

Just two very brief examples occur, both in *Forgive*, 38, and in the mouth of the same speaker: (1) ' "Well, Mr George," said the landlord . . . , "a sight of you's guid for sair een. It's o'er lang since you've been doon among the fells." ' (2) ' "He [Mr George] was always one of them cankery chiels as never have a kindly word for man or beast," . . .'

k) Wiltshire

Only in *Vicar*, and only twice, in Chapters 3 and 52. I transcribe the first and longer of the two.

'Who be there?' said the voice of the farmer.

'Is that you, Mr Trumbull? It is I, – Mr Gilmore. I want to get round to the front of the parson's house.'

'Zurely, zurely,' said the farmer, coming forward and opening the gate. 'Be there anything wrong, about, Squire?'

'I don't know. I think there is. Speak softly. I fancy there are men lying in the churchyard.'

'I be a-thinking so, too, Squire. Bone'm was a growling just now like the old 'un' . . . 'What is't t'ey're up to? Not bugglary.'

'Our friend's apricots, perhaps. But I'll just move round to the front. Do you and Bone'm keep a look-out here.'

'Never fear, Squire, never fear. Me and Bone'm together is a'most too much for 'em, bugglars and all.'

l) Yorkshire

Ralph, 20: ' "There won't be any place of business agait[1] that [election] day." '

1. 'Open to customers.' *OED* spells it 'agate'. 'Percycross [the borough where, in *Ralph*, Sir Thomas Underwood stands for Parliament] and Beverley [where

A lodge-keeper's wife in *Bertrams*, 43:

'Be you she what sent the letter?' . . .
'Then my lord says as how you're to send up word what you've got to say.' . . .
'Yees [*sic*]. Just send up word.' . . .
'I'm telling you no more than what the lord said his ain sell. He just crawled down here his ain sell.' . . .
'I didna know nothing aboot it.' . . .
'Mither,' said the woman's eldest son, 'you'll cotch it noo.'
'Eh, lad; weel. He'll no hang me.'[1]

Trollope himself uses one Yorkshire word, *shandy*, in *Love*, 6: 'Could there be anything more moonstruck, more shandy, more wretchedly listless, than for . . . a penniless girl . . . to indulge in dreams of an impossible lover?' All the citations of this adjective given by Joseph Wright, *English Dialect Dictionary* (Oxford University Press, 1898–1905), are from Yorkshire. Several meanings were apparently current there (perhaps in different parts of the county) at different times, including 'boisterous' and 'dissipated', but the only one that clearly fits the context in the sentence quoted above is 'Visionary, empty-headed, crackbrained, half crazy'. Why this Yorkshire word popped into Trollope's head here I have not the slightest idea. Even if Yorkshire were the setting of *Love* (it is Hampshire), it would be contrary to Trollope's rigorous exclusion of dialectal words from authorial language.[2]

4. URBAN (MAINLY LONDON) UNEDUCATED AND HALF-EDUCATED

This is richly and variously illustrated, and in a large number of the novels (besides being probably both more interesting to most readers and also probably more accurately recorded by Trollope than at least some of the provincial dialects), and I give a correspondingly large number of examples.

Orley, 47. A London housemaid.

Trollope stood] were, of course, one and the same place.' (*Autobiography*, Chapter 19.) Beverley is in the East Riding.

1. The scene is laid in the North Riding 'on the borders of Westmorland'.
2. Some exceptions are mentioned under 'Scots', below.

'Did she marry at last against [her parents'] wishes?'

'Oh dear, no; nothing of that sort. She wasn't one of them flighty ones, neither. She just made up her own mind and bided. And now I don't know whether she hasn't done about the best of 'em all. Them Oliphants is full of money, they do say – full of money. That was Miss Louisa, who came next. But, Lord love you, Mr Graham, he's so crammed with gout as he can't ever put a foot to the ground; and as cross; – as cross as cross. We goes there sometimes, you know. Then the girls is all plain; and young Mr Oliphant, the son, – why he never so much as speaks to his own father; and though they're rolling in money, they say he can't pay for the coat on his back. Now our Mr Augustus, unless it is that he won't come down to morning prayers and always keeps the dinner waiting, I don't think that there's ever a black look between him and his papa. And as for Miss Madeline, – she's the gem of the four families. Everybody gives that up to her.'

Orley, 9. A commercial traveller.

'I don't want to insult no one, . . . and those who know me best, among whom I can't as yet count Mr Johnson, though hopes I shall some day, won't say it of me . . . Mr Snengkeld and Mr Gape, they're my old friends, and they knows me. And they knows the way of a commercial room – which some gentlemen don't seem as though they do. I don't want to insult no one; but as chairman here at his conwivial meeting, I ask that gentleman who says he is a solicitor whether he means to pay his dinner bill according to the rules, or whether he don't?'

Ralph, 24. A prosperous London tradesman.

'Not as I want to interfere. You're on the square, there's nothing I won't do. I ain't a-blaming you, – only stick to her. . . Only stick to her, Captain, and we'll pull through. I'll put her through her facings to-night. She's thinking of that orkard lout of a fellow just because he's standing to be a Parl'ment gent.'

Scarb, 11.

'Come, come, come! If he have more to get than I, he mush be pretty deep. There is Mishter Tyrrwhit. No one have more to get than I, only Mishter Tyrrwhit. Vy, Captain Scarborough, the little game you wash playing there, which wash a very pretty little game, is as nothing to my game wish you. When you see the money down, on the table there, it seems to be mush, because the gold glitters; but it is as noting to my little game where the gold does not glitter, because it is pen and ink. A pen and ink soon writes ten thousand pounds. But you think much of it when you win two hundred pounds at roulette.'

This is spoken by a Jewish money lender to his debtor at Monte Carlo. All but one of Trollope's Jews (except one or two who are mentioned but do not appear) are money lenders,[1] and they all speak in this way. I doubt somehow whether the representation is very accurate. It also tends to be inconsistent – in this speech, *eg*, we have both 'mush' and 'much'. The virtual absence of any Jewish characters but money lenders, all of them rapacious, the regular use of 'the Jews' meaning money lenders, and the occasional pseudo-polite 'Hebrews' all make it clear that Trollope was not free of what is (but should not be) called anti-Semitism.

Scarb, 36. The same speaker. This time he drops his *h*'s (though it must be acknowledged that in the preceding speech he had by chance little opportunity of doing so), as, however, all lower-class Londoners in Trollope, and many lower-class provincials, do.[2]

'By George!' continued Mr Hart, 'we come forward to 'elp a shentleman in his trouble and to wait for our moneys till the father is dead, and then when 'e's 'ad our moneys the father turns round and says that 'is own son is a —— [*ie*, bastard]!'[3]

1. Mr Mahomet [!] M. Moss, in *Land*, is an opera-house manager. He is an American, and revolting.
2. And in later speeches he puts in *h*'s where they don't belong. ' "Hare you a bastard, or haren't you?" ' ' "Then pay us what you h'owes us. You h'ain't h'agoing to say as you don't h'owe us." ' ' "H'angry! By George! I h'am h'angry! I'd like to pull that h'old sinner's bones h'out of the ground!" ' Why Trollope here (except at the beginning), and here only, inserts apostrophes after the false *h*'s I don't know.
3. It is odd that Trollope should here, and here only – not even in the nearly adjacent passage quoted in n. 2 above – represent this word by dashes – without even the initial letter; he consistently spells it out when he is speaking in his own words and on the rare occasions when he puts it into the mouths of gentlemen. He must have unreflectingly felt as he wrote this speech that the word was, so to speak, vulgar and indecent only in a vulgar and indecent man's mouth. It is here, as always, used in its literal, legal sense, not as an indecent and insulting figure of

Oh! it's too shocking! I 'aven't slept since I 'eard it, – not a regular night's rest. Now it's my belief that the captain 'as no 'and in it.'

Trollope's uneducated townsmen do not only speak; occasionally they write. In *Castle*, 39, *eg*, there is a letter covering two pages and not worth quoting *in extenso* but full of illiterate misspellings, most of which do not represent a non-standard pronunciation, but many of which do: *eg*, initial *h* used where it does not belong and omitted where it does, 'respictit', 'Fitsjerrals', 'comanment', 'horphand', 'a gitten', 'confounedly', 'barronnite', 'befrindin' – the writer is not only illiterate, but Irish – 'wint', 'hunraffel', 'agrebbel', 'niver', 'alivin', 'worse' (for *worth*) 'sein' (for *seeing*), 'haskin', 'fine' (for *find*), 'at presence' (for *present*), 'someat', 'a backin', 'un'. A final *s* is oddly attached to *over* meaning 're-peatedly' – ' "I was at the guvnor hovers and hovers agin." ' The grammar is almost as illiterate: ' "I new as Appy Ouse Fitsjerral was the orse as ort to win," ' ' "you was ther," ' ' "as I does hall this," ' ' "wat I has to say," ' ' "I opes," ' ' "sein as how I comes forward," ' ' "no one coodent be the wiser," ' ' "I advises you," ' ' "go there immejat," ' ' "I looks," ' ' "see as I gits someat." ' In reproducing the *speech* of the writer of this letter, Trollope uses standard *spelling* (except for the initial *h* business) so that the speaker's other actual departures from standard English pronunciation are not indicated. Probably Trollope assumed that they would be mentally and automatically supplied by his readers. He does, however, reproduce the non-standard *grammar*.

In a second illiterate letter (*Finn*, 17) Trollope forgets to make the spelling and punctuation match the grammar and style:

'Dear and Honoured Sir,
    'Bunce is getting ever so anxious about the rooms, and says as how he has a young Equity draftsman and his wife and baby as would take the whole house, and all because Miss Pauncefoot said a word about her port wine, which any lady might say in her tantrums, and meaning nothing after all. Me and Miss

---

speech. Later (*Scarb*, 60) the same speaker is given the same word, spelt out – and in addressing the 'bastard' himself (as he also is doing in the passage quoted in n. 2 above) – who has turned out to be no bastard at all.

Pauncefoot's knowed each other for seven years, and what's a word or two as isn't meant after that? But, honoured sir, it's not about that as I write to trouble you, but to ask if I may say for certain that you'll take the rooms again in February. It's easy to let them for the month after Christmas, because of the pantomimes. Only say at once, because Bunce is nagging me day after day. I don't want nobody's wife and baby to have to do for, and 'd sooner have a Parliament gent like yourself than any one else.

'Yours 'umbly and respectful,
'Jane Bunce.'

Finally, in *Fay*, 26, there is a letter not exactly illiterate, but thoroughly and amusingly vulgar. It is written by Samuel Crocker, a Post Office clerk, a snob and a social climber, who thinks he is educated and a gentleman, neither of which he is, and who has managed to force his acquaintance on Lord Hampstead. One need not understand all the background and the allusions in order to enjoy the comic stylistic mixture of the 'elegant' and the half-educated, both liberally seasoned with the equally comic substantive mixture of syncophancy and presumption.

'My dear Lord Hampstead,
'I hope I may be excused for addressing your lordship in this familiar manner. I take occasion of this happy day [Christmas Day] to write to your lordship on a message of peace. Since I had the honour of meeting you at your noble uncle's mansion, Castle Hautboy, I have considered it one of the greatest delights of my life to be able to boast of your acquaintance. You will not, I am sure, forget that we have been fellow sportsmen, and that we rode together on that celebrated run when we killed our fox just over the Airey Force. I shall never forget the occasion, or how well your lordship went over the rough country. To my mind there is no bond of union so strong as that of sport. "Up strikes little Davy with his musical horn."
'I am sure you will remember that, my lord, and the beautiful song to which it belongs. I remember, too, how, as we were riding home after the run [and when Lord Hampstead had given Crocker the choice between leaving him and being left], your lordship was talking all the way about our mutual friend,

George Roden. [Actually, Crocker did the talking, and Lord Hampstead tried in vain to stop him.]

'He is a man for whom I have a most sincere regard, both as being an excellent public servant, and as a friend of your lordship's. It is quite a pleasure to see the way in which he devotes himself to the service, – as I do also. When you have taken the Queen's shilling you ought to earn it. These are my principles, my lord . . .

'But as I was saying to your lordship about George Roden, there has something come up which I don't quite understand, which seems to have turned him against me. Nothing has ever given me so much pleasure as when I heard of his prospects as to a certain matter – which your lordship will know what I mean. [(Pure Sairey Gamp.) Roden is engaged to Lady Frances Traffle, Lord Hampstead's sister, against the will of her whole family – even including Roden's friend, the Radical and theoretically egalitarian Lord Hampstead.] Nothing could be more flattering than the way I've wished him joy ever so many times. So do I also your lordship and her ladyship, because he is a most respectable young man, though his station in life isn't so high as some people's. But a clerk in H. M. S. has always been taken for a gentleman which I am proud to think is my position as well as his.

'But, as I was saying to your lordship, something seems to have gone against him as to our mutual friendship. [Roden, who *is* a gentleman, resents Crocker's insistent harping on his engagement, of which he himself has never spoken to Crocker.] He sits there opposite and won't speak a word to me, except just to answer a question, and that hardly civil. He is as sweet as sugar to those fellows who ain't at the same desk with him as I am, – or I should think it was his future prospects were making him upsetting. Couldn't your lordship do something to make things up between us again, – especially on this festive occasion. I'm sure your lordship will remember how pleasant we were together at Castle Hautboy, and at the hunt, and especially as we were riding home together on the day. . . .

'It could have been a joke of mine; and I do joke sometimes, as your lordship may have observed. But I shouldn't think Roden would be the man to be mortally offended by anything of that sort. Anyway, I will leave the matter in your lordship's hands, merely remarking that, – as your lordship may remember, – "Blessed are the peace-makers, for theirs in the Kingdom of Heaven."

> 'I have the honour to be,
> 'My dear Lord Hampstead,
> 'Your lordship's most obedient,
> 'Very humble servant,
> 'Samuel Crocker.'

This is answered exactly as it deserves:

> 'Dear Mr Crocker,
> 'I am afraid I cannot interfere with Mr Roden, who doesn't like to be dictated to in such matters.
> 'Yours truly,
> 'Hampstead.'

5. SCOTS

The only Scots in the novels covered in this book is in one speech in *Clerks*, 8 and in several chapters of *Eustace*.[1] The first is notable for being the only instance of a gentleman not speaking Standard English: Lord Gaberlunzie says, ' "Ye maun be a puir chiel, gin ye'll be worth less than ten thoosand poond in the next market o' marriage; and ten thoosand poond is a gawcey grand heritage!" '

---

1. This does not count four Scots words (six, if we include *Gaberlunzie* and *Cantrip*, for which see Chapter V, Section 4) used once or more in Trollope's own language or in that of non-Scottish characters. (1) *Bairn(s)* is decidedly the most frequent. It occurs perhaps half a dozen times, usually, at least, in characters' language. It had a considerable vogue among the educated classes in England in Trollope's time (I suspect the influence of Balmoral), and perhaps both earlier and later, as a sentimental substitute for *child(ren)*, most often in the mouths of their parents, especially in speaking to each other. (2) *Greet* ('weep'). Though Joseph Wright's *English Dialect Dictionary*, gives this as exclusively Scots, Border-country, and Irish, Trollope puts it into the mouth of a 'Barset' (*ie*, Somerset) peasant – quite wrongly, if Wright is correct, as he almost certainly is. See 'Barsetshire', 3 *a*, above. (3) *Forby* ('besides'). This occurs once in a speech by a (non-Scottish) character in *Bertrams*, 21: ' ". . . their income will be tight enough, forby what you can do for them." ' (4) *Umquhile* ('formerly'). This, though not exclusively Scots, remained in use in Scotland (and perhaps also somewhat south of the Border) longer than elsewhere, but I believe it is now obsolete everywhere. The contexts of the two instances that I have noted make it clear that Trollope is using it rather as a literary archaism than as specifically Scots, and I therefore mention it again under that heading (Chapter V, Section 1).

All the rest occur in the speech of Andrew Gowran, Lady Eustace's steward at her country seat in Ayrshire. I give two examples: a conversation with Lady Eustace from Chapter 22, and Gowran's longest uninterrupted speech, in Chapter 54. Together they constitute about half of his utterances.

'Andy,' [Lady Eustace] said, 'I shall want to get a pony for the gentlemen who are coming to the cottage. It must be there by Tuesday evening.'

'A pownie, my leddie?'

'Yes, a pony. I suppose a pony may be purchased in Ayrshire, though of all the places in the world it seems to have the fewest of the comforts of life.'

'Them as find it like that, my leddie, needn't bide there.'

'Never mind. You will have the kindness to have a pony purchased and put into the stables of the cottage on Tuesday afternoon. There are stables, no doubt.'

'Oh, ay, there's shelter, nae doot, for mair pownies than they's ride. When the cottage was biggit, my leddie, there was nae cause for sparing nowt.' . . .

'And I needn't spare my cousin the use of a pony,' she said grandiloquently . . . 'You'll have the goodness to procure one for him on Tuesday.'

'But there ain't aits nor yet fother, nor nowt for bedding down. And wha's to tent the pownie? There's mair in keeping a pownie than your leddyship thinks. It'll be a matter of auchten and saxpence a week, will a pownie.' . . .

'Very well. Let it be so.'

'And there'll be the beastie to buy, my leddie. He'll be – a lump of money, my leddie.'

'Of course, I must pay for him.'

'He'll be a matter of – ten pound, my leddie.'

'Very well.'

'Or may be twal; just as likely.' . . .

'You must give the proper price – of course.'

'There ain't no proper price for pownies – as there is for jew'ls and sich like.' . . .

'We shall see about that afterwards.'

'Ye'll never leave him there to eat his head off there a' the winter! He'll be to sell. And the gentles'll ride him may be,

ance across the hillside, out and back. As to the grouse, they can't cotch them with the pownie, for there ain't none to cotch.' . . .

'Do you mean to tell me that my cousin cannot be supplied with an animal to ride upon?'

'My leddie, I've said nowt o' the kind. There ain't no useful animal as I kens the name and nature of as he can't have in Ayrshire – for paying for it, my leddie; horse, pownie, or ass, just whichever you please, my leddie. But there'll be a seddle –'

'A what?'

There can be no doubt that Gowran purposely slurred the word so that his mistress should not understand him. 'Seddles don't come for nowt, my leddie, though it be Ayrshire.'

'I don't understand what it is that you say, Andy.'

'A seddle, my leddie,' said he, shouting the word at her at the top of his voice – ' and a briddle. I suppose as your leddyship's cousin don't ride bareback up in Lunnon?'

'Of course there must be the necessary horse-furniture,' said Lady Eustace, retiring to the castle.

'What I saw wi' my ain twa e'es . . . I saw, and nane the less because his lairdship may nae find it jist tasteful, as your leddyship was saying. There were them twa a-colloguing, and a-seeting ilk in ither's lap a' o'er – yes, my leddy, a-keesing as females, not to say males, ought nae to keess unless thay be mon and wife – and then not amang the rocks, my leddy; and if his lairdship does nae care tell o' it, and finds it nae tasetful, as your leddyship was saying, he should nae ha' sent for Andy Gowran a' the way from Portray, jist to tell him what he wanna hear, now I'm come to tell 't to him!'

6. IRISH ENGLISH[1]

I have given about two-thirds as much space to Irish English as to all the other non-standard dialects together. This is not so much because the material is abundant as because this dialect differs

1. This section is based entirely on the first three of the Irish novels, *Macd*, *Kellys*, and *Castle*. The fourth, *Eye*, was written eleven years after Trollope had left Ireland, is set partly in England, and contains very little Irish English – and all in the mouth

more than any of the others from Standard English since it has been influenced by a foreign language, Irish Gaelic, in vocabulary, syntax and idiom, as well as in pronunciation.

Trollope was a close and loving observer of Irish speech, and on the whole, at least apparently faithful in his representation of it, but, through carelessness, far from invariably consistent, even in reporting the speech of a single character in a short conversation with the same hearers.

He must have heard a good many local varieties of Irish English, but with one possible exception (mentioned below) he did not, so far as I have observed, differentiate among them in representing them. Probably many slight differences escaped his ear. He *does* distinguish urban from rustic, and uneducated from both half-educated and educated – two distinctions that overlap. Presumably he was most familiar with the speech of the districts where he lived, though he travelled out of all of them so often and so widely that the presumption is perhaps not very strong. His first station (1841–45) was at Banagher, King's County, just across the Shannon from County Galway; his second (1845–51), at Mallow, County Cork; his third (after some time in England) at Belfast (1853–54); his last, at Donnybrook, then near and now in Dublin, where he settled in 1854. From 1857 to 1859 he was for most of the time in England or Scotland or abroad; he returned briefly to Donnybrook in 1858, but left Ireland for good (except for two brief visits in 1882) in 1859. It is indicative either of his conviction that at least rustic Irish English was pretty much of a piece or of his carelessness whether it was or not that when he wrote *Macd* (1843–45), set in Leitrim, he was living in King's, and had visited Leitrim only briefly, and that when he wrote *Kellys*

---

of a single person, a priest, whose language is only faintly Irish; the fifth, *Land*, was written twelve years after *Eye*, and, though it contains a good deal more Irish English, furnishes no considerable addition to what can be gathered about Trollope's Irish English from the first three. I know nothing of Irish English at first hand, and have throughout depended chiefly on P. W. Joyce, *English as We Speak It in Ireland* (London: Longmans, Green Ltd, 1910), Jeremiah H. Hogan, *The English Language in Ireland* (Dublin: Educational Company of Ireland, 1927), P. L. Henry, *An Anglo-Irish Dialect of Roscommon* (Dublin: Department of English, University College, 1957 – though the study was made in 1945–48). (The dialect referred to is that of Cloongregan, in the hinterland of the village of Cootehill some seven miles from Boyle in County Roscommon. It could hardly be closer to the locale of *Macd*.) *OED* and (even more) Partridge have also been very useful for vocabulary.

(1847), set in Dublin, he was living in Cork, and probably seldom visited Dublin. *Castle* is an exception; though when he began it (1859) he was living on the outskirts of Dublin, he had had (some years earlier, indeed) almost seven years' residence at Mallow, which is only a few miles away from the setting of that novel.

The *social* differences in the English that Trollope represents Irishmen as speaking are marked. The speech of the uneducated (most of them peasants) departs conspicuously from Standard English in pronunciation, grammar (in the narrow sense), syntax (including word order), idiom, and vocabulary, all of which are discussed below in turn; the speech of the urban half-educated (found chiefly in *Kellys*) departs notably from Standard English only in pronunciation; the same is true of the rustic half-educated, except under the influence of strong feeling, when they tend to lapse into peasant language; the educated (mostly but not exclusively Protestants), even those educated in Ireland instead of in England, as some of them are, only once in a while show Irish traces of any kind. To be sure, it is probable that many of them pronounced their preconsonantal *r*'s, as Irishmen of all classes and all degrees of education still commonly do, but one cannot tell from the spelling used by Trollope (who certainly did *not* pronounce his preconsonantal *r*'s).

A good example of educated speech is that of Father John McGrath, a principal character in *Macd*. His very first utterance (*Macd*, 5), to be sure, does not promise as much: his maid-servant has interrupted him at breakfast to tell him he has a visitor, and he says, 'with his mouth full', ' "Why, then, Judy . . . , bad manners to them; mayn't I eat a breakfast in peace and quiet? There was I at the widow Byrne's all night, destroyed with the cold, and now I must lose my breakfast, as well as my sleep." ' But even here, though the diction, the phrasing, and the lilt are peasant, the grammar and the pronunciation (always excepting, presumably, the business of the preconsonantal *r*) are not; and for the rest of the book, he speaks Standard English – and very good Standard English – in all respects, with only rare and trivial exceptions, even to his peasant parishioners. He must have felt uniquely at home with Judy. Father John, Trollope tells us, was, unlike most Irish priests, of good family, was educated at St Omer, and was a bookworm.

What I have called the rustic half-educated ordinarily speak, in the main, Standard English, but, as I have said, lapse into peasant speech under the stress of strong emotion. Such lapses are shown in the speech of Thaddeus Macdermot, heir of the Macdermot estate, Ballycloran. (Though the estate is now ruinously encumbered, he still ranks as a gentleman.) One example occurs at the end of a conversation of his with Father John (*Macd*, 5), Thaddeus's part of which has been (except for pronunciation) in English as standard as his collocutor's. But at the end, his feelings overcome him, and he says:

'It's little heart I have now to be saying to you what I was going to do, for my soul's sick within me, with all the throubles that are on me. An' av it warn't for Feemy [his sister] then, Father John, bad as I know I've been to her, laving her alone there at Ballycloran, with her novels and her trash, – av it warn't for her, it's little I'd mind about Ballycloran. There is them still as wouldn't let the ould man want his stirabout, and his tumbler of punch, bad as they all are to us; and for me, I'd sthrike one blow for the counthry, and then, if I were hung or shot, or murthered any way, devil a care. But I couldn't bear to see the house taken off her, and she to lose the rispect of the counthry entirely, and the name of Macdermot still on her!'

The language of this speech is hardly, if at all, distinguishable from that of the speeches of the peasants. In order to give a reasonably full impression of what these are like, I will quote one long dialogue *in extenso*. This is a conversation in *Kellys*, 6 between a lower-middle-class Dublin woman and a transplanted peasant girl, and has the special usefulness of illustrating some of the differences between urban half-educated and rustic language.

'I'm Biddy, please ma'am – from Lynch's, and I'm wanting to spake to yerself, ma'am – about Miss Anty [her mistress]. She's very bad intirely, ma'am.'

'What ails her – and why d'you come here? Why don't you go to Dr Colligan, av' she's ill; and not come knocking here?'

'It ain't bad that way, Miss Anty is, ma'am. Av' you'd just be good enough to open the door, I'd tell you in no time.'

It would, I am sure, be doing injustice to Mrs Kelly to say that her curiosity was stronger than her charity; they both, however, had their effect, and the door was speedily opened.

'Oh, ma'am!' commenced Biddy, 'sich terrible doings up at the house! Miss Anty's almost kilt!'

'Come out of the cowld, girl, in to the kitchen fire,' said the widow . . . and [Biddy] followed the woman into . . . the . . . kitchen. 'And now, tell me what it is ails Miss Anty? She war well enough yesterday, I think, and I heard more of her then than I wished.' . . .

'Oh, Misthress Kelly, ma'am, there's been disperate doings last night up at the house. We were all hearing, in the morn yesterday, as how Miss Anty and Mr Martin, God bless him! – were to make a match of it, – as why wouldn't they, ma'am? for wouldn't Mr Martin make her a tidy, dacent, good husband?'

'Well, well, Biddy – don't mind Mr Martin; he'll be bether without a wife for one while, and he needn't be quarrelling for one when he wants her. What ails Miss Anty?'

'Shure I'm telling you, ma'am; howsomever, whether it's thrue or not about Mr Martin, we were all hearing it yesther-day; and the master [Anty's brother], he war afther hearing it too, for he came into his dinner as black as tunder; and Terry says he dhrunk the whole of a bottle of wine, and then he called for the sperrits, and swilled away at them till he was nigh dhrunk. Well, wid that, ma'am, he sent for Miss Anty, and the moment she comes in, he locks to the door, and pulls her to the sofa, and swears outright that he'll murdher her av' she don't swear, by the blessed Mary and the cross, that she'll niver dhrame of marrying no one.'

'Who tould you all this, Biddy? was it herself?'

'Why, thin, partly herself it war who tould me, ma'am, and partly –; you see, when Mr Barry war in his tantrums, and dhrunken like, I didn't like to be laving Miss Anty alone wid him, and nobody nigh, so I and Terry betook ourselves nigh the door, and partly heard what was going on; that's the thruth on it, Mrs Kelly; and, afther a dale of rampaging and scolding, may I niver see glory av' he didn't up wid his clenched fist, strik [*sic*] her in the face, and knock her down – all for one as 'av he wor a dhrunken blackguard at a fair!'

'You didn't see that, Biddy?'

'No, ma'am – I didn't see it; how could I, through the door?

– but I heerd it, plain enough. I heerd the poor cratur fall for dead amongst the tables and chairs – I did, Mrs Kelly – and I heerd the big blow smash agin her poor head, and down she wint – why wouldn't she? and he, the big blackguard, stricking at her wid all his force! Well, wid that, ma'am, I rushed into the room – at laist, I didn't rush in – for how could I, and the door locked? – but I knocked agin and agin, for I was afeard he would be murthering her out and out. So, I calls out, as loud as I could, as how Miss Anty was wanting in the kitchen: and wid that he comes to the door, and unlocks it bould as brass, and rushes out into the garden, saying as how Miss Anty war afther fainting. Well, in course I goes in to her, where he had dragged her upon the sofa, and thrue enough, she war faint indeed.'

'And did she tell you, Biddy, that her own brother had trated her that way?'

'Wait, Mrs Kelly, ma'am, till I tell yer how it all happened. When she comed to herself – and she warn't long coming round – she didn't say much, nor did I; for I didn't just like then to be saying much agin the masther, for who could know where his ears were? – perish his sowl, the blackguard!'

'Don't be cursing, Biddy.'

'No, ma'am; only he must be cursed, sooner or later. Well, when she comed to herself, she begged av' me to help her to bed, and she went up to her room, and laid herself down, and I thought that at any rate it was all over for that night. When she war gone, the masther he soon come back into the house, and begun calling for the sperrits again, like mad; and Terry said that when he tuk the biling wather into the room, Mr Barry war just like the divil – as he's painted, only for his ears. After that Terry wint to bed; and Judy and I weren't long afther him, for we didn't care to be sitting up alone wid him, and he mad dhrunk. So we turned in, and we were in bed maybe two hours or so, and fast enough, when down came the misthress – as pale as a sheet, wid a candle in her hand, and begged me, for dear life, to come up into her room to her, and so I did, in coorse. And then she tould me all – and, not contint with what he'd done down stairs, but the dhrunken ruffian must come up into her bed-room and swear the most dreadfullest things to her you iver heerd, Mrs Kelly. The words he war afther using, and the things he said, war most horrid; and Miss Anty wouldn't for her dear life, nor for all the money in Dunmore, stop another night, nor another day in the house wid him.'

'But, is she much hurt, Biddy?'

'Oh! her head's cut, dreadful, where she fell, ma'am; and he shuck the very life out of her poor carcase; so he did, Mrs Kelly, the ruffian!'

'Don't be cursing [!], I tell you, girl. And what is it your misthress is wishing to do now? Did she tell you to come to me?'

'No, ma'am; she didn't exactly tell me – only as she war saying that she wouldn't for anything be staying in the house with Mr Barry; and as she didn't seem to be knowing where she'd be going, and av' she be raaly [*sic*] going to be married to Mr Martin – '

'Drat Mr Martin, you fool! Did she tell you she wanted to come here?'

'She didn't quite say as much as that. To tell the thruth, thin, it wor I that said it, and she didn't unsay it; so, wid that, I thought I'd come down here the first thing, and av' you, Mrs Kelly, wor thinking it right, we'd get her out of the house before the masther's stirring . . . I hope I warn't wrong, ma'am, in coming down and throubling you so arly? I thought maybe you'd be glad to befrind Miss Anty . . .'

'No, Biddy – for a wondher, you're right, this morning. Mr Barry won't be stirring yet?'

'Divil a stir, m'am! The dhrunkenness won't be off him this long while. And will I go up, and be bringing Miss Anty down, ma'am?'

'Wait a while. Sit to the fire there, and warm your shins . . . I must go up wid you myself, and ask yer misthress down, as she should be asked. They'll be telling lies 'av she don't lave the house dacently, as she ought.'

'More power to you thin, Mrs Kelly, this blessed morning, for a kind good woman as you are, God bless you!' whimpered forth Biddy, who, now that she had obtained her request, began to cry, and stuff the corner of her petticoat into her eyes.

We may now proceed to deal with the features of Irish English (most of them illustrated in the passages above) under the headings of pronunciation, grammar (in the narrow sense), syntax and word order, idiom, and vocabulary.

A. PRONUNCIATION

Modern[1] Irish English was imported into Ireland in the seventeenth century,[2] and it preserves some features of the pronunciation of seventeenth-century English that lasted even in England into the eighteenth century and sporadically even into the early nineteenth. Of these the four chief ones are as follows: (1) 'ay' (in some words) where Standard English now has 'ee'. (2) 'eye' where Standard English now has 'oy'. (3) 'ahr' for Middle English 'air' (with retained *r*) where Standard English now has 'uh(r)', usually spelt *er* (though Standard English preserves the pronunciation 'ah(r)' in *clerk* and *sergeant* – the latter even in the United States; in *parson* (differentiated in meaning and spelling from *person*, which was earlier pronounced in the same way); in the quasi-slang *varsity* (this also in the United States); and in many family and place names). (And cf. the name of the letter *r*, and *Barn(e)y* as the nickname for *Bernard*.) 'Air', spelt *er*, became 'ahr' in London English in the fifteenth century, and the commonest words (*eg, sterre* and *bern(e)*, which became *star* and *barn*) came to be spelt *ar* (except, again, in *clerk* and *sergeant* – but cf. *Clark(e)* and *Sargent*) then or in the sixteenth. Words (all 'learned') of later introduction from Latin were spelt, as they have continued to be, *er*, and probably pronounced 'air' (with retained *r*) and later 'uh(r)'. This pronunciation has been restored, in Standard English, by analogy with most earlier words pronounced 'air' that escaped the spelling change to *ar*. (4) '-in' ' (or '-en') for the suffix *-ing*.

(1) 'ay' for 'ee'. Middle English spelling denoted two distinct

1. One MS (Harley 913 in the British Museum) of *c.* 1300 containing sixteen poems, probably written or at least collected at Kildare, testifies to the existence then of a distinctive Irish English, but it seems to have died out, and not to have been the ancestor of modern Irish English. See G. L. Brook, *English Dialects* (London: Deutsch, 2nd ed. 1965), pp. 111, 112.
2. This should remind us that Irish English differs from provincial English dialects (and Scots) not only in being heavily influenced by a (practically) unrelated language, but in having split off from Standard English, and at a comparatively recent date, whereas the others have existed as independent entities continuously since at least not long after the Anglo-Saxon invasion of Britain in the fifth century – some of them probably from even before it; no less continuously than modern Standard English, which is just as properly called a dialect – specifically, the dialect of London – as they are. This has, to be sure, unlike them, become, from a local dialect, a class dialect in speech, and then the national standard literary dialect in writing; all literate speakers of English write it, and many of them (in all parts of England) speak it, or something very like it (or try to or think they do).

long vowels by *e* (often *ee*). One, called 'close *e*', /e:/ was approximately the same as modern 'ay'; the other, called 'open *e*' /ɛ:/ was pronounced with the front of the tongue slightly lower – approaching the position of the *a* in modern English *hat*, but still closer to that of the close *e*. In modern Standard English, with two or three exceptions, these two sounds have fallen together into /i:/. In Ireland, however, and in England up into the eighteenth century, only the close *e* underwent this development, whereas the open *e* became close *e* – *ie*, 'ay'; *eg*, 'spake', 'plaze', 'dacent', and 'crater' above. (There is one instance of a socially ambitious Irishwoman's 'overcorrecting' this pronunciation: ' "He's managed to get you a lovely steak . . . ," said Fanny [inn-keeper's daughter and barmaid], pronouncing the word as though it were written "steek".')

(2) 'eye' for 'oy'. The only example above happens to be 'biler', but the feature is at least nearly universal. The most frequent example is probably 'jine'.

(3) 'ahr' for Middle English 'air' (modern Standard, 'uh(r)'). This happens to be illustrated above only by 'arly', 'war', and 'warn't'. But the feature is universal; common examples are 'sartin', 'sarvint', 'itarnal', 'consarn(ed)', ' 'arth', ' 'arn' (for *earth* and *earn*), 'parfict', and 'varmin(t)'.

(4) '-in' ' (or '-en') for *-ing* (in the present participle and the gerund). To judge from Trollope's spelling, his Irish said regularly '-ing'; he 'drops the *g*' (as it is inexactly described) in only a few places. I feel almost certain, however, that his Irish regularly did, as the uneducated Irish (and English and Americans) still do. The natural development everywhere is '-in' ' (or '-en') the restoration of '-ing' is a nineteenth-century spelling pronunciation. Trollope very probably himself at least usually said '-ing', but '-in' ' (or '-en') must have been common in his day not only among the uneducated, but also among people from the opposite end of the educational, or perhaps rather social, scale; indeed, 'huntin', shootin', 'n' fishin' ' can still occasionally be heard from them. Trollope was, I take it, familiar enough with *-ing* in writing for '-in' ' in speech in England for it seldom to occur to him to write '-in' ' (or '-en') in reproducing Irish speech. In somewhat the same way, he only now and then writes 'me' for unstressed *my*, but I think Irish peasants said it regularly – as many Englishmen of all classes did, probably including Trollope himself. Until fifty years ago, at least, it could still be heard from old Shakespear-

ian actors, and if 'me lord' and 'me lady' are not, a development of them – 'm' lord' and 'm' lady' – certainly is.

The preceding features are Irish survivals of earlier general English usage; those that follow are at least for the most part Irish developments. (I continue the series of numbers begun above.)

(5) Two of these Irish developments, at least, are transfers from Gaelic. They are (a) the *usual* writing of 'th' for 't' and of 'th' (or, less commonly, 'dh') for 'd' before *r*, either vocalic (usually spelt *er*) or consonantal, and (b) the *occasional* writing of 't' or 'd' for 'th'. In modern Standard English, *t* and *d*, though commonly called dentals, are not dentals, but alveolars; *ie*, they are produced by the tip of the tongue just above and behind the upper front teeth – the region called the alveolus. In most other languages (at least European ones), including Gaelic, *t* and *d* are true dentals; *ie*, they are produced by the tip of the tongue against the edges of the upper front teeth (usually also touching the lower front teeth lightly). The two sounds /θ/ and /ð/ written 'th' in English (as in *thin* and *then*) are produced in the same way, but they are fricatives not stops. In short, English has alveolar stops and dental fricatives; Gaelic has dental stops but no dental (*or* alveolar) fricatives. The result is (a) that the native speaker of Gaelic, in speaking English, tends to substitute his native dental stops for *both* alveolar stops *and* dental fricatives, and (b) that the native speaker of English tends to hear the *dental* stops substituted for *alveolar* stops as fricatives, and (though less commonly) the dental *stops* substituted for *dental fricatives* as stops, and hence, in trying to write Irish English, often writes 'th' for 't' and 'd' (or sometimes 'dh' for 'd'), and (though less commonly) 't' for the sound in *thin* and 'd' for that in *then*. Trollope makes the latter substitutions only sporadically, and much less often than he makes the former; thus he never, I believe, writes, as many English writers, particularly earlier ones, do, 'dis', 'dat', 'den', 'dere', 'dey', etc., and rarely 'dese' and 'dose' – though he usually writes 'wid'. Either he did not want to clutter up the page, or, more probably, he *usually* apprehended the substitute for 'th' as closer to 'th' than to *t* or *d*, especially when initial, and, to a lesser degree, medial. On the other hand, when *t* or *d* is followed by *r* (consonantal or vocalic), he most of the time writes 'th' for 't', and 'th', or, less often, 'dh', for 'd', *eg*, above, 'throubles', 'sthrike', 'murther', 'betther', 'masther', 'afther', 'murdher', 'dhrame', 'dhrunk(en)', 'misthress',

'thruth', 'wondher'. That is, when *t* and *d* are followed by *r* (spelt *er* when vocalic), Trollope *always* apprehended the substitute as 'th' (in both values), though he now and then forgot to *write* it; cf. above 'trash', 'tunder' (where he perversely does *not* make the substitution he usually makes and, by compensation, as it were, *does* make the one he usually does *not* make), 'tantrums', 'stricking', 'dragged', 'trated'. But these are mere careless inconsistencies. It is not surprising that Trollope, or any native speaker of Standard English, should be uniquely likely to apprehend the dental stops followed by *r* as fricatives; for *r* is a fricative, and, so to speak, tends to infect the preceding stop.

(6) Short *i* for short *e*. This is especially common before nasals, but occurs elsewhere. Some examples above are 'intirely', 'wint', 'contint', 'befrind', and 'disperate'.

(7) 'ou' and 'ow' for long *o* before *l*. 'Ould,' 'cowld,' and 'tould' alone appear above, but all words containing the sequence almost always have the 'ou' or 'ow' spelling too.

(8) A multitude of miscellaneous words, most of them not illustrating any general principle, and only some of them exemplified above. Typical instances are 'harum', 'coorse', 'ketch', 'yz' (for *yes*), 'mortial', 'jist', 'fust', 'tuk', 'shuck', 'leddy', 'oncet', 'saxpence' (oddly enough, *penny* and *pence* are never 'pinny' and 'pince'), 'fur' (for *far*), 'p'lice', 'b'lieve', 'ongineer', 'heerd', 'widdy', 'sperrits', 'forrard', 'hoss', 'kilt' (for *killed*), 'ax(ed)' (for *ask(ed)*, 'st(h)ri(c)k', 'afeard' – and dozens more. Some of these, of course, are not peculiarly Irish. On the other hand, the pronunciation of *if* as [əv] is characteristic of Irish English. Trollope represents it by *av*, with or without a mysterious apostrophe, sometimes before and sometimes after.

He now and then falls into two traps always awaiting the writer of regional (or substandard) dialects. (1) Once in a while he makes (at least half-educated) Irishmen *write* Irish English – 'sthrong' and 'throuble' in letters, and 'lodging and enthertainment' on an inn sign. (2) Somewhat oftener he pointlessly uses 'phonetic' spellings for words pronounced identically (except for the pre-consonantal *r*) in Irish and Standard. 'Shure(ly)' (see above) is much the commonest of these, and all but universal; others that appear now and then (some only once) are 'honer' (and, more surprisingly, 'honor'), 'tho' ', 'vittles', 'rispect' and the like, 'inisheated', 'morgidges', and 'blagguard' (but usually 'blackguard').

Trollope never himself makes fun of Irish pronunciation, though he makes three of his educated characters do so – once 'rints' and twice 'ay' for 'ee'. One example (including also a kind of bull) is funny enough to quote:

'O'Leary was seen walking down Regent Street with a parson . . . Phil Mahon saw him, and asked him who his friend in the choker was. "Is it my friend in black you mane?" says [O'Leary], "thin, my frind was the Honourable and the [*sic*] Reverend Augustus Howard, the Dane." "Howard the Dane," says Mahon, "how the duce [*sic*] did any of the Howards become Danes?" "Ah, bother!" said [O'Leary], "it's not the Danes of Schwaden [!] I mane, at all, man; but a rural Dane of the Church of England!" '

B. GRAMMAR (IN THE NARROW SENSE)

In uneducated speech, the third-person-singular present of the verb is almost always used with subjects in both numbers and all persons. An important exception to this is *be*, which, in the present, follows Standard use (but see *ain't* below). In the frequent 'thim is' (for *those are*, but not for *they are*), the objective for the nominative is a translation of an illogical but idiomatic Gaelic use. (The corresponding uses of *them* in substandard English outside of Ireland are presumably independent developments.) In the preterite, the plural verb ('war', 'wor', 'were') is usual also with a singular subject. *Ain't* is used with both numbers and all persons by the uneducated, but also once in a while by the educated as well except for the third-person singular. *Don't* for *doesn't* is usual among the uneducated, but now and then appears also among the educated. Neither of these is peculiarly Irish; see Chapter I, c. 2, a) and c). *Him and me* for *he and I* is fairly common in peasant speech; *between him and I* somewhat less so. These too of course are universal substandard, as are the very common *as* and *as how* for *that* (conj.) and *as* (without *such*) as a relative pronoun.

C. SYNTAX

Several frequently occurring syntactic features are all literal translations from Gaelic:

(1) *To be after doing.* This familiar Irish English construction is oftener misinterpreted and misused by the non-Irish than not. It properly means 'to have (*just*) done' (a '*recent* perfect'), *not* 'to be doing', and still less 'to be about to do'; and Trollope did not learn this fact till part way through his first Irish novel (and did not always remember it later). He misuses it, *eg*, in ' "Denis McGoverty is afther going to get married . . ." ' (*Macd*, 5), but correctly, *eg*, in ' "I am afther taking a little [punch] just now . . ." ' (*Macd*, 13.) Thereafter he ordinarily uses it correctly, but once in a while lapses, *eg*, in ' ". . . we did not . . . know whether yer honer'd be afther beginning [to have us dig] at the top or the bothom [of the hill]." ' (*Castle*, 17.) Instances of both the correct and the incorrect uses are sometimes found in the speech of a single person; *eg*, in the long dialogue quoted above, Biddy says ' ". . . he war afther hearing it too, for he come into his dinner as black as tunder . . ." ' (correct) and ' "The words he war afther using, and the things he said, war most horrid . . ." ' (incorrect).

(2) *. . . and he doing.* This would be, but for the *and*, almost an absolute phrase. An instance above is ' "down she wint – why wouldn't she? and he . . . stricking at her wid all his force!" '

(3) Expletive *it's* at the beginning of a clause. Two instances from *Macd*, 5 will illustrate this: ' "It's little heart I have" ' for 'I have little heart', and ' "It's little I'd mind" ' for 'I'd mind little'. It is especially common with the progressive form of the verb (cf. (5) below): ' "Maybe it's wanting tay in the shop he is." ' (*Kellys*, 6.)

(4) Initial position of predicative adjective. A typical instance is ' "hard it was upon them" ' for 'it was hard upon them' (*Macd*, 1; in the first piece of Irish English Trollope wrote).

(5) Tendency to use progressive instead of simple form where Standard uses the latter (especially in the present). This is illustrated no fewer than nine times in the long passage above alone.

D. IDIOM

The following list is far from exhaustive. All the items in it but the first are, like the syntactical uses just above, literal translations from Gaelic.

(1) As in most popular spoken dialects outside of southeastern England, *will* is universal in all but educated speech for *shall* in the first person of the future declarative. But *will I* for *shall I* in questions appears to be peculiarly Irish, *eg*, from above ' "will I go up . . .?" '.

(2) Unidiomatic use of prepositions. Some examples, all in *Macd*, 5, above, are ' "all the throubles that are on me" ', ' "the name of Macdermot still on her" ', and ' "I couldn't bear to see the house taken off her" '.

(3) *This day* for *today*. Nearly universal.

(4) *In it* for *in the house*, especially *in this house*. Extremely common throughout.

(5) *He* for *my husband*, *eg*, Irish peasant woman of her husband (who has not been called that, or by his name), in *Kellys*, 33, ' "She warn't that way when he went away." ' This use is related to *himself* meaning 'the master of the house', of which I have seen, but carelessly neglected to record, instances in Trollope's Irish novels.

(6) 'Intirely', especially at the end of a sentence, for *indeed* or *decidedly* or the like – *eg*, in the first speech in the long dialogue above: ' "She's very bad intirely, ma'am." '

E. VOCABULARY

The following list, unlike the one just preceding, is at least close to exhaustive. It is divided into two parts, 1, Gaelic words, and 2, English words used in Irish senses. Perhaps unexpectedly, 2 is longer than 1. The words are italicized and alphabetized. Single quotation marks (only) around a word (or phrase containing it) indicate (not necessarily exclusive) occurrence in Trollope's own language.

1. GAELIC WORDS

' "Kathlees, *agra* . . ." ' (Spoken by man to barmaid.) My love.

' "Well, *alanna*, how's yourself?" ' (Spoken to young woman.) My child.

' "*Arrah*, nonsense, man! . . ." ' An expostulation, of unknown etymology, but Gaelic, and meaning something like 'oh, really, now', or 'come, now', or 'come off it!'

' "You'll not be so long, *avick* . . ." ' Priest to male parishioner, *Macd*, 12. 'My son.' Also *avich* (*Kellys*, 5).

'. . . a small *boreen* or path . . .'

' ". . . there war no use in letting every little *bostthoon* see her crossing with a lot of baggage . . ." ' 'A worthless, spiritless fellow.'

'*dudheen*'. 'A short clay tobacco pipe.'

'. . . donkeys carrying turf . . . in double *kishes* . . .' 'Baskets.'

' ". . . *musha*, thin, can't you be quiet with the big horse?".' Literally, 'if it be so', but commonly used like *what of it?*

' "*Ochone, ochone*, and it's ruined we'll be . . ." ' A lamentation, of unknown etymology, but Gaelic; equivalent to *alas*. Also *o-hone, o-hone*. (Apparently at least usually doubled.)

'*potheen*'. Illicitly distilled whiskey. (If Scotch were referred to, I should write 'whisky'.)

'. . . Denis looked on [them] as paupers and *rapparees*.' *OED*, 'Originally a short pike; then an Irish pikeman or irregular soldier; then an Irish bandit, robber, free-booter.' But Trollope's meaning here seems to be nothing worse than 'good-for-nothing', or at worst 'rascal'.

' "*shebeen (shop)*" '. An unlicensed public house; an illicit still cabin.

' "*spalpeen*" '. *OED*, 'Originally a labourer, especially agricultural; then a rascal [so used in Trollope]; then a youngster.'

' ". . . not that I care a *thrawneen* for him and his company." ' A long slender grass stalk. (Cf. Standard *straw*.)

2. ENGLISH WORDS

' "Father John, there's Denis McGovery wanting to see yer riverence, below then." People in Connaught always call the hall, door, and passage "below"; the parlour, or sitting room, "*above*"; though, in nine cases out of ten, they are on the same floor.' (*Macd*, 5.) And later in the same novel, 'It will be remembered that the "above" and "below" in the priest's house were only terms of compliment.'

' "*Begad*" '. Obsolete in England but still current in Ireland at least in Trollope's time. *Not* peasant use; cf. *begorra, by Dad, Egad*, and *faix* below.

' *"Begorra"* '. Unlike *begad*, a peculiarly Irish euphemistic distortion of *by God*. Peasant use.

' *"below"* '. See *above* above [!].

' *"By Dad"*.' Like *begad* above, *qv*, and cf. *begorra* above and *Egad* and *Faix* below.

'*car*'. A carriage (of any kind).

An Irish gentleman (*Castle*, 15) addresses his grown son as 'my darling', and Father John (*Macd*, 7) so addresses a grown man (a Protestant, to boot); and in *Kellys*, 1, an onlooker shouts to the defendants in a political trial, ' "Success to every mother's son of you, my darlings!" ' (Cf. Chapter II, 4, a.)

' *"Egad"* '. Like *begad*, *qv*, and cf. *begorra*, *by Dad*, and *faix*.

'He . . . had heard through the servants that she was ill – very ill – "not *expected*", as the country people call it . . .'

' *"Faix"* '. A very frequent asseverative or oath in the mouths of peasants, ordinarily at the beginning of a sentence, and commonly followed by *and*. A euphemistic distortion of *faith*, which only the educated Irish use, the peasants regarding it as offensively profane; almost all their oaths are similarly disguised. Cf. *begad*, *begorra*, *by Dad*, and *Egad*.

' ". . . hauling and pulling like a *gossoon* at a pig's hind leg." ' *OED* gives this as '*chiefly* [italics mine] Anglo-Irish', defines it as a lackey, derives it from French *garçon*, and dates it from 1684. French nasalized *-on* was regularly anglicized as *-oon* in seventeenth-century spelling; cf. *saloon*. The absence of *r* from the first syllable of *gossoon* makes me think that it originated in southern England.

' "There are only a few *gripes*" – Irish for small ditches . . .' See *OED*, 'Bial. var. of GRIP sb.²' This *OED* now classifies as 'Only'.

' "I don't know that they ever said death or murder; av they were going to hole [*qv*] a chap, it's giving him his quiatus or *gruel* they'd be talking about." '

' ". . . we'll *hole* him till there ar'nt a bit left in him to hole." ' Now, for the benefit of the ignorant, I may say that, "holing a man," means putting a bullet through him.'

'An *inside-covered car* [elsewhere 'inside car'] is an equipage much given to shaking, seeing that it has a heavy top like a London cab, and that it runs on a pair of wheels. It is entered from behind, and slopes backward. The sitter sits sideways . . .'

'. . . a one-horse car – or *jingle*, as such conveniences were then called in the south of Ireland.'

' ". . . and there'll be *kidneys* biled . . ." ' *OED*, 'An oval variety of potato (1796).'

'. . . in Ireland a *schooling-match* means the amusement of teaching your horse to jump.'

' "*sib*" '. Akin.

'. . . a *squireen* of three or four hundred a year . . .' This is of course the English word *squire*, but plus the Gaelic diminutive suffix *-een* (of which several examples occur in section E. 1 above).

(Spoken to a murderer.) ' ". . . shure, you're betther off still than the gay man you *stretched* the other night." ' Killed.

' "*Tare an' ages!*" ' For *tare*, see next entry; *ages*, Partridge suggests, is for *aches*. This is much more possible – and probable – than it may seem. The noun was till into the eighteenth century pronounced 'aitch' and spelt *ache*; the verb, pronounced 'ake', and so spelt. Later English adopted the spelling of the noun, and the pronunciation of the verb, for both parts of speech. The *aches* refer blasphemously to Christ's sufferings.

' "*Tear and 'ouns* Misther Lord Chief Justice! . . . and are ye niver going to open thim big doors ?" ' (*Kellys*, 1.) *Tear* (cf. *tare* in the preceding entry) is pretty certainly (Christ's) *tears* (though the absence of the final *s* is puzzling), and *'ouns* quite certainly *wounds*.

A man engaged to be married is urged to set up an inexpensive household, ' "and not to be *taring* [*sic*] *and tatthering* away, as av' money had no eend [*sic*] . . ." ' (*Kellys*, 8.) Partridge quotes Goldsmith (significantly), 1766, as writing 'tatter a kip' in the sense 'wreck a brothel'. In the passage from *Kellys* the whole expression seems to mean 'living extravagantly and perhaps riotously'. In a later chapter (27) we have ' ". . . there'll be tearing and fighting, and tatthering about that money . . ." ' Here the sense is closer to 'making a row'. Goldsmith's sense is closer to the latter in Trollope than to the former, but the two are not far apart.

'. . . earning their pittance of "*yellow meal*". . .' Applied by the Irish peasants (who pronounced it 'yally male') to the maize meal imported for them during the potato famine.

There are a few instances of Irish bulls, or something nearly allied. Only the first is in indirect discourse:

A witness in a breach-of-promise case has, for no good reason, 'a very strong objection to inform the jury whether he was engaged [to be married] . . . whereupon it was decided that the witness need not answer the question, as he could not be called on to criminate himself.' (*Macd*, 28.)

A peasant woman says of her approaching marriage after her collocutor has said that the woman's husband-to-be is a hard-working man who will never let the (as yet, of course, wholly supposititious) children starve, ' "Oh, the children, the little dears! it's of them I'm thinking. God knows, it's chiefly along of them as makes me do it . . ." ' (*Macd*, 8.)

' "I'll tell them that it isn't Betsy Cane's cow, who wouldn't have the calf, though she was engaged." ' (*Macd*, 5.)

' "She was my favourite sister, Doctor Colligan – that is, I had no other." ' (*Kellys*, 23.)

' "Poor cratur! . . . it's all up with her now; the Lord be praised for all his mercies. She's all as one as gone, glory be to God and the Blessed Virgin." ' (*Kellys*, 23.)

(Said of famine victims.) ' "Glory be to God, the poor creatures!" ' (*Castle*, 17.)

Of what are possibly recognitions of local differences, apart from differences between urban and rural, I have observed very few. They all occur in *Castle* only, and, for what they are worth, distinguish the dialect of Cork from those of Leitrim (*Macd*) and Dublin and its vicinity (*Kellys*). (1) 'Leddy' for *lady*. (2) 'Yz' for *yes*. (3) 'Uz' for *us*. (4) 'Yez' for *ye* or *you* – but several times both forms are found in the same sentence – 'yez' objective only, but so also *ye* sometimes.

Only one character (a very minor one) is represented as knowing no English. Trollope gives a translation of a short conversation involving him, saying that it was in Gaelic – but translating it into *Irish* English! The only Gaelic phrase (Trollope italicizes it, unlike the words in E. 1 above) that appears is the following (*Macd*, 3): ' "By dad, if he'd take the house, and leave the ground, he's my welcome, and *ceade mille faltha*, Pat." ' This phrase, as many visitors to Ireland know, means 'a hundred thousand welcomes'. Trollope's spelling may have been current in his time, but the spelling according to the present-day official orthography is '*céad míle fáilte'* – pronounced approximately, I am reliably informed, 'kaid meeluh falltyuh'.

7. AUSTRALIAN[1]

Australian English is found in only two novels, *Caldig* and *Gangoil*, and is exemplified in them only by vocabulary. The words are italicized and alphabetized.

'. . . Jerry slowly . . . brought forth a modicum of spirits, which he called *Battle-Axe*, but which are supposed to be brandy.' Pretty certainly not made from grapes. References to its potency are frequent.

'During all this [conversation] . . . there was a large portion of the art which in the colony is called *"blowing."* Jerry, Boscobel, and Nokes all boasted, each that on the first occasion he would give Harry Heathcote such a beating that a whole bone should hardly be left in the man's skin.'

'. . . *"buggies,"* – so always called in the bush, open carriages on four wheels . . .'

The Bush. '. . . according to common Australian parlance, all sheep stations are in the bush, even though there should not be a tree or shrub within sight. They who live away from the towns live a "bush life." Small towns, as they grow up, are called bush towns – as we talk of country towns. The "bush," indeed, is the country generally . . . There are Australian pastures which consist of plains in which not a tree is to be seen for miles; but others are forests, so far extending, that their limits are almost unknown.'

Chum. A fellow worker; but a *'new* chum' is a recent immigrant, and not necessarily a fellow worker.

Damper. OED, *'Australia.* 'A kind of cake or bread made, for the occasion, of flour and water and baked in hot ashes. 1833.'

Heathcote has derided his hand, Jocko, for almost falling off his horse in jumping a fence. ' "Why don't you sit in your saddle, you stupid young *duffer*?" Jocko replies, ' "Sit in my saddle! Why don't he jump proper? . . . I don't know that I'm a duffer. Duffer, indeed! My word!" ' *Duffer* in entered in *OED* in the sense 'an incompetent' as colloquial or slang, first recorded in 1842. It has

1. Trollope picked up his knowledge of Australian English chiefly during his first visit down under, from July 1871 to November 1872. He may have added something during his later but very brief visit, from June to August 1875.

since, as everyone knows, become (informal) Standard English. But Jocko's resentment of the epithet seems a little excessive. The reason is possibly that the word had Australian overtones: Partridge says of it, 'In Australia, a cattle-stealer (or illicit brander); . . . from 1870, though unrecorded before 1889.'

Free-selector. See *Squatter.*

'There was always "*grub*" [*ie*, a meal] at one, and "grub" at seven, and "grub" at eight in the morning.' Now commonly, I think, 'food' generally rather than 'a meal'.

'In colonial phrase he was a "*lag*," – having been transported; but this was many years ago . . . ; and he had now been a free man for more than thirty years.'[1]

'. . . the owner of the [gold mine] took them through the crushing-mill attached, [and] showed them the stone or *mulloch*, as it was thrust into the jaws of the devouring animal . . .' *OED*, "Mullock [*sic*] . . . late ME . . . 1. Rubbish, refuse matter. Now only *dial*. 2. *Austral.* Rock which does not contain gold; also, the refuse from which gold has been extracted [.] 1864.'

' "In the name of charity, give me a *nobbler*." ' A glass of spirits – especially or perhaps only 'brandy' (see *Battle-Axe*) and water.

'Mrs Heathcote had twisted round Harry's hat a long white scarf, called a *puggeree*, – though we are by no means sure of our spelling.' Trollope probably thought this a native Australian word; but *OED* gives it ('pugg(a)ree') as from a Hindustani word meaning 'turban', dating it in English in this sense from 1665, and in the sense used by Trollope from 1859. Similar in purpose, though not in form, to a havelock.

'Jerry had unblushingly declared that he himself had "*shaken*" the horse, – Anglicé, had stolen him . . .'

'After dinner . . . Dick Shand "*shouted*" for the company. Dick had quite learned by this time the mystery of shouting. When a man "stands" drinks all round, he shouts; and then it is no more than reciprocal that another man should do the same.' '. . . the whisky was brought, and Mick insisted on "shouting" for it out of his own pocket.'

1. Partridge dates *lag* in the sense '*transported* convict' from before 1811; in the sense '*any* convict' from *c*. 1830; in the sense 'a one-time convict' (preceded by *old*) from before 1856 (although strictly speaking it is this term applied to a ticket-of-leave man that is expressly so dated). Trollope's meaning seems to be narrower than any of these – 'a *one-time transported* convict'.

Squatters (and *free-selectors*). A squatter was not a man using land illegally (though he had no title to and paid no taxes on it), and was by no means necessarily poor; he was indeed often richer than a free-selector – in sheep, but not in cash. Harry Heathcote is a squatter; but he owns 30,000 sheep, and is 'master, as far as his mastership went, of 120,000 acres'. These acres, however, were 'by no means his own property. He was simply a tenant of the Crown, paying a rent computed at so much a sheep. He had indeed purchased the land on which his house stood – but this he had done simply to guard himself against other purchasers.' The other purchasers, the free-selectors, 'were the bane of his existence, the one great sorrow which, as he said, broke his heart.' Free-selectors seem to have been free to acquire title to land from the state, even land fenced and grazed – quite legally – by squatters. Heathcote himself, indeed, held 'the land on which his house stood' by free selection. It would seem that he and other squatters who required enormous ranges of land to graze their great flocks could not profitably acquire title to enough of it, and were constantly threatened with the loss of its use, and with the consequent reduction in their flocks, by the encroachments of free-selectors – encroachments perfectly legal, but regarded by squatters, with some reason, as inequitable, and even unconscionable. Would-be free-selectors, and established free-selectors desirous of enlarging their holdings, often set fire to squatters' grazing land, thus rendering it useless – for a time only, to be sure, but for long enough to drive the impecunious squatters out of business and thus eliminate them as competitors for free selection, even to the limited extent to which they might otherwise have competed. Sometimes even the squatters' buildings were burnt. The more substantial free-selectors commonly grew sugar-cane and manufactured sugar.

'Every miner has his *swag*, – consisting of a large blanket which is rolled up, and contains all his personal belongings.'

Swagsman. An itinerant labourer.

' "I don't care a damn for that sort of *tucker* [*ie*, food]," he said, as though he despised potatoes from the bottom of his heart.'

8. AMERICAN

A number of American characters appear in several novels, and two or three scenes are set in the United States, but the number of Americanisms that the Americans use, or that now and then Trollope or his English characters use in mockery, is small. And the mockery is always good-natured: if one may judge by the American characters in his novels, Trollope on the whole liked Americans, and did not despise their speech, though he was amused by it. The two locutions most often found are *have a good time* ('enjoy oneself') and *I guess* (' believe' or the like – neither, incidentally, an American invention, but a peculiarly American survival of what was once general English usage. The latter is common in Chaucer.). The former is exemplified at least nine times, not always in Americans' mouths. Trollope himself uses it three times with a reference to its provenience: 'An American, when he has had a pleasant day, will tell you he has had "a good time." ' 'They had . . . not . . . on the whole what our American friends call a good time of it.' 'It is [an American girl's] acknowledged right to have what she calls a good time with young men.' Only once is it included in an American's actual utterance: ' "I do have a good time pretty much . . ." ' Once it is what may be called a quotation from an American's thoughts otherwise reported in indirect discourse: 'Should she allow him to have amused himself with her love, to have had "a good time," and then to roam away like a bee . . . ?' Once it is what the American spoken of would presumably have said: '. . . Mr Fisher had "a good time" in London.' Three times it is used without explicit reference to its provenience of the actions of English men or women, once without quotation marks: 'Miss Mackenzie seemed to be having "a good time" with her neighbours . . .' '. . . he seemed to be intent only on "having a good time" like some schoolboy out on a holiday.' 'He intended to . . . have a good time.' I think Trollope rather fancied the expression.

I guess I have noted ten times in six novels. I quote only those instances otherwise interesting. ' ". . . would they pick her to pieces?" [says an American lady]. ' "I guess they would, – as you say," ' her English fiancé replies. ' "Then, I guess, the thing's about as good as done." These words were spoken with a fine, sharp, nasal twang by a brilliantly dressed American gentleman . . .' ' "I guess I've got to fit myself for that sort of life." And Nora [who is English, speaking to an American], pronounced her words with something of a nasal twang, imitating certain countrymen of her friend's.' ' "I guess we have [got something to say to each other]," said Rachel, "so if you'll wait here we'll come to you when the [railway] cars¹ are fixed." ' ' "I guess you [English] are pretty particular," said Miss Petrie ['the American Browning'], "and it seems to me you don't have much regard to intellect or erudition, – but fix things up straight according to birth and money." ' ' "I guess I shall [remain in Italy for the summer]; or, perhaps, locate myself in the purer atmosphere of the Swiss mountains." ' ('The American Browning', again.)

Further Americanisms without *I guess* follow. 'Mr [Hamilton J.] Fisker [an American] had "struck 'ile" when he induced his partner . . . to give him a note to the great man.' 'Mr Gotobed [an American Senator] declared that everything was "fixed convenient." ' ' "You think he's a rascal, Mister?" ' 'Mr Morton . . . showed [the American Senator] the buildings which had once been the kennels of the Rufford hounds. "All that for dogs!" exclaimed Mr Gotobed. "All for dogs," said Mr Morton. "Hounds, we generally call them." "Hounds, are they? Well, I'll remember; though 'dogs' seems to me more civil [!]." ' ' '. . . American buncom of a high order of eloquence.' ' "I don't want to talk buncum . . ." ' (An Englishman, and without reference to Americans; the term was apparently getting naturalized by 1874, when Trollope wrote these words.) 'There has come up among them a general feeling that it's just as well to let things slide, – as the Yankees say.' ' "He knows I'm a lost sheep – a gone 'coon, as the Americans say . . ." ' ' "I won't stay here to be questioned this way," said the boy [who has told a lie], feeling that his blushes would betray him, and his incapacity to "lie square," as the Americans say.' 'We do not know here that special season which across the Atlantic is called the Indian summer . . .'

1 *Anglice*, 'carriages'.

CHAPTER V

Ornaments — Mostly Bad[1]

🔲🔲🔲🔲🔲🔲

1. 'LITERARY' ARCHAISMS

I have dealt with usages still common in both speech and writing in Trollope's day, but not so any longer, under the heading of 'Out-of-mode Usage' (Chapter III). The present section concerns usages already obsolete or nearly so, at least in conversation and written prose, in Trollope's time, but intelligible to him and his contemporary readers, as they are to us, from their occurrence in old books still read, and used by him almost always because he thinks them amusing.

Of these archaisms I think I have recorded every instance except for *thou*, etc., probably, and *would fain* and *was fain to* possibly, and I do not believe I have missed any considerable number of those. Supposing my figures to be substantially correct, what is striking – and very striking indeed – is that after 1873 – *ie*, in the last thirteen novels, produced over the last nine years of Trollope's life – I have recorded no instances whatever of any of them (except possibly a few *thou's* and *fain's*), and only three in the eleven produced after 1866 and before 1874. I am sure I did not suddenly and utterly stop being observant. Of the seventeen[2] novels finished before 1867, in only four have I recorded no instances (still not counting perhaps a few *thou's* and *fain's*) – *Thorne* (1858), *Ray* (1863), *Mack* (1864), and *Belton* (1865). These I take to be accidental exceptions; what is clear is that after 1866

1. It would be helpful to the reader if, before reading this chapter, he would read the summary treatment of the subject in the Introduction.
2. Not counting *Struggles*, which is crammed with exaggeratedly stilted language, including many 'literary' archaisms. I omit these altogether from this section; the style is not Trollope's, but a combination of what one would imagine 'Robinson's' to be and that of 'one of Smith and Elder's young men'. Robinson, the *persona*, uses 'literary' archaisms because he thinks them elegant, not, as Trollope almost always does when writing as Trollope, in mockery of 'elegance'.

Trollope virtually stopped using archaisms, and, after 1873, completely (yet once more except for possibly a few *thou's* and *fain's*). This can hardly be an accident. It is certainly due to his having come to feel, by the middle sixties, that archaisms are not a very good joke after all – and virtually all of them are meant to be jokes, or at least amusingly quaint and old-fashioned. As is to be expected, only two, I am pretty sure, appear in dialogue: Trollope never thought archaisms in the speech of contemporary ladies and gentlemen either funny or credible (except Mr Crawley, whose archaisms are not affected or 'literary').

My register (in chronological order, but deferring *thou*, etc.) is as follows: *wax wroth, ribands, his affianced, aught (Macd); wight, sable habiliments (Kellys); full large (Warden); 'twas* (in dialogue – *Towers); weasand, umquhile* (Scots as well as archaic), *I trow (Clerks); wot, umquhile, 'twas* (in dialogue), *holden (Bertrams); wot, 'twas, the son of his loins, would fain, tithe* (literally 'a tenth'), *it boots not (Castle* – in this novel Trollope really let himself go, as he did with *thou*, etc. – see below); *such an one* (in dialogue), *would fain (Framley); was a-hungered (Orley); aught (House); methinks (Claver); nay, was fain to (Chron); whether* (used to introduce an independent question – *Finn); would fain (Way)*.

Of passages containing one or more instances of *thou*, etc. (except in provincial dialects and Mr Fay's Quaker speech), I have bothered to record only eleven, though I am sure there are a good many more. But I am equally sure that such as there are occur, as all the recorded ones do, either in the author's addresses to the reader, or – much oftener – in apostrophes to a character, and sometimes serious (solemn, indeed) but much oftener comic – almost always so when the reader is addressed. *Castle* contains no fewer than six of the solemn kind; cf. the list above. But the most insistent and protracted example (it is of the solemn kind), painfully reminiscent of Dickens's farewell to Tom Pinch, is in *Clerks*, 47:

And to thee, Gertrude – how shall we say farewell to thee, excluded as thou art from that dear home, where those who love thee so well are so happy? Their only care is now thy absence. Adversity has tried thee in its crucible, and thou art found to be of virgin gold, unalloyed; hadst thou still lapped in prosperity, the true ring of thy sterling metal would never have been heard. Farewell to thee, and may those budding flowers of thine break forth into golden fruit to gladden thy heart in thy coming days!

The whole style of this passage is mannered and florid and high-flown and self-consciously 'literary', and the tone sentimental; despite Trollope's perfectly serious intention, it strikes the modern reader as almost as ludicrous as 'Robinson's' style in *Struggles*, where Trollope is poking fun at it.

2. PLAYFUL LANGUAGE

Up to 1869, Trollope often plays with language; thereafter, almost never. He does so most often by inventing words; and below these are shown in context, italicized and alphabetized. All but three of them occur in authorial language (cf. Section 1).

'. . . she had a leash [itself not playful, but mischievous – see Section 3] of baronets and their *baronettes* . . .' (*Towers*, 35.)

'She had some mysterious acquaintances with the *county-ocracy* . . .' (*Bertrams*, 29.)

' "Mr Harding might have been a dean . . . if he'd liked. They did offer it to him." "And he refused it?" "Indeed he did, sir." "Nolo *decanari*. I never heard of that before." ' (*House*, 16.)

'. . . I began to see evident signs on the part of the road of retrograding into *lane-ism* . . .' (*Macd*, 1.)

' "A man can't drive four horses because he's a philanthropist, – or rather a *philhorseophist*, and is desirous that the team should be driven without any hurt to them." ' (*Forgive*, 21.)

Frank Gresham 'went down to dine . . . with sundry other *philogeants* [*sic*].' (*Framley*.) The Giants were the Tories in Parliament, and the Gods the Liberals.

' "A poet doesn't want to marry a poetess [*pace* Browning], nor a philosopher a *philosopheress*." ' (*Redux*, 29.)

'Whatever immediate effect such symposiums might have had on his inner mind – symposiums indeed they were not; *posiums* I will call them, if I may be allowed; for in later life, when he drank heavily, he drank alone . . . his body suffered greatly.' (*Thorne*, 9.)

Two gentlemen, for fighting a duel, 'were spoken of [in a radical newspaper] as glaring examples of that aristocratic *snobility*, – that was the expressive word coined . . . for the occasion, – which

the rotten state of London society in high quarters now produced.'
(*Finn*, 40.)

There are other kinds of playful language. There is one
portmanteau word – 'There was [in the G.P.O. clerk] . . .
thorough confidence in himself *postofficially*.' (*Caldig*, 48.) There
are two facetious formations of the degree of the adjective: (1)
' "I'm ruined, but you're *ruinder*." ' (*Forgive*, 5.) (2) 'Julia was
the . . . *cherry-cheekedest* of the lot.' (*Caldig*, 1.) There are facetious
analogical verbs: (1) Dr Thorne '. . . painted . . . he papered,
and *mirrored*, and *linened*, and *blanketed* . . .' (*Thorne*, 3.) (2)
'. . . Chaldicotes . . . had . . . fallen into their hands and been
newly furnished, and newly decorated, and newly *gardened*, and
newly *greenhoused* and *hot-watered* by them . . .' (*Chron*, 2.) There
are plays on the multiple meanings of words: (1) '. . . a bog
stream which *ran*, or rather crept, across the road.' (*Macd*, 1.) (2)
Having mentioned 'Bragg's End' as a part of a parish, Trollope
says, 'How Bragg came to have an *end* . . . no one in the parish
knew.' (*Ray*, 1.) (3) '. . . he was still of opinion that the Dean was
a *child* of wrath, and poor Mary [the Dean's daughter], therefore,
a grandchild.' (*Popenjoy*, 49.) (4) 'He was . . . already a *Bachelor* of
Arts. In a very few years he would probably assume the higher
title of a married man of arts . . .' (*Castle*, 5. (4) '. . . he now was
a director [of a railway company] of a week's *standing*, or perhaps
we should say sitting.' (*Clerks*, 24.) Finally, there are two instances
of humorous syllepsis: (1) '. . . you [while hunting] lose your
stirrup leather, or your way . . .' (*Fay*, 39.) (2) 'So . . . they
started from the vicarage door with many farewell kisses, and a
large paper of sandwiches.' (*Bertrams*, 35.)

3. MISCHIEVOUS LANGUAGE

This section, like the preceding one, deals with humorous
language, but with a quite different and greatly superior kind.
The humour consists in the choice or placement of words (always
Trollope's, never his characters'). It is not easy to classify some
of the examples, or rather to find appropriate names for them; but
to this there are at least three exceptions (the only ones I have
noted more than twice): grotesque or startling anticlimax (seven
instances), other kinds of incongruity (four), and what I will call

straight-faced impudence (four). They are not only Trollope's favourites; they bear a family likeness. (However infelicitous my class names may sometimes be, the point is always clear.)

1) Grotesque or startling anticlimax.
'The bishop . . . felt that John Bold . . . would . . . distribute all tithes among Methodists, Baptists, and other savage tribes . . .' (*Warden*, 3.) '. . . a soft, greasy voice made up of pretence, politeness, and saliva . . .' (*Ralph*, 20.) 'It was ten thousand pities that a [clergyman and headmaster] should be disturbed by unnecessary questionings who could not only preach, but play cricket as well.' (*Wortle*, 4.) 'Then he blew out a great cloud of smoke, and went into bed lost amidst poetry, philosophy, love, and tobacco.' (*Right*, 25.) 'The Duchess [of Omnium] . . . declared to herself that her husband was the truest nobleman in all England. She revered, admired, and almost loved him.' (*Prime*, 18.) 'It is easy for a man to say that he will banish care, so that he can enjoy to the full the delights of the moment. But this is a power which none but a savage possesses – or perhaps an Irishman.' (*Prime*, 25.) 'Dogs have turned against their masters, and even Neapolitans against their rulers, when oppression has been too severe.' (*Towers*, 3.)

2) Other kinds of incongruity.
A gentleman has been almost fatally hurt at a hunt. The hunt ball in the evening, preceded by dinner, must still go on. The gentlemen sit at their wine. 'Even while drinking their wine they could not keep themselves from the subject, and were convivial in a cadaverous fashion.' (*Senator*, 23.) The same gentlemen on the same occasion '. . . all took their places [at the ball] with a lugubrious air, as aware that they were sacrificing themselves in the performance of a sad duty.' 'The three ladies knelt on their hassocks in the most becoming fashion, and sat during the sermon without the slightest sign either of weariness or of attention.' (*Way*, 21.) '. . . if one has to be hung in a given week, would not one wish to be hung on the first day, even at the risk of breaking one's last Sabbath day in the world?' (*Way*, 39.) '. . . a leash of baronets . . .' (*Towers*, 35.)

3) Straight-faced impudence.
'The bishop did not whistle [in astonishment]; we believe that

they lose the power of doing so on being consecrated . . .'
(*Warden*, 3.) '. . . one hand ensconced within [Archdeacon
Grantly's] pocket, evinced the practical hold which our mother
church keeps on her temporal possessions; . . . and below . . .
the decorous breeches, and great black gaiters showing so
admirably that well-turned leg, betokened the outward beauty and
grace of our church establishment.' (*Warden*, 5.) '. . . a certain
quiet clerical hotel . . . much patronized by bishops and deans
of the better sort . . .' (*Chron*, 70.) 'This narrative is supposed to
commence immediately after the installation of Dr Proudie. I will
not describe the ceremony, as I do not precisely understand its
nature. I am ignorant whether a bishop be chaired like a member
of parliament, or carried in a gilt coach like a lord mayor, or sworn
in like a justice of the peace, or introduced like a peer to the upper
house, or led between two brethren like a knight of the garter, but
I do know that everything was properly done . . .' (*Towers*, 3.)

4) Comic euphemism.
' "I know that young Talbot is to leave [Dr Wortle's] school,"
said Mrs Staniloup . . . This happened to be altogether untrue.
What she probably meant was, that the boy should not go back to
school if she could prevent his doing so . . . It may be remembered that she had declared . . . that young Talbot was not
to go back [to school]. But this had been a figure of speech, as has
been already explained.'

5) Jocose pathetic fallacy.
'. . . the ravens [in the cathedral close] cawed with a peculiar
reverence as [Archdeacon Grantly] wended his way . . .' (*Warden*,
5.)

6) Oxymoron.
'. . . then there were Captain Gunner and Major Pountney, two
middle-aged young men . . .' (*Prime*, 20.) (Such are frequent
objects of Trollope's raillery.) '. . . there had been knights bearing that name, some of whom had been honourably beheaded for
treason . . .' (*Orley*, 2.)

7) Sarcasm.
'. . . let it be observed of [a barrister] that in perverting the

course of justice – which may be said to be the special work of an advocate, – he never condescended to bully anybody.' (*Caldig*, 41.)

This sort of thing is about as frequent in Trollope's later novels as in his earlier ones, and in novels prevailingly serious in subject and sombre in tone as in those not so, unlike what I have called 'playful language' (Section 2, above). The reason is, I suppose, that the former is an ancient, standard, and familiar rhetorical device, genuinely witty and usually funny, and almost always appealing and effective, whereas the latter is much more likely to be easy, mechanical, weakly or cheaply humorous, and wearisome to the reader.

4. FACETIOUS NAMES

Trollope, as all his readers know to their sorrow, was excessively and incurably given to inventing facetious (and usually allusive) names (chiefly surnames) for his characters and for other fictitious persons mentioned. I say 'to their sorrow' because the facetious names are extremely numerous, but seldom either very funny or very clever, and are most of them given to characters that appear in serious or at least realistic passages along with characters with credible names, to the weakening of the reader's 'willing suspension of disbelief'.

Trollope was also given as incurably to inventing such names for peerages, Parliamentary boroughs, villages, residences, periodicals, and a few other things, but this strain of the malady, though as incurable as the other, was milder in that he suffered from it a good deal less often, and less irritating to readers in that instances of it tend to be repeated less often, so that it less often detracts from their feeling of an incongruous mixture of the credible and the incredible. To avoid anticlimax, I will deal with these names before the first kind. All but a few of them are place-names.

I am not speaking here at all of place-names invented but wholly plausible. The most familiar examples of these are of course Barset(shire) and Barchester; almost as familiar are some other place-names in the Barsetshire novels – *eg*, Silverbridge, Framley, Greshamsbury, and even Plumstead Episcopi. There are others outside the series; *eg*, Bullhampton and Loring in *Vicar*. Nor am I speaking of the other English counties than Barsetshire invented by Trollope – Ufford and Rufford (both in *Senator*) – whose names he took from villages in Suffolk and Lancashire respectively. And there is a third, Brothershire (in *Popenjoy*) – not, like the foregoing, a real place-name, and not very plausible; but the name of its county town, Brotherton, is not only plausible, but existent, as that of villages in Suffolk and Yorkshire. All such are fictitious, at least in application, but they are not facetious at all.

Between them and the wholly facetious come the names of three places that are real enough, but that Trollope makes funny by making them Parliamentary boroughs, which it is hardly conceivable they could be: Crewe Junction (*Clerks*), Mile End (*Framley*), and The Essex Marshes (*Orley*).[1] From these the transition is easy to the wholly facetious names of non-existent places made Parliamentary boroughs by Trollope: Sticinthemud [*sic*] and Porcorum, both in *Way*. He was so fond of this tasteless and rather pointless parody of *Canonicorum* that he also has a village of Busby Porcorum, in *Fay*. There are half a dozen parishes with such names, of which two examples will suffice: St Judas Without (which in a way anticipates Beerbohm and which I find really rather amusing), in *Clerks*, and St Peter's-cum-Pumkin [*sic*], in *Right*. Residences do not escape: Gatherum Castle, which first appears in *Towers* (and which of course depends for such amusement as it may afford on remembering that its owner is the Duke of Omnium); Castle Reekie (first in *Forgive*) which depends in a somewhat similar way on the Marquis of Auldreekie; Cauldkail Castle (first in *House*) – situated, of course (as, equally of course, is Castle Reekie), in Scotland; Killancodlum (also first in *House*), Mr Montacute's Scottish seat (the name, which sounds Scottish enough, is actually a wretched quasi-pun based on the estate's being devoted to the preservation of birds for shooting); and the (perfectly pointless) Tumour Castle, the Marquis of Trowbridge's seat in *Vicar*. Smaller and humbler dwellings are Creamclotted Hall (in *Framley*) – inevitably situated in Devon; Oileymeed (in *Forgive*), the rich farm of a rich farmer, Mr Cheesacre; and, in the same novel, Nethercoates (like Tumour Castle, perfectly pointless). Even periodicals suffer. The best-known example is of course *The Jupiter* (ie, *The Times* – first in *Warden*, but in several later novels

---

1. Essentially like these are the Marquis of Kensington Gore and the Bishop of Belgravia. Lazarus College (Oxon) is of a rather different kind; and the First Lord of the Stannaries and the Lord Petty Bag are two varieties of yet a third.

also), but there are others: *eg, Clerks* has ' "The Scalping Knife," got up in dead opposition to "The Lancet" ', and *Caldig, The Daily Tell-tale*, what we should now call a scandal sheet.

From facetious names of places and things we may pass to those – much the most numerous – of persons. Propriety, I suppose, requires that we should start with the peerage. I give only a selection.

The Duke of Omnium and the Marquis of Auldreekie have necessarily already been mentioned above, along with their castles; but a character in *Redux* refers to the Duke of Discount, who ' "retains his interest in the [public] house in Lombard Street" ', and the Marquis of Maltanops, who ' "has a share in a bitter beer house at Burton" '; and in *Popenjoy* we get Lord Parachute, Lord Giblet, and the Earl of Plausible (all pointless except perhaps the last), as well as Lord Grassangrains, 'that well-known breeder of bullocks'. The names of two Scottish peers are funny (so far as they are) only to people who know a little Scots: Lord Gaberlunzie ('a strolling minstrel'), in *Clerks*, and Lord Cantrip ('a necromancer's trick'), in *Finn*. Neither title can be said to be allusive to its bearer's character or anything else about him, except his nationality. The title of the Duke of St Bungay, a prominent, estimable, and perfectly serious character in *Forgive* and later novels in the Parliamentary series, is funny only because of the 'St'; there is undeniably a Bungay (though even by itself it would hardly be a likely name for a peerage, or at least a dukedom), but there certainly never was a *St* Bungay.

Descending to the commonalty, we find that facetious surnames are most often allusive to the occupations of their bearers. I will be merciful, and give only a few examples; and I will save space by omitting the names of the novels in which they appear, as being of little interest. Sir Alexander McSilk, Q.C.; Dr Fillgrave and Dr Rerechild; Mr Cantabili, music-master; Mr Wutsanbeans, a livery stable keeper; Hayanotes, a groom; Mr Shortribs, a butcher; Mr Cutcote, a tailor; Mr Binns, a butler; Mr Wobytrade, an undertaker; and Captain Cuttwater, a retired naval officer. A special case is Mr Du Boung, a brewer (in *Prime*), who ' "used to be plain English Bung before he got rich and made his name beautiful." ' Trollope almost never misses an opportunity to give allusive names to legal and commercial firms – allusive usually to the occupations, but sometimes to the faults conventionally attributed to those who follow them (especially lawyers). Thus we have, *eg*, Messrs Slow and Bideawhile, Messrs Dry and Stickabit, and Messrs Sharpit and Longfite, all attorney's firms; Messrs Leadham and Loiter, publishers; Messrs Piles, Sarsnett, and Gingham, drapers; Messrs Blocks, Piles, and Cofferdam, bridge-builders; and Messrs Stewam and Sugarscraps, caterers. And this is a better place than any other in which to mention the Shadrach Fire Assurance Office (in *Mack*). (In the immediate context of this, we have the Abednego *Life* Assurance Office, which, unlike the former, has at best a very blunt point, and is typical of Trollope's occasional failure to let well enough alone. But at least he spares us Meshach.)

Though facetious personal names most often allude to occupation, they do not always. They may allude to avocations (*eg*, Sir Harkaway Gorse, devoted to hunting, and Mrs King Guarded, equally devoted to whist); to opinions (*eg*, the Rev. Dr Hyandry and his natural enemy had they ever met, the Rev. Mr Lowlad; Sir Nicholas Fitzwhiggin, a Liberal politican; the (Bavarian) Baroness Banmann, an enthusiast for women's rights, and Mr Philogunac Cœlebs, a male supporter of them – bearing, incidentally, the only name reminiscent of Peacock; to foibles (*eg*, Mrs Lookaloft, the socially ambitious wife of a tenant farmer; Mr Everbeery, who was 'always drunk'; Baron (of the Exchequer) Brawl, captious and contentious; and – if to be a prosperous pluralist is a foible – the Rev. Canon Holdenough; to age (*eg*, Mr Younglad, a junior barrister – aged between forty and forty-five! – and Dr Century, a very old physician); and to personal circumstances (*eg*, the Rev. Mr Quiverful, with twelve children in *Warden* and fourteen in *Towers*).

Finally, (1) there are at least two names that do not allude to the bearers' callings or characters or anything about them, but are merely all but incredible – and yet, like many Dickensian names (*eg*, Chuzzlewit), only all but: Sir Timothy Beeswax, Solicitor General, and Mr Mainsail, a barrister – not, as one might expect, a sea captain; and (2) two that are not only not allusive, but wildly fantastic and utterly impossible – more so, if that could be, than the Duke of Omnium and his Gatherum Castle: Sir Lamda [*sic*] Mewnew and Sir Omicron Pie, eminent physicians who come down from London to attend Bishop Grantly in his last illness.

Though Trollope is merciless in contriving facetious names, he extremely seldom bestows them on prominent characters, especially admirable ones. I think there are only three exceptions (unless we count the Duke of St Bungay), and all, I believe, can be explained. (1) The (old) Duke of Omnium first appears in *Thorne*, and as a very unimportant (and not very attractive) character, whom I think Trollope had no intention of using again, at least as prominent and attractive. But in *Finn*, he becomes both (though even here he is prominent only in a secondary plot), and Trollope, having decided to reintroduce him, could not get rid of his facetious title. Nor could he, of course, when Plantagenet Palliser succeeded to it. 'Planty Pall' is first introduced in *House*, and as the old Duke's heir presumptive, but in a secondary plot (in which he plays no very creditable part), and I think that here Trollope had no intention of reintroducing him, at least as prominent and estimable, or perhaps even of killing off the old Duke and hence making Palliser succeed him. But again, having done both, in *Finn*, Trollope – and the young Duke – are stuck with the facetious name. (2) The Earl of Persiflage (in *Fay*), who is anything but a fool, still less a knave, does not become prominent till near the end of the novel, and, I think, at the beginning was not meant to become so. (3) Mr Neefit (in *Hotspur*), a maker of hunting breeches, is prominent throughout, but only in a secondary plot, and is a fool (though a genuinely pathetic one).

This list may seem a long one, but it gives only a faint idea of how common facetious names are. Not counting names of either the Barchester kind or the Ufford–Rufford kind, which are not facetious at all, I have recorded over 280 facetious and usually allusive names in the forty-two novels covered in this book. Several of them in the Barsetshire and Parliamentary series (only, I think) appear in more than a single novel in one or the other, and a few of those in at least one novel in both series; each of these I have counted only once, and the figures below for individual novels represent the names *first appearing* in each – an average of nearly seven *new* names to a novel. Only four contain none, and they range in date from *Kellys* (1847) through *Claver* (1864) and *Eye* (1870) to *Gangoil* (1873). The four have no characteristic in common that each has not with others; there is nothing about the subject or tone of any of them that would make the appearance of facetious names less appropriate than in many others. And such names in the remaining thirty-eight show no tendency to increase

or decrease in number steadily, or to be more or less numerous for
any period of years; the numbers vary from one, in *Castle* (1860),
Hotspur (1869), *Anna* (1871), and *Wortle* (1879), to *forty-two* in
Clerks (1857), the novels just before and just after that (*Towers*,
1856, and *Thorne*, 1858) having respectively eleven (new ones) and
sixteen. The second highest number is seventeen, in *Popenjoy*
(1875!) – a very poor second indeed to the forty-two in *Clerks*.
Half the 280-odd in the forty-two novels is reached in *Mack* (1864),
the fifteenth to be written, leaving about 140 for the remaining
twenty-seven; and the first twenty-one (ending with *Hotspur*,
1869) contain about 160, leaving about 120 for the last twenty-
one. These facts at first sight suggest that Trollope *did* tend to use
fewer facetious names in his later years, but that appearance is
almost wholly owing to the egregious *Clerks*, with its forty-two.
Most other 'ornaments' are most numerous in *Towers*, and some
of them are next most numerous in *Clerks*, the next novel (written
only a year later), which in these cases is often a good second to
Towers, the third being a poor third; but in facetious names, neither
Towers nor any other novel is within hailing distance of *Clerks*. It
is a solemn thought that if every novel had introduced as many
facetious names as *Clerks*, we should have, not about 280 – which
is too many – but 1764.

Trollope once laughs at his own improbable or impossible
names – and does so, with singular propriety, in *Clerks*. In
Chapter 22, Charley Tudor's unpublished novel *Crinoline and
Macassar* is being read aloud in his family circle, and the title
proves to be the names of his heroine and hero. Captain Cuttwater
says he has never heard such names, and his great-niece Katie says,
' "At any rate, uncle, they are as good as Sir Jib Boom and
Captain Hardaport" ' – names of persons mentioned by her uncle
as among his naval friends. Trollope is implicitly reminding us
that his book is a piece of fiction, as he so often does in other ways
usually explicit, in many of his earlier novels.

5. LATIN TAGS AND LEGAL TERMS

A. Latin Tags

Though Trollope quotes a great many times from Latin poetry
(see Chapter VI, Section 6), he makes comparatively little use of

non-literary Latin tags, of which (other than legal ones, treated of
under B, below), I have recorded only thirty-nine instances – an
average of less than one to a novel – of thirty-two phrases. And
unlike French words and phrases, a good two-thirds of these,
though they cannot be called necessary, or even invariably handier
than an English equivalent, are in contexts where they give at
least no marked impression of having been lugged in by the ears
as comic or otherwise 'ornamental'.[1] But some certainly do; and
these (together with some that do not) are strikingly more
numerous in *Towers* (8) and *Clerks* (7) than in any of the rest of the
novels, which show a total of twenty-four among them. It is
precisely these two novels that contain markedly more comic or
otherwise 'ornamental' instances of French (in Trollope's own
language) than any of the rest. Trollope, that is, suffered a mild
and brief fever of Latin tags as a humorous device at exactly the
climax of the severer and more protracted fever of French words
and phrases used for the same ends.

And yet even the Latin tags that seem more or less pointless or
only faintly funny, besides being both absolutely and relatively
much less numerous than the French ones, impress me, at least, as
on the whole much less distasteful and much less jarring than the
French. I can only suppose that I find foppish humour less to my
taste than donish humour. And though Trollope was hardly a don,
he was much further from being a fop, so that his Latin tags
sprang to his mind more spontaneously, I think, than the French
ones.

A register of the recorded instances follows, with contexts and
comments where they seem worth giving.

alma mater, à tergo,[2] *casus belli* (2 – both times of private quarrels),
censor morum, cui bono?, currente calamo, detur digniori(bus) (3),[3] *Deus*

---

1. They do not, therefore, belong, at least very clearly, in a chapter called 'Ornaments
   – mostly bad', but it seems best to treat them along with those that do; and they
   are not sufficiently numerous to deserve a main section to themselves, let alone a
   chapter.
2. '. . . the vicar having thoroughly warmed himself, as far as this might be done
   by facing the fire, turned round and began the operation *à tergo*.' (*Framley*, 1.) I
   find this genuinely, if only mildly, amusing.
3. Eg, '. . . *detur digniori* is a fearful law for such a profession as the Civil Service.'
   (*Clerks*, 6.) The other two instances (*Towers*, 43 and *Orley*, 3), like this one, reflect
   Trollope's bitter, life-long aversion to filling posts on the basis of examinations.
   This subject is a *Leitmotiv* of *Clerks*, in which Trollope draws heavily on his own
   youthful experience as a G.P.O. clerk.

[*sic*] *ex machina*(2), *facile princeps* (3), *festina lente* (a barrister to clients in a hurry), *in articulo mortis*, '. . . his evidence was published *in extenso*', *In Memoriam* (chapter heading of *Chron*, 67; Mrs Proudie has died in the preceding chapter), *ipsissima verba*, *lapsus naturæ*, *locus pænitentiæ* (2),[1] *lusus naturæ*, 'That she was a lady . . . I hereby state as a fact, *meo periculo*', *nolo episcopari*, *per fas et nefas*,[2] *pro bono publico*, *pro hac vice*,[3] *quid pro quo*, *Quieta non movere*,[4] 'The *statu* [*sic*] *quo* of the university', *status pupillaris*, *sub dio*,[5] *toga virilis*,[6] *Vale, Valete* (chapter heading of *Bertrams* 10 – neither pretentious nor humorous), *Victrix* (chapter heading of *Finn*, 61; cf. preceding item).

B. Legal Terms[7]

Trollope was well up in the language of the law. I have found eighteen legal terms, seven of them used twice. All but four occur in legal contexts and most commonly in the mouths of lawyers; the four that are used outside of such contexts and humorously are given at the end of the following list, in context. The other fourteen naturally appear only in those novels that deal with legal matters (and not in all of those), and they appear throughout

1. *Eg*, 'There was within him the means of repentance, could a *locus pænitentiæ* have been supplied to him.' (*Framley*, 44.) The Rev. Mark Robarts has sinned gravely, at least in Trollope's eyes, and the Latin tag here is not pretentious or humorous, but technically correct and highly appropriate.

2. '. . . it had become her own religion to assert her daughter's right, – *per fas et nefas*, – to assert it by right or wrong . . .' (*Anna*, 1.) A good example of what might be called Trollope's occasional compulsive resort to Latin tags, even when the idea is expressed all over again in English. It is not meant to be funny.

3. '. . . they had imbarked [*sic*] in a sort of partnership, *pro hac vice* . . .' (*Clerks*, 15.) A good example of the ludicrously incongruous use of what might be called the language of state in connexion with a trivial transaction of private – and humble – life. Cf. *casus belli* above.

4. '*Quieta non movere* was the motto by which the rector governed his life . . .' (*Senator*, 1.) Rather successfully mischievous; the Latin is appropriate to a *sanctæ theologiæ professor*, but the rector is lazy. (This probably belongs rather in Chapter VI, Section 6 than here; but I do not know its source.)

5. '. . . a . . . board was to be spread *sub dio* for the . . . lower class of yokels . . .' (*Towers*, 35.) Cf. n. 3 above. But there Trollope is laughing at the rather absurd clerk-partners; here he is laughing, I think, not so much at 'the lower class of yokels' as at the people who call them that.

6. 'The very lads who had eaten his father's dinners at Eton . . . knew much better than to associate with him at Cambridge now that they had put on the *toga virilis*.' (*Thorne*, 24.) The sort of thing a nineteenth-century English writer with a classical education falls blamelessly into in a light-hearted moment.

7. See n. 1, p. 135, under 'Latin tags'; it applies even more to this section.

Trollope's career – as early as 1847 and as late as 1881. The list follows.

corpus delicti, commission de lunatico, distraining, felo de se, femme couverte, in formâ pauperis (2), *laches* (2), *latitat, ne exeat (regno)* (2), *non compos (mentis)* (2), *notice* (*ie,* 'give legal notice to') (2), *onus probandi* (2), *prima facie* (2), *traverser* (OED, 'one who traverses'; *traverse,* v., 'to contradict formally (a matter of fact alleged in the previous pleading); to deny at law.').

'Sunday was always a *dies non* with the Greshamsbury [post-boy] . . .' (*Thorne,* 43); '. . . the girl told her that Miss Todd was regarded, *ex parte* Stumfold [an Evangelical clergyman], as being the old gentleman [*ie,* Satan] himself . . .' (*Mack,* 3); Archdeacon Grantly condemns Eleanor Bold for being the addressee of a letter from Mr Slope 'as though she was necessarily a *particeps criminis.*' (Towers, 28); '. . . Mr Trevelyan took his leave, declaring to himself that he was worse off than the foxes, who have holes in which to lay their heads; – but it must be presumed that his sufferings in this respect were to be by attorney, as it was for his wife, and not for himself, that the necessary hole was to be required.' (*Right,* 29; there is an additional comic force in the repetition of 'hole'.) And for good measure, there is, of course, a biblical echo – not in quite the best taste.

6. FRENCH WORDS AND PHRASES

Though I am not certain that I have made a complete register, I have made, I think, a nearly complete one, or at least one that furnishes a sufficient basis for generalizations, of the French words and phrases in the novels dealt with in this book (omitting *Struggles,* which is completely un-Trollopian). In those forty-one novels, I have recorded 169 instances of the use of 112 words and phrases (and a sentence or two). Of the 169, 125 – nearly three-quarters – occur in Trollope's own language (*ie,* he makes himself speak French much oftener than he does his characters). These 125 I have classified, necessarily somewhat arbitrarily, impressionist-ically, or even perhaps now and then perversely, but as judiciously as I could, as (1) what I will call natural or sometimes almost un-avoidable, serious, unaffected, and unpretentious in the context, and (2) what I should say lacked one or more of those qualities, and might better (except perhaps a very few of the humorous ones) have been put into English. Again almost three-quarters (ninety) belong to the latter class.

Typical examples of class 1 are '. . . how can melodramatic *dénouements* be properly brought about . . . while [Dr Gwynne] is laid up with the gout?' 'Mr Harding evinced a lamentable want of *esprit de corps* . . .' 'Such *liaisons* have the interests of intrigue . . .' 'Thus [Mr Slope] made sure that this act of self-jurisdiction [by Bishop Proudie] should be as nearly as possible a *fait accompli.*' '. . . one noble lord had become "the earl" *par excellence* . . .' Typical examples of class 2 are '. . . George was somewhat afflicted by a *tête montée* on this matter [of choosing a profession].' 'The august secretary received him on his promotion without much *empressement* . . .' 'One gets home [from a morning party] fagged and *désœuvré* . . .' '. . . a cheque was the most useful [wedding] *cadeau.*' '. . . now she was *au désespoir* because that result had been reached.' It will be observed that all the French words and phrases given as examples of class 1 are now, as they probably were in Trollope's time, pretty freely and unselfconsciously used among educated speakers of English, whereas those given of class 2 are not – and pretty certainly never were.[1]

The figures given above would be of little interest or importance by themselves, but an analysis of their chronological distribution reveals a striking, sudden, significant, and surely conscious and deliberate alteration in Trollope's practice. Of the 90 instances in class 2, no fewer than 53 – well over half – occur in the five novels written before 1858, and of those 53, 39 occur in the fourth and fifth – *Towers* (19) and *Clerks* (20). The next four – *Thorne*, *Bertrams* (both 1858), *Castle*, and *Framley* (both 1860) show a decided falling off (with one backsliding), having respectively 6, 12, 5, and 3 instances of class 2, making a total of 79 in the nine novels written before 1861, and leaving only 11 for the later thirty-two – *ie*, an average of about nine instances to the novel before 1861 and of about one-third of an instance (a rather metaphysical concept, I admit, but statistically useful) – twenty-seven times fewer – to the novel written after 1860. Of these

---

1. I have not extended this classification to the forty-four instances in the speech (or writing or reported thoughts) of characters, because it can be reasonably presumed that the results would reflect not Trollope's habits, but those of the several characters as he conceived them.

thirty-two, three contain two instances each, five contain one each, and the remaining twenty-four none. The conclusion seems to me inescapable that as early as 1858 Trollope came to think – suddenly – that sprinkling his language with unnecessary French was neither pleasingly tasteful or ornamental nor richly comic, but tawdry and tiresome. From 1858 to 1860 he tried, with marked but uneven success, to taper off; by 1861 he had got rid of the addiction almost entirely. I think some critic, friendly or unfriendly, must have given him some good advice, which he took. (Even instances of what I have called class 1 in his own language and of both classes in that of his characters become fewer, and become so even a little earlier, on the average, but not if we discount, as we should to keep the averages from being deceptive, the altogether exceptional cases of *Towers*, which has the incomparably exceptional number of 13 in 'Trollope class 1', and *Kellys*, which has the likewise incomparably exceptional number of 9 instances (of both classes) in the language of characters.) The first eleven novels contain some French (though the last three of these contain very little); of the later thirty, fourteen contain (but cf. my caveat at the opening of this section) none at all.

Below is a register of the observed French words and phrases, with some notes on a few.

abandon (n.), *agrémens* (*sic*), *à la Russe*,[1] ' ". . . the hair dressed *à l'imperatrice*" ' (*sic*), *amende* (*honorable*) (2), *amour propre* (2), *à outrance*, *au cinquième* [*étage*], (*au*) *désespoir* (3), *au fait, au fond, au marvel, au pied de la lettre, au première* [*étage*], *au ravier* (*sic*!), *avant-courier, bandeaux* (4), *beau monde, beaux yeux, billet doux, blasé, bon gré* (*mal gré*) (2), *bonhomie, bon vivant, cadeau* (2), *carte blanche, cause célèbre* (2), *cela depend* (*sic*), (*cela va*) *sans dire* (2), *chef d'œuvre, ci-devant* (2), *congé* (3), *contretemps, cordonnier, cortège* (3), *couleur de rose, coup de main, coup d'œil, débonnaire*,[2] *débris, décolleté, de haut en bas, déjeuner, dénouements, désœuvré, détour, de trop* (4), *distingué(e)* (3), *éclat, embonpoint, empressement* (3), *enceinte*,[3] *en déshabille* (*sic*),[4] *en garçon,*

1. A dinner *à la Russe* (*Mack,* 5), it is clear from the context, was one consisting of an inordinately long parade of small and fussy dishes (mostly 'made') – and in this case pretentious, penny-pinching, and unappetizing.
2. The spelling, the accent, and the italics (which last Trollope does not commonly use, but does once) are surprising in view of the fact that *debonair* has been thoroughly naturalized in English for centuries, though they might not be if the word occurred in an (affected) character's writing rather than in Trollope's own.
3. This is used because it is a euphemism, not because it is French, in *Macd,* 27 where Trollope says of an Irish peasant woman that 'she declared her suspicions

en grand seigneur, en masse (3), *ennuyé, en règle, entêtée, entrée, esprit de corps, exigeant,*[1] *façon de parler, fainéant* (2), *fait accompli, faute de mieux* (2), *faux pas, fête champêtre* (2),* (Mollet) *fils, finesse, fracas, gage d'amour, hors de combat, insouciance, jeunesse dorée, la grace* (sic),[2] '. . . the signora ['La Signora Madeline Vesey Neroni – Nata Stanhope', as her card reads] . . . had quite a *levée* round her couch' at her parents' afternoon party (*Towers*, 46); *liaisons, malgré lui* (2), *malgré moi, mauvaise honte* (3), *mauvais suget* (sic), *ménage* (2), *métier* (3), *par excellence, parti* ('eligible husband') (2), [*le*] *pas, pas si mal,* (Mollet) *père, pied à terre, pis aller, pour passer le temps, première ieunesse, preux chevalier* (2), *preux chevalier sans peur et sans reproche, sans reproche, protégée, recherché, retroussé, robe de nuit,*[3] *roué* (2), *ruse, sang-froid* (3), *selon les regles* (sic), *soidisant* (sic), *soupçon* (5) *tapis* (2), *tête-à-tête* (2 n., 1 adv.), *tête montée, the* (sic) *dansant, tout ensemble* (2), *triste, trousseau.*[4]

German Trollope never uses; of Italian, besides the single word

---

that Fanny was *enceinte*' – a word that she herself, of course, would never have been represented by Trollope as understanding, let alone using.

4. This occurs in *Kellys*, 26. In *Warden*, 2 appears the English spelling '*dishabille*' – italicized as if it were French. Trollope would seem to have forgotten in 1853 what he knew (though imperfectly) in 1847.

1. This is, oddly, Trollope's invariable spelling (and he uses the word often), but only in *Land* 28 does he italicize it. It looks as if it had dawned upon him only late in life that it was not the English spelling.

2. ' "The Miss O'Joscelyns have been expecting you . . . to play *la grace* with them. They didn't give up the sticks till it was quite dark . . ." ' (*Kellys*, 30.) This is not an affectation; no English name was current. According to *The Encyclopædia Britannica* (11th edition), 'LA GRÂCE, or LES GRÂCES, [is] a game invented in France during the first quarter of the nineteenth century and called there *le jeu des Grâces*. It is played with two light sticks about 16 inches long and a wicker ring, which is projected into the air by placing it over the sticks crossed and then separating them rapidly. The ring is caught upon the stick of another player and thrown back, the object being to prevent it from falling to the ground.'

3. Archdeacon Grantly (*Warden*, 2), preparing to go to bed with his wife, 'exchanged . . . [his] shining black habiliments for his accustomed *robe de nuit* . . .' This is not pretentious or affected, but rather mock decorum; lesser men, perhaps even humbler clergymen, may wear nightshirts (first recorded in *OED*, incidentally, from 1857; what on earth *did* people call them before?), but not an archdeacon, or at least this archdeacon.

4. A fair number of these words and phrases are now so thoroughly naturalized that we did not italicize them. They include none that Trollope does not italicize at least once; all of them, *ie*, he at least usually thought of as not completely naturalized.

nata on Madeline Neroni's card, he uses only three[1] phrases – *con amore* and (*dolce*) *far niente* twice each, and *sotto voce* a good many times. The Portuguese *auto-da-fé* occurs once – 'The sin of bribery . . . is the one sin for which, in the House of Commons, there can be no forgiveness . . . It is a heresy which requires an *auto-da-fé.*' (*Thorne*, 22.)

1. Not counting an entire sentence – ' "Che va piano va sano" ' – in the mouth of an Italian in the midst of an English conversation. (*Scarb*, 11.)

CHAPTER VI

Trollope's Reading

🔷🔷🔷🔷🔷🔷

I. INTRODUCTION

A striking feature of Trollope's style is the multitude of literary allusions, quotations, and echoes, of which there are, I think, proportionately (and perhaps, considering his output, absolutely) more in his novels than in those of Dickens or Thackeray or Meredith. Unquestionably Trollope read a great deal, he remembered (*verbatim* as well as in substance) much of what he had read, and he seems to have been spontaneously reminded of his reading as he wrote his novels and often as it were irresistibly driven to reflect his reading in his writing. Obviously, to do so gave him pleasure, he obviously regarded the practice as a respectable literary device, and he did not employ it to show off, but to give pleasure to his readers – an object that he could of course not have hoped to attain if he had not expected them to recognize his literary references.

These generalizations, however, require several amplifications, qualifications, and limitations.

(1) I have recorded over a hundred literary allusions and over 250 quotations and phraseological echoes. Though I am sure I have neglected to record some – at least some allusions consisting of the mere isolated mention of a literary or mythological figure or echoes so slight and faint that I have not recognized them – I am equally sure that the proportions are essentially right. Why Trollope quoted or echoed two and a half times as often as he alluded I do not know, nor do I know whether the same proportions would be found in other nineteenth-century novelists, or for that matter in writers (particularly of prose fiction) generally.

(2) By pure coincidence, the references (taking all three kinds together) occur also about two and a half times as often in Trollope's own language as in that of his characters. This is easier

to understand; the collocutors in a conversation both in real life and in realistic fiction, speaking without reflection about their daily concerns, fall less readily into literary allusions, quotations, and echoes than a novelist (or almost any kind of writer), and especially a novelist who intrudes so often as Trollope does in dialogue and straight narrative with analyses of his characters' states of mind, discursive comments on the conduct of life, apostrophes to characters and addresses to readers, and other divagations from a straightforward account of a series of fictitious happenings. (See Chapters VII and VIII.)

(3) Of literary references of all kinds, the first three novels (*Macd*, 1845; *Kellys*, 1847; and *Warden*, 1853) contain fewer than twenty among them. Between 1853 and 1856, Trollope, for what reason I do not know, must have consciously and designedly conceived the idea of filling – indeed, overfilling – a novel with literary references; for the fourth novel (*Towers*, 1856) contains over seventy – about a fifth of the total in all forty-one[1] novels.[2] No other novel remotely approaches this number; Trollope would seem to have decided immediately that he had overworked the device. The first novel after *Towers* (*Clerks*, 1857) has considerably fewer than half as many instances, and the next (*Thorne*, 1858) hardly more than a tenth. In the next three (*Bertrams*, 1858, and *Castle* and *Framley*, both 1860), there is a slight relapse, the first two having about twenty each, and the third about fifteen. In the next (*Orley*, 1861), there is a reduction to about the level of *Thorne*. Then up again in *House* (1863), to about a dozen, and then, later in the same year, drastically down to one (*Ray*), followed by an average of about four in *Forgive*, *Mack*, and *Claver* (all 1864), and *Belton* (1865), when a reader of all the novels in the order of publication[3] (which happens to be, with the single inconsiderable

1. I exclude *Struggles*; the style is not Trollope's at all, but what he imagined would be that of a semi-literate bill-sticker (as polished by a publisher's hack editor), with no acquaintance with literature, who, further, sticks to his narrative. For both these reasons, the book contains, and would be expected to contain, almost no literary references.

2. This is chiefly, though by no means wholly, owing to the number of *non*-biblical allusions and of *biblical* quotations and echoes (a paradoxical oddity in itself): *Towers* contains slightly more of each of these two kinds of references than all the rest of the novels together.

3. I suspect that strictly speaking there were only four such readers other than the author, *viz.*, the publisher's reader, the compositor, the proof-reader, and Mrs Trollope; *Macd* and *Kellys* sold almost no copies, and Trollope was so discouraged that he did not try again (except in *La Vendée*, written 1849 and published 1850,

exception of *Claver*, finished a year earlier than *Belton*, but published a year later) the same as that of the order in which they were written (or rather finished – as is not always true later) – a reader, *ie*, who read them with the particular kind of attention that I have read them with, as I very much doubt whether any did – would have said that Trollope had finally 'kicked the habit' – only to have to revise his opinion in 1866 with *Chron*, which, with about twenty references, reverts to the level of *Bertrams* and *Castle*, finished respectively eight and six years earlier. But this proved not to be a forecast of things to come: of the twenty-four later novels (1867–1882), only six have more than five references (*Scarb* has most – about a dozen), and these six, furthermore, do not occur close together, but are scattered over the fifteen years from 1867 to 1881 – *Finn* (1867), *Redux* (1872), *Way* (1873), *Children* (1876), *Fay* (1879), and *Scarb* (1881). The intervening (and following) eighteen have an average of fewer than three references.

(4) The numbers of literary references given in the preceding paragraph for the several novels show on the whole, though with some interruptions, even some late ones, still a very definite decline, and the reader is excusable if he is led to the conclusion that the decline involves, and involves more or less equally (a) both allusions, and quotations and echoes, and (b) all the sources – (secular) English literature, the Bible, the Book of Common Prayer, and classical literature and mythology. Analysis, however, shows this to be decidedly untrue. The *general* decline is almost wholly owing to the virtual disappearance after 1866 of *allusions* to the Bible and to classical literature and mythology (allusions to secular English literature also fall off, and quotations and echoes of the Bible, but not so suddenly or so markedly); *quotations and echoes* of both English and Latin authors are on the whole pretty evenly distributed throughout Trollope's career, at least after 1860. The only explanation I can suggest for Trollope's coming to use fewer allusions but continuing to use about as many quotations and echoes is a combination of three facts: (a) Though the

---

not covered in this book – see Introduction) for five years. Indeed, in his last years there may have been only three such readers. Up to 1878, Mrs Trollope transcribed all her husband's novels (out of compassion for the compositor); but in that year, after finishing *Ayala*, Trollope began to suffer from writer's cramp, and dictated all the later novels (except the last, *Land*) to his niece Florence Bland (see Sadleir, p. 316), and it seems improbable that her aunt read her manuscripts.

majority of both allusions, and quotations and echoes, are used more or less lightly – many of them facetiously – this is markedly truer of the allusions, especially of those to the Bible and to classical literature and mythology. (b) In the course of the years, the novels tend – admittedly with several exceptions here and there, but still on the whole – to become more serious, even sometimes sombre, in subject and theme, and Trollope's style becomes correspondingly less humorous and light-hearted. (c) It also becomes less given to most kinds of deliberate ornaments (see Introduction and Chapter V), *ie*, more businesslike, and generally speaking the allusions – often elaborate – give the impression of calculated contrivance – even now and then of ostentation, whereas the quotations and echoes much oftener sound as if they had sprung unbidden from Trollope's excellent verbal memory as he wrote. Even when they are light-hearted, even when they are humorous, even when they are facetious, they seem spontaneous.[1]

Let us now turn to the several sources of Trollope's literary allusions, quotations, and echoes.

2. ENGLISH AUTHORS

Trollope both alludes to and quotes or echoes at least five English writers; he alludes to, without quoting or echoing, at least fifteen; he quotes or echoes, without alluding to, at least sixteen. Following is a list of all thirty-six, showing first the number of allusions recorded and second the number of quotations and echoes.

Shakespeare – 11, 54; Milton – 0, 14; Dickens – 15, 1; Scott – 7, 2; Pope – 0, 8; Byron – 5, 1; Thackeray – 5, 0; Sterne – 1, 3; Dryden – 0, 3; Wither – 0, 3; Sir Henry Taylor – 0, 3. Two allusions, no quotations or echoes: Canning, Chaucer (?), Richardson, Sheridan, Tennyson. Two quotations or echoes, no allusions: Charles Maturin, Gray, Prior, Thomas Morell, Burns. One allusion, no quotations or echoes: Bunyan, Carlyle, Disraeli, Fielding, Goldsmith, Nicholas Rowe, Samuel Warren, Sir David

---

1. I suppose I hardly need say – but I think it will be well to say – that this chapter could not possibly have been produced – at least by me – without constant reference to John Bartlett, *Familiar Quotations* (Boston: Little, Brown and Company, 14th edition, revised and enlarged, 1968); *The Oxford Book of Quotations* (Oxford University Press, 2nd edition, 1953); and Burton Stevenson, *The Home Book of Quotations* (New York: Dodd Mead and Company, 9th edition, 1958).

Brewster, William Whewell. One quotation or echo, no allusions: Thomas Campbell, Cowper, Nathaniel Lee, Shelley, Thomas Tusser, Isaac Watts.

The most striking facts revealed by a cursory inspection of these figures are (1) that Shakespeare supplies slightly more than half the quotations and echoes;[1] (2) that he supplies far more allusions than any other writer but Dickens; (3) that next to Shakespeare, Milton supplies by far the largest number of quotations and echoes – but *no* allusions; (4) that Dickens supplies somewhat more allusions than Shakespeare – but only one quotation (or rather echo); and (5) that Trollope quotes or echoes English writers almost twice as often as he alludes to them (though this is very largely accounted for by the number of quotations and echoes of Shakespeare).

But there is much of interest not revealed by these figures.

Shakespeare. (1) The usual preponderance of allusions in Trollope's own language over those in his characters' is here reversed: seven are characters' and only four Trollope's. This is all but wholly owing to Madeline Neroni's part in the wonderful conversation with Mr Slope in *Towers*, 27 – one of Trollope's masterpieces of character-revealing dialogue. During this conversation Madeline mentions Cleopatra's resolute faithfulness to Antony, Imogen's faithfulness, Ophelia's, Desdemona's, and Juliet's; and says, ' "A man may love and yet not be a Troilus. All women are not Cressidas." ' For good measure she goes beyond Shakespeare and throws in a reference to Dido and adds Byron's Haidée to her catalogue of 'Cupid's saints'. And finally she baptizes the whole thing, so to speak, by quoting 'spiritual pastors and masters' from the Prayer Book Catechism. Madeline, usually confined to her father's house and often alone, must have spent a good deal of time reading – and to good purpose. Of Trollope's own allusions, the only notable (and only comic) one is also in *Towers*, 33: '. . . had [Mrs Proudie] married Petruchio, it may be doubted whether that arch wife-tamer would have been able to keep her legs out of those garments which are presumed by

1. This is perhaps partly owing to the fact that Trollope took to Shakespeare young. He says in his *Autobiography*, Chapter 1, that between 1827 and 1830, when he was at Winchester, he 'passed one set of holidays . . . in my father's chambers in Lincoln's Inn. . . . On this occasion my amusement consisted in wandering about those old deserted buildings and reading Shakespeare . . . it was not that I had chosen Sheakespeare, but that there was nothing else to read.'

men to be particularly unfitted for feminine use.' (2) Of the fifty-four Shakespeare quotations and echoes, more than two-thirds are in Trollope's own language. There is nothing in this figure to suggest that Trollope quoted or echoed one play much more than another. But he decidedly did; of the fifty-four, fifteen are from *Macbeth* and thirteen from *Hamlet* – together over half the total. Thirteen other plays are quoted or echoed, but only one (*Twelfth Night*) as many as five times, and six (plus *Venus and Adonis*) only once. Clearly Trollope had read *Macbeth* and *Hamlet* far oftener than any other play, and he was correspondingly far oftener reminded of passages from them – but often, with *Macbeth*, the same passages again and again: 'But screw your courage to the sticking point [*sic*]' occurs twice, as do 'The labour we delight in physics pain,' 'Stand not upon the order of your going', and 'Canst thou not minister to a mind diseased?'[1] With *Hamlet*, repetition is not so frequent, but what is notable is that of the thirteen quotations and echoes, five are from 'the' soliloquy, and three from Hamlet's rebuke to his mother (III.iii), including two uses of 'Look here, upon this picture and on that'. The only other plays from which a single passage is quoted or echoed more than once is *Twelfth Night* (three 'ginger shall be hot i' the mouth' out of five) and *As You Like It* (two 'Men have died and worms have eaten them – but not for love' out of four). (3) Generally speaking Trollope's quotations and echoes of Shakespeare tend to be oftener used in serious contexts and with serious application than those from other English writers – though this may possibly be only because *Macbeth* and *Hamlet* are tragedies.

Milton. Though references to Milton make him second (a very poor second, to be sure) to Shakespeare, the whole number – all quotations or echoes, and no allusions – on the face of it does not suggest that the quotations or echoes of Milton are not from a proportionate range of works. Nothing could be less true. Of the fourteen quotations or echoes, eleven are from *Lycidas*.[2] Further, five of the eleven quote or echo 'To sport with Amaryllis in the shade,/Or with the tangles of Neæra's hair' (twice accompanied by

1. This and the later Shakespeare quotations I give in the authentic form, but some of the occurrences in Trollope are echoic, not literal.
2. Pope-Hennessy speaks (p. 287) of *Lycidas* as Trollope's 'favourite poem', and Trollope himself tells in his *Autobiography*, Chapter 3, which deals with his early G.P.O. days in London, of 'throwing out of the window . . . a volume of Johnson's *Lives of the Poets*, because he spoke sneeringly of *Lycidas*.'

Phoebus's touching the trembling ears), and four quote or echo 'He tricks his beams, and with new spangled ore/Flames in the forehead of the morning sky'. Only two other passages from the poem are quoted or echoed: in *Towers*, 1 we are told that 'Our archdeacon . . . was ambitious – who among us is ashamed to admit "that last infirmity of mortal minds [*sic*]"?', and in *Towers*, 51, when Mr Slope considers his future on leaving Barchester, Trollope quotes, with a sartorially allusive 'variant reading', ' "At last he rose, and twitched his mantle blue (black),/Tomorrow to fresh woods and pastures new." ' From outside of *Lycidas* there is nothing but two echoes of *Paradise Lost* – 'all the world before them where to choose', adapted to the bright prospects of a young heir – the opening sentence of *Right*, and 'Better to reign in Hell than serve in Heaven', quoted to herself by Arabella Trefoil in *Senator*, 75, when she contemplates exchanging impoverished spinsterhood in London for marriage to the Minister to 'Patagonia'; and one quotation from *Samson Agonistes* by Mr Crawley to his daughter in *Chron*, 62 – 'Ask for this great deliverer now, and find him/Eyeless in Gaza, at the mill with slaves.' (This is one of the few Miltonic quotations or echoes that Trollope does not apply humorously or at least lightly.) In short, Trollope gives no evidence of having at his fingers' tips anything of Milton's but *Lycidas*, and little but two passages from that.

Dickens. The situation with Dickens is in strong contrast in two ways: (1) Trollope knew at least seven of Dickens's novels well, and (2) only one of his references to them is an echo, the other fifteen being allusions. He started reading Dickens early: in his first novel, *Macd* (1845), he mentions 'Bardell *v.* Pickwick' – eight years after the completed publication of *Pickwick Papers*. The next two references – to *Martin Chuzzlewit* and *Bleak House* – appear in *Warden*, 15 (1853); but unlike any of the others, they occur in the context of a long and above all discriminating critique of Dickens. In this chapter Trollope amuses himself by parodying the ways in which Mr Harding is charged by *The Jupiter* (*ie, The Times*), Dr Pessimist Anticant (*ie,* Carlyle), and Mr Popular Sentiment (*ie,* Dickens) with moral, though not legal, guilt in drawing, from the greatly enhanced value of the land whose rents had been left (in 1434) by John Hiram for the maintenance of his hospital, £800 a year, plus a commodious house, while the twelve bedesmen who were to have been the essential and primary beneficiaries of

Hiram's bounty get only a cottage and 1s. 6d. a day (raised by Mr Harding from Hiram's 1s. 4d.).

'You see,' said [Tom] Towers [a leader-writer for *The Jupiter*, to John Bold, who has read Towers's attacks, and to whom Towers shows Dr Anticant's], 'that this affair has been much talked of . . . Have you seen the first number of the "Almshouse?" '

No; Bold had not seen the 'Almshouse.' He had seen advertisements of Mr Popular Sentiment's new novel of that name, but had in no way connected it with the Barchester Hospital . . .

'It's a direct attack on the whole system,' said Towers.

On leaving Towers, Bold buys a copy of the first number, and proceeds 'to ascertain what Mr Popular Sentiment had to say to the public on the subject . . .' Before telling us, Trollope pauses for a disquisition on Dickens generally.

In former times great objects were attained by great work. When evils were to be reformed, reformers set about their heavy task with grave decorum and laborious argument . . . We get on now with a lighter step, and quicker: . . . monthly novels convince, when learned quartos fail to do so. If the world is to be set right, the work will be done by shilling numbers.

Of all such reformers, Mr Sentiment is the most powerful. It is incredible the number of evil practices he has put down: it is to be feared he will soon lack subjects, and that when he has made the working classes comfortable, and got bitter beer into proper-sized pint bottles, there will be nothing further left for him to do. Mr Sentiment is certainly a very powerful man, and perhaps not the less so that his good poor people are so very good; his hard rich people so very hard; and the genuinely honest so very honest. Namby-pamby in these days is not thrown away if it be introduced in the proper quarters. Divine peeresses are no longer interesting, though possessed of every virtue; but a pattern peasant or an immaculate manufacturing hero may talk as much twaddle as one of Mrs Ratcliffe's [*sic*] heroines, and still be listened to. Perhaps, however, Mr Sentiment's great attraction is his second-rate characters. If his heroes and heroines walk upon stilts . . . their attendant satellites are as natural as though one met them in the street: they walk and talk like men and women, and live among our friends a rattling, lively life; yes, live, and will live till the names of their callings shall be forgotten in their own, and Buckett and Mrs Gamp will be the only words left us to signify a detective officer or a monthly nurse.

Though the concluding prediction has not been literally fulfilled – and Trollope doubtless knew he was exaggerating – no one today would disagree with his judicious appraisal of Dickens's strengths and weaknesses. Every lover of Dickens nowadays loves him for the 'attendant satellites' of his 'heroes and heroines . . . upon stilts'; for them, and for most of his febrilely and unfairly exaggerated attacks on social abuses, they forgive him. Or the latter, perhaps, they rather endure once, but do not return to: I, at least, in re-reading Dickens (as I have long done) have never for years re-read an entire novel (except *Pickwick* – which, any-way, is perhaps not a novel at all, but which I am combatively convinced is the greatest piece of prose fiction in the language). I do not re-read *Martin Chuzzlewit*, but the quarrel between Sairey Gamp and Betsey Prig, and the dinner for the Pecksniffs at Todgers's; I do not re-read *Our Mutual Friend*, but Silas Wegg's reading to the illiterate Boffins of what Mr Boffin calls 'Decline-and-Fall-Off-The-Rooshan-Empire', and Mrs Wilfer's pompous mock-martyr allocutions to her long-suffering family. These are the sort of thing in Dickens that stick in one's mind and that, if one is a true Dickensian, one returns to with ever-fresh delight. At any rate, to judge from Trollope's allusions, that was true of him.

But before we look at some of them, let us return to Trollope's outline[1] of the first number of *The Almshouse*.

The 'Almshouse' opened with a scene in a clergyman's house. Every luxury to be purchased by wealth was described as being there; all the appearances of household indulgence generally found amongst the most self-indulgent of the rich were crowded into this abode. Here the reader was introduced to the demon

1. That is what it is; it is not, like the preceding mockery of *The Times* or of Carlyle, a stylistic parody. And yet till I re-read *Warden* (for at least the tenth time) for the purposes of this book, I should have said that it *was* a stylistic parody, so perfectly does it reproduce (with only a little exaggeration) Dickens's characterization, and so naturally in consequence are we charmed into inaccurately remembering it as reproducing his diction as well.

of the book . . . the clerical owner of this comfortable abode.
He was a man well stricken in years, but still strong to do evil:
he was one who looked cruelly out of a hot, passionate, blood-
shot eye, who had a huge red nose with a carbuncle, thick lips,
and a great double, flabby chin, which swelled out into solid
substance, like a turkey cock's comb, when sudden ire inspired
him; . . . his husky voice told tales of much daily port wine,
and his language was not so decorous as to become a clergyman. [Mr Harding!] . . .

The second chapter of course introduced the reader to the
more especial inmates of the hospital. Here were discovered
eight old men; and it was given to be understood that four
vacancies remained through the perverse ill-nature of the
clerical gentleman with the double chin. The state of these
eight paupers was touchingly dreadful: sixpence-farthing a-day
had been sufficient when the almshouse was founded; and on
sixpence-farthing a-day were they still doomed to starve,
though food was four times as dear, and money four times as
plentiful. It was shocking to find how the conversation of these
eight starved old men in their dormitory shamed that of the
clergyman's family in his rich drawing-room. The absolute
words they uttered were not perhaps spoken in the purest
English, and it might be difficult to distinguish from their
dialect to what part of the country they belonged; the beauty
of the sentiment, however, amply atoned for the imperfection
of the language; and it was really a pity that these eight old men
could not have been sent through the country as moral
missionaries, instead of being immured and starved in that
wretched almshouse.

Let us now turn to the remaining allusions to Dickens. (1) In
Towers, 43 we are told that Bishop Proudie 'read the last number
of the [*sic*] "Little Dorrit" of the day [*sic*] with great inward
satisfaction.' I have no doubt that Trollope thought of *Little
Dorrit* specifically here because he was himself pretty certainly
reading it at the same time; it was being written, and appeared,
during 1855 and the two following years, and Trollope finished
Towers in 1856. At the same time, by saying '*the* "Little Dorrit" of
the day', he manages to suggest, with good-natured mischievous-
ness, that he means 'whatever novel the indefatigable Dickens

happened to be publishing at the time in monthly parts'. (In a very
few years, we should have to say 'the pot and the kettle'.) *Little
Dorrit* was not unnaturally still fresh in Trollope's mind in the
next year, 1857, when in *Clerks*, 1 he writes that the Department
of Weights and Measures 'is exactly antipodistic to the Circumlocu-
tion office . . .' (2) From *Pickwick*, besides the reference already
mentioned, come '. . . there was no drop of the Leohunter [*sic*]
blood in Miss Thorne's veins . . .' (*Towers*, 37 – 1856); 'Dodson
and Fogg' (*Chron*, 32 – 1866); and 'He [the – questionably – Rev.
Mr Emilius] was about as near an English mitre as that great man
of a past generation, the Deputy Shepherd' (*Eustace*, 72 – 1870).
(3) *Oliver Twist* (1837–38) is alluded to three times: 'Alaric Tudor
was now a rogue; . . . a Bill Sykes [*sic*] without any of those
excuses which a philanthropist cannot but make for wretches
brought up in infamy.' (*Clerks*, 29 – 1857); 'It is Bill Sikes before
conviction that I have ever pitied.' (*Castle*, 43 – 1860); and 'The
Liberals . . . would . . . have half the patronage in beadles,
bell-ringers and bumbledom in general.' (*Ralph*, 20 – 1869). (4)
Nicholas Nickleby (1838–39): ' "Her dresses were made at the
exclusive establishment of Madame Mantalini . . ." ' (*Clerks*,
22 – 1857; from Charley Tudor's mock-fashionable novel *Crinoline
and Macassar*, of which parts are embodied in *Clerks*). (5) From
Martin Chuzzlewit (1843), besides the reference already mentioned,
come ' "You will at once have run the whole gamut of humanity
from St Paul to Pecsniff [*sic*]." ' (*Bertrams*, 26 – 1858), and ' "Miss
Spruce, do let me send you a little more gravy?" . . . Mrs Roper
[the landlady] was probably thinking of Mrs Todgers.' (*House*, 29 –
1863.) (6) *David Copperfield* (1848–1850): ' "The long and the
short of it is this: is Barkis willing?" ' (*Struggles*, 8 – 1861; this is
the only instance of a Dickensian echo as distinct from a mere
allusion, and pretty nearly the only literary allusion in *Struggles*.
Both the speaker and 'Robinson', the fictitious author, are of the
lower middle class – an evidence of Dickens's appeal to almost all
ranks of society.) (7) *Bleak House* (1852–53) supplies, besides the
reference already mentioned, ' "Turveydrop and deportment will
suffice for us against any odds." ' (*Children*, 26 – 1876; spoken by
Phineas Finn in the House of Commons. Another reference to
'Turveydrop and deportment' in Chapter 76 of the same novel is
cited in the Introduction.)

The dates given above do not demonstrate that Trollope read

any novel of Dickens's except *Bleak House* and *Little Dorrit* less than eight years after its publication, but he probably read most of them when they were published (as most people who read light fiction at all apparently did). And he apparently re-read them, or remembered them very well, or both: his first and last allusions to *Martin Chuzzlewit* are separated by eleven years, to *Oliver Twist* by thirteen, to *Bleak House* by twenty-four, and to *Pickwick* by twenty-six. He plainly – and justly – expected as good an acquaintance with Dickens of his own readers as he had himself.

Pope. All the quotations are, and had become long before Trollope's day, commonplaces, and indeed so nearly proverbial that they have been and are often quoted by people ignorant of their source (though I doubt whether Trollope was). Only one or two of them are serious or half-way serious in context or application. They all appear in novels finished from 1856 to 1858, except one in 1867. 'Leather and prunella' occurs three times, and one other phrase from the same poem (*Essay on Man*), 'all the blood of all the Howards', once; in *Towers*, 21 Mr Arabin quotes 'damn with faint praise' (*Epistle to Dr Arbuthnot*) – but follows it not with "assent with civil leer", but with 'crush with open calumny'; Trollope says of a flirt in *Clerks* that ' "A feast of reason and a flow of soul" [from the 'imitation' of Horace's *Satire* 1, Book 2 – where Pope wrote 'the' in both places] were not the charms by which Clementina . . . essayed to keep her admirers spellbound . . .'; and 'Welcome the coming, speed the parting guest', from the translation of the Odyssey, is quoted appositely enough by a character in the same novel. Finally – and mentioned last for a good reason – a character in *Bertrams* 9 quotes, from the 'imitation' of Horace's *Epistle* 1, Book 2: ' " 'Praise undeserved is satire[1] in disguise,' " said Mr Cruse, *not quite understanding, himself, why he made the quotation.*' (Italics mine.) There is a yet more pointed comment by Trollope on quoting for quoting's sake in *House*, 2: ' " 'As sweet an musical as bright Apollo's lute,' "[2] said Mr Crosbie, *not meaning much by the quotation.*' (Italics mine.) Mr Cruse is not much one way or the other; but Adolphus Crosbie, who jilted Lily Dale, is, besides being self-seeking and cynical, also vain and ostentatious, and shows these qualities here, by quoting what

---

1. Pope wrote 'scandal'; and incidentally, he lifted the line from an anonymous epigram in *The Grove*, 1721.
2. From *Love's Labour's Lost*, IV. iii. 42.

he quotes merely because, on hearing someone say 'Apollo' – and hearing nothing more – as he joins a conversation, he intrudes, for purposes of display, and not to make a relevant or even amusing contribution to the conversation, the subject of which he cannot even guess, the first line of poetry containing 'Apollo' that occurs to him – and possibly the only one he knows.

This kind of literary reference, pointless and inapposite, and lugged in by the ears solely to impress the hearers with the speaker's familiarity with literature, exhibits just the sort of vanity and dishonesty that would excite aversion and contempt in one given, as Trollope was in an exceptionally high degree, to quoting, and to quoting always appropriately and spontaneously, if not *quite* always in good taste, and out of a genuine and wide acquaintance with literature – itself a demonstration of his love of it. In *Eustace*, 21, he ridicules the other kind of quotation severely and at length. Lizzy, Lady Eustace (probably the most abominable character Trollope ever invented), has lost, by death, which she has hastened, and lost even earlier than she had hoped, the sickly husband she had married for his money. She sits down in her garden with a copy of *Queen Mab* with the deliberate intention of enhancing spuriously her intellectual charms by memorizing some poetry to quote in company, exactly as she might try to enhance her physical ones by finding a more durable and deceptive rouge. And the less definite the meaning of the poetry to her or to anyone, the more frequent its usefulness.

She had often talked of 'Queen Mab' and perhaps she thought she had read it. This, however, was in truth her first attempt at the work. 'How wonderful is Death, Death and his brother Sleep.' Then she half-closed the volume, and thought that she enjoyed the idea. Death – and his brother Sleep! She did not know why they should be more wonderful than Action, or Life, or Thought; but the words were of a nature which would enable her to remember them, and they would be good for quoting. 'Sudden arose Ianthe's soul; it stood All beautiful in naked purity.' The name of Ianthe suited her exactly. And the antithesis conveyed to her mind by naked purity struck her strongly, and she determined to learn the passage by heart. Eight or nine lines were printed separately, like a stanza, and the labour would not be great, and the task, when done, would

be complete. 'Instinct with inexpressible beauty and grace,
Each stain of earthliness Had passed away, it reassumed Its
native dignity, and stood Immortal amid ruin.' Which was
instinct with beauty, the stain or the soul, she did not stop to
inquire, and may be excused for not understanding. [An
incidental, and just, criticism of Shelley.] 'Ah,' she exclaimed
to herself, 'how true it is; how one feels it; how it comes home
to one! – "Sudden arose Ianthe's soul." ' And then she walked
about the garden, repeating the words to herself, and almost
forgetting the heat. ' "Each stain of earthliness had passed
away." Ha; yes. They will pass away and become instinct with
beauty and grace.' A dim idea came upon her that when this
happy time should arrive, no one would claim her necklace
from her, and that the man at the stables would not be so
disagreeably punctual about sending in his bill. ' "All beautiful
in naked purity!" ' What a tawdry world was this in which
clothes and food and houses are necessary. How perfectly that
boy poet had understood it all. ' "Immortal amid ruin!" ' She
liked the idea of the ruin almost as well as that of the im-
mortality, and the stains quite as well as the purity. As im-
mortality must come, and as stains were instinct with grace,
why be afraid of ruin? But then, if people go wrong – at least
women – they are not asked out anywhere. ' "Sudden arose
Ianthe's soul; it stood all beautiful – ." ' And so the piece was
learned, and Lizzie felt that she had devoted her hour to poetry
in a quite rapturous manner. At any rate she had a bit to quote;
and though in truth she did not understand the exact bearing of
the image, she had so studied her gestures and so modulated
her voice, that she knew that she could be effective.[1]

Later on the same day Lizzie sits with her old companion, Miss
Macnulty, watching the mouth of the Clyde from her drawing-
room window, and professes to be reminded of looking over the
Bay of Naples with her late husband (whom she has driven into
his grave).

1. Trollope could hardly have had a copy of *Queen Mab* beside him when he wrote
this passage. 'How wonderful is Death,/Death and his brother Sleep!' are the first
two lines of the first 'stanza' of eight lines, whereas all the rest of the poem
Trollope quotes here is from the nine-line 'stanza' beginning with line 130 of the
first section; but he leaves one with the impression that all the lines quoted are
consecutive.

'There are scenes there which ravish you, only it is necessary that there should be some one with you that can understand you. "Soul of Ianthe!" ' she said, meaning to apostrophize that of the deceased Sir Florian. 'You have read "Queen Mab?" . . . I know of nothing in the the English language[1] that brings home to one so often one's own best feelings and aspirations. "It stands all beautiful in naked purity," ' she continued, still alluding to poor Sir Florian's soul. ' "Instinct with inexpressible beauty and grace, each stain of earthliness has passed away." I can see him now in all his manly beauty, as we used to sit together by the hour, looking over the waters. Oh, Julia, the thing itself has gone, the earthly reality; but the memory of it will live forever . . . I see him now,' she went on, still gazing out upon the shining water. ' "It reassumed its native dignity and stood primeval among ruin." Is that not a glorious idea, gloriously worded?' She had forgotten one word and used a wrong epithet; but it sounded just as well. Primeval seemed to her to be a very poetical word.

The only other English writers referred to by allusion, quotation, or echo more than three times (Sterne doesn't count – see below on the Bible) are Scott, Byron, and Thackeray. With all three, the allusions are more numerous than the quotations (Scott, 7, 2; Byron, 5, 1; Thackeray, 5, 0) – another indication of the reading public's familiarity with them. Two instances of the use of the name Caleb Balderstone (*Castle*, 43 and *Redux*, 10), as if it meant anybody's butler, testify to Trollope's confidence that his readers were familiar with *The Bride of Lammermoor* (cf. his probably not serious prediction that we should come to speak of Mrs Gamps rather than of monthly nurses); of a young lady in *Vicar*, 8 Trollope says that 'with such a one as Flora MacIvor she had no patience; – a girl . . . who of all flirts was to her the most nauseous' (*Waverley*); in *Towers*, 22 Miss Thorne, who shares her brother's belief in their descent from a pre-Conquest noble Saxon family and his consequent contempt for Normans as parvenus, was, says Trollope, 'not unlike Scott's Ulrica, and had she been given to cursing, would certainly have done so in the names of Mista, Skogula, and Zernebock' (*Ivanhoe*); and in the next chapter,

1. Impudent and overreaching baggage! She wishes to be supposed to know not only *Queen Mab*, but at least a considerable part of English literature.

Trollope, animadverting upon what he regards as an excessive and unseemly lack of diffidence in young clergymen preaching their first sermons, says that 'we must own that the deep affection which Dominie Sampson felt for his young pupils has not more endeared him to us than the bashful spirit which sent him mute and inglorious [an incidental echo of Gray] from the pulpit when he rose there with the futile attempt to preach God's gospel' (*Guy Mannering*). A single paragraph in *Ralph*, 56 – part of a long disquisition on the didactic function as proper to the novelist – mentions Jeanie Deans (*The Heart of Midlothian*) and Richard Varney (*Kenilworth*) as types respectively of the perfect heroine and the perfect villain. As against these, there are only two quotations, both from 'Lochinvar' in *Marmion*, and both implicitly comparing bold and dashing lovers to Lochinvar (*Orley*, 74 and *Finn*, 54). Much the same thing is true of Byron; the only quotation is Lucy Toogood's ' "Fancy a love 'Who thundering comes on blackest steed, with slackened bit and hoof of speed' " ' (*Chron*, 40), quoted without mentioning the source (*The Giaour*). In her next speech she speaks of Conrad and Medora, but again does not mention the poem in which they figure (*The Corsair*). 'The Corsair' is also the name Lizzy Eustace aptly applies (in her thoughts) to one of her suitors, whose near-savagery both fascinates and frightens her. Finally, there are three allusions to Haidée (two in dialogue, including one by Madeline Neroni mentioned above).

Thackeray is represented by the mention of Henry Esmond, Colonel Newcome, Barry Lyndon, Becky Sharp, and Fitzjeames – all but the last (which is in *Towers*, 1) in the disquisition in *Ralph*, 6 cited above under Scott, and with the same purpose. Considering Trollope's well-known admiration, not to say veneration, of Thackeray, reflected in his *Autobiography* and in his *Life of Thackeray* (1879), and even by his well-meant but dismal imitation of Thackeray's early (and worst) style in *Struggles*, it seems strange that his novels contain so few allusions to his hero's – and those few so concentrated. (Contrast Dickens.) There is one reference of a special kind. In *Forgive* (written 16 August 1863–28 April 1864) Trollope introduces a minor character, Lord Cinquebars, a peer's heir devoted to hunting. At the first occurrence of the name, Trollope subjoins this footnote: 'Ah, my friend [Thackeray], from whom I have borrowed this scion of the nobility! Had he been left with us he would have forgiven me my little theft, and now that he has gone I will not change the name.' This name (but spelt 'Cinqbars') first occurs in *A Shabby-Genteel Story* (1840) and later in several others of Thackeray's books – not clearly always designating the same person. Thackeray died on 24 December 1863, in the midst of Trollope's composition of *Forgive*.

To deal in similar detail with references to all the other English writers listed above would hardly be worth either the reader's time or mine, but there are several of special interest of one kind or another.

Carlyle. The only so to speak unmasked allusion to Carlyle occurs in *Fay*, 2 (1879): 'Then our noble Republican [the heir to a marquisate with Radical opinions, and a special aversion to shooting] would quote Teufelsdröch [*sic*] and the memorable epitaph of the partridge-slayer.' But much earlier (in 1853) in *Warden*, 15, Trollope delivers a reasoned opinion of Carlyle (under a transparent pseudonym) followed by three parodies of Carlyle's style, the last being what Carlyle might be imagined as saying about Mr Harding and Hiram's Hospital. (Cf. the similar castigation of Dickens – 'Mr Popular Sentiment' – in the same chapter, quoted above under Dickens.)

Dr Pessimist Anticant was a Scotchman, who had passed a great portion of his early days in Germany, and had learnt to look with German subtlety into the root of things . . . No man ever resolved more bravely than he to accept as good nothing that was evil . . . Returning from Germany, he had astonished the reading public by the vigour of his thoughts, put forth in the quaintest language. He cannot write English, said the critics. No matter, said the public; we can read what he does write, and that without yawning. And so Dr Pessimist Anticant became popular. Popularity spoilt him for all further real use, as it has spoilt many another. While, with some diffidence, he confined his objurgations to the occasional follies or shortcomings of mankind; while he ridiculed the energy of the squire devoted to the slaughter of partridges, or the mistake of some noble patron who turned a poet into a gauger of beer-barrels, it was all well; we were glad to be told our faults and to look forward to the coming millennium, when all men, having sufficiently studied the works of Dr Anticant, would become truthful and energetic. But the doctor mistook the signs of the times and the minds of men, instituted himself censor of things in general, and began the great task of reprobating everything and everybody, without further promise of any millennium at all . . . We all of us could, and many did, learn much from the doctor while he chose to remain vague, mysterious, and cloudy; but when he became practical, the charm was gone.

Then comes the parody.

'Heavens, what a sight! Let us with eyes wide open see the godly man of four centuries since, the man of the dark ages; let us see how he does his godlike work, and, again, how the godly man of these latter days does his.

'Shall we say that the former one is walking painfully through the world, regarding, as a prudent man, his worldly work, prospering in it as a diligent man will prosper, but always with an eye to that better treasure to which thieves do not creep in? Is there not much nobility in that old man, as, leaning on his oaken staff, he walks down the high street of his native town, and receives from all courteous salutation and acknowledgment of his worth? A noble old man, my inhabitants of Belgrave Square and such like vicinity, – a very noble old man, though employed no better than in the wholesale carding of wool.

'This carding of wool, however, did in those days bring with it much profit, so that our ancient friend, when dying, was declared, in whatever slang then prevailed, to cut up very well. For sons and daughters there was ample sustenance, with assistance of due industry; for friends and relatives some relief for grief at this great loss; for aged dependants comfort in declining years. This was much for one old man to get done in that dark fifteenth century. But this was not all: coming generations of poor woolcarders should bless the name of this rich one; and a hospital should be founded and endowed with his wealth for the feeding of such of the trade as could not, by diligent carding, any longer feed themselves.

' 'Twas thus that an old man in the fifteenth century did his godlike work to the best of his power, and not ignobly, as appears to me.

'We will now take our godly man of latter days. He shall no

longer be a woolcarder, for such are not now men of mark. We will suppose him to be one of the best of the good, – one who has lacked no opportunities. Our old friend was, after all, but illiterate; our modern friend shall be a man educated in all seemly knowledge; he shall, in short, be that blessed being, – a clergyman of the Church of England.

'And now, in what perfectest manner does he in this lower world get his godlike work done and put out of hand? Heavens! in the strangest of manners. Oh, my brother! in a manner not at all to be believed but by the most minute testimony of the eyesight. He does it by the magnitude of his appetite, – by the power of his gorge; his only occupation is to swallow the bread prepared with so much anxious care for these impoverished carders of wool, – that, and to sing indifferently through his nose once in a week some psalm more or less long – the shorter the better, we should be inclined to say.

'Oh, my civilised friends! – great Britons that never will be slaves, – men advanced to infinite state of freedom and knowledge of good and evil – tell me, will you, what becoming monument you will erect to an highly-educated clergyman of the Church of England?'

The contemporary reading public's familiarity with Disraeli's novels almost as much as with Dickens's is reflected in *Towers*, 9: 'This Sidonia . . . did not take so strong a fancy to [Bertie Stanhope] as another of that family did to a young English nobleman.' The allusion is to *Tancred*, published in 1847, eight years before *Towers* was begun. It is Trollope's only reference to Disraeli as a novelist, though it is pretty generally believed that Mr Daubeny in *Finn* and *Redux* is a portrait of Disraeli the politician. The only other contemporary novelist alluded to, and with the same implication that he was widely read, is Samuel Warren (1807–1877), who wrote (not very copiously) in several genres, including a number of short stories published in *Blackwood's* from 1830 to 1837 which were extremely popular, and two novels, one a failure, but the other, *Ten Thousand a Year* (also for *Blackwood's*, 1839–1841), a novel that almost everyone seems to have read, and for which Warren is alone remembered today, so far as he is remembered at all. All Trollope draws from it (*Chron*, 32) is the name of a scoundrelly solicitors' firm, Quirk, Gammon, and Snap, whose names he obviously expected his readers to recognize, even after fifteen years.

There is one instance of Trollope's evidencing his acquaintance (and his expectation of his readers' acquaintance) with other popular works than fiction, and works almost exactly contemporary. In *Towers*, 19, Charlotte Stanhope, accompanied by her brother Bertie, is making conversation with Eleanor Bold:

> 'Are you a Whewelite or a Brewsterite, or a t'othermanite, Mrs Bold?' said Charlotte, who knew a little about everything, and had read about a third of the books to which she alluded.
>
> 'Oh!' said Eleanor: 'I have not read any of the books, but I feel sure that there is one man in the moon, if not more.'
>
> 'You don't believe in the pulpy gelatinous matter?' said Bertie.
>
> 'I heard about that,' said Eleanor; 'and I really think that it's almost wicked to talk in such a manner. How can we argue about God's power in the other stars from the laws which he has given for our rule in this one?'
>
> 'How indeed!' said Bertie. 'Why shouldn't there be a race of salamanders in Venus? and even if there be nothing but fish in Jupiter, why shouldn't the fish there be as wide awake as the men and women here?'
>
> 'That would be saying very little for them,' said Charlotte. 'I am for Dr Whewell myself; for I do not think that men and women are worth being repeated in such countless worlds.'

Here we have a reference to what was clearly a widely discussed controversy of the day, but a reference that now probably mystifies almost everyone. William Whewell (1794–1866), a philosopher with an interest in natural science, published anonymously in 1853 and with his name in the next year *Of the Plurality of Worlds*, in which he controverted the notion of extraterrestrial life. The book provoked another in the same year (1854) defending the idea, *More Worlds than One*, by Sir David Brewster (1781–1868), a sort of polymath of the natural sciences, and a prolific writer on most of them. Bertie's 'pulpy, gelatinous matter' was Brewster's name for at least approximately what we now call protoplasm (though *OED* records that word from as early as 1848), which Brewster believed to be probably distributed throughout the solar system – or even more widely. How long the controversy excited the public interest I do not know, but it was still certainly doing so in 1856. (It may well have been submerged by the much greater controversy aroused by the publication of *The Origin of Species* three years later.) The dialogue quoted above incidentally exemplifies first Eleanor's modest reluctance to discuss subjects above her, then her orthodox but thoughtful piety, then Bertie's constitutional levity, and finally Charlotte's misanthropy.

Another long-popular work, but now hardly ever heard of, a blank-verse play, Trollope clearly knew extremely well and admired highly. This is Sir Henry Taylor's (1800–1886) *Philip van Artevelde*, inspired by Southey, begun in 1828, published in 1834, praised by Lockhart in *The Quarterly*, long popular on the stage, and yet longer among readers. Taylor was a distinguished editor, literary critic, and civil servant, whom Trollope met during his G.P.O. days in London, and who tried to entice the young clerk into improving company, but was rebuffed by the youthful Trollope's bashful and self-conscious gaucherie.[1] But if he was stand-offish, he was probably grateful, and certainly admiring, to the end of his life. In *Towers*, 30, when Mr Arabin begins almost to think of himself as a rival of Mr Slope's for Eleanor Bold's hand, Trollope makes him quote to himself some ten lines of *Philip*, beginning, 'When we think upon it,/How little flattering is woman's love,/Given commonly to whosoe'er is nearest/And propped with most advantage.' In the next novel, *Clerks* (1857), *Philip* is still in Trollope's mind: in Chapter 3 he observes sententiously that 'The assertion made by Clara van Artevelde, that women "grow upon the sunny side of the wall," is doubtless true . . .' The play is not referred to again for many years, and one might suppose that it had faded in Trollope's memory and perhaps sunk in his esteem (and in his estimate of its continued familiarity), but not so; in his very last novel, *Land* (1882), in Chapter 32 he makes a stubborn victim of the boycott by the Landleaguers say, ' "You remember what Van [*sic*] Artevelde said – 'They shall not make me go the way, that is not my way for an inch.' " '

To pass from a contemporary (though older) writer to a very early one, Trollope twice may be alluding to *The Canterbury Tales*. *Towers*, 25 recounts the heroic measures Mrs Quiverful takes, out of concern for her fourteen almost starving children, to retrieve

1. See Escott, p. 27, n. 1.

for her husband the lucrative Wardenship of Hiram's Hospital. 'Medea and her children,' says Trollope, 'are familiar to us, and so is the grief of Constance. Mrs Quiverful . . . felt within her bosom . . . the fury of the tragic queen, and the despair of the bereaved mother.' I somehow find it a little hard to think of Trollope being much interested in Chaucer, especially in such a tale as the Man of Law's, though from where else he is likely to have come to know the story I cannot think. Again, in *Towers*, 33, we are told that Bishop Proudie 'slept as quietly as though Mrs Proudie had been Griselda herself.' This gives one less temptation to suppose that Trollope had read the Clerk's Tale; 'the patient Grizel' had long been a proverbial figure, doubtless often mentioned by people ignorant of *The Canterbury Tales*. And both they and Trollope could have learnt the story from the *Decameron*, as Chaucer did (though through Petrarch's Latin translation of the last tale).

One other allusion, and at least three quotations, had become so proverbial and commonplace that Trollope, like many people familiar with them, may not have known the sources. The allusion occurs where Trollope says (*Towers*, 30) that 'Eleanor understood [Mr Arabin] as thoroughly as though he had declared his passion with all the fluency of a practiced Lothario.' I rather doubt whether Trollope had read Nicholas Rowe's (1674–1718) *The Fair Penitent*, where 'the haughty, gallant, gay Lothario' is a leading character. The three quotations are (1) ' "When Greek meets Greek, then comes the tug of war," ' (*Thorne*, 12) cited inaccurately from *The Rival Queens or the Death of Alexander the Great* (IV.ii) by Nathaniel Lee (1653–1692), who actually wrote 'When Greeks joyned Greeks, then was the tug of war'. (2) ' "See the conquering hero comes" ' is the heading of *House*, 36, and is also quoted by a speaker in *Bertrams*, 2, where it is preceded by ' " "Sound the timbrels, beat the drums.' " ' The original is 'See the conquering hero comes!/Sound the trumpets, beat the drums!', which almost certainly owes its universal familiarity to its occurrence in the text of Handel's *Judas Maccabæus* (1746), supplied by that learned divine, Dr Thomas Morell (1703–1784). (He first wrote it for Handel's *Joshua* (1747), but later transferred it – or rather Handel transferred it along with the music – to the earlier but much more popular oratorio.) (3) From a much better-known writer than these three, namely Matthew Prior, comes a quotation that Trollope uses twice: (1) ' "Nor need we precisely name the bootmaker to whom is confided the task of making those feet 'small by degrees and beautifully less.' " ' (*Clerks*, 22), and (2) '[Mr Bertram] went on sending his half-yearly statements, which became anything but "small by degrees." ' (*Bertrams*, 5.) In *Henry and Emma*, Prior wrote 'fine', not 'small'; the usual misquotation, shared by Trollope, is not an improvement.

Two final quotations used by Trollope at least three times each are (1) ' " 'The lovely Thais sits beside you. Take the goods the gods provide you.' " ' (from Dryden's *Alexander's Feast*, which Trollope may or may not have known he was quoting – he quotes nothing else of Dryden's), and (2) ' "Shall I, wasting in despair,/ Die because a woman's fair?/If she be not fair for me [*sic*: the poet wrote 'so to me']. What care I how fair she be?" This is the upshot of the question which Withers [*sic*], the poet, gave to the matter, and Withers was doubtless right.' (*Clerks*, 23.) (Here, clearly, Trollope did know whom he was quoting, and presumably what – *The Shepherd's Resolution*.) One of the other quotations of this passage (though of the second couplet only – and with 'fair' for 'so' again, as indeed here is necessary) Johnny Eames sings to himself in *House*, 58 on his final (in this novel!) rebuff by Lily Dale.

I have noted only two references to modern foreign literature. One is an allusion: '. . . as Don Quixote's heart grew strong when he gripped his lance, so did Mrs Proudie look forward to fresh laurels, as her eyes fell on her husband's pillow.' (*Towers*, 26.) The other is a quotation by Bishop Proudie (*Towers*, 32), speaking to himself, of Mme du Deffand's celebrated *mot*, '*Il n'y a que le premier pas qui coûte*,'[1] when, having for the first time in his life triumphed (with Mr Slope's assistance, to be sure) over his wife, in the matter of who shall be Warden of Hiram's Hospital, he begins to 'hope that he was now about to enter into a free land' and 'felt himself every inch a bishop'.

3. THE BIBLE

A. Allusions

Trollope knew his Bible, and expected his readers to know it, as

---

1. I doubt whether Trollope, or most people (at least non-Frenchmen) who have been quoting this for two centuries, could identify the source. Incidentally, what the bishop is actually represented as saying is '*Ce n'est que*,' etc.

most people (except many of the urban poor – a large exception) did – and no longer do. But he knew it, and (rightly) expected his readers to know it not at least mainly for sanctimonious or even pious reasons, but rather because it was a part of the common culture of educated people much as Shakespeare was, and not so much from reading it privately as from hearing it read in church. I doubt very much whether many non-Evangelical Anglicans, including Trollope, were much given to private and diligent searching of the Scriptures 'in their closets', as people used to say, but they certainly were in the habit of going to church; and I think it very likely that the frequent inexactness of Trollope's quotations is due to his knowing the Bible much better from hearing it read in church than from reading it himself.

He shows his knowledge and his expectations in three ways: by allusion, by quotations, and by verbal echoes. Let us take allusions first, and in the order of the books of the Old Testament, the New, and the Apocrypha.

Trollope demands the reader's familiarity with the sacrifice of Isaac (*Chron*, 51); Joseph and Potiphar's wife (*Chron*, 51, and *Popenjoy*, 32); Jacob's waiting for Rachel (*Claver*, 33); the Promised Land of milk and honey (*Towers*, 32); Jael and Sisera (*Chron*, 24 ff.); Jephthah's sacrifice of his daughter (*Warden*, 11); Samson's destruction of the Philistines (*Framley*, 9); Bildad the Shuhite (*Towers*, 43); God's feeding the ravens (*Warden*, 18); Ahab's coveting the vineyard of Naboth (*Framley*, 2 and *Belton*, 13); Jezebel (*Towers*, 11); Obadiah and Elijah (*Towers*, 4); the gulf fixed between Dives and Lazarus (*House*, 32); the unjust steward and the mammon of unrighteousness (*Towers*, 39); 'He was, perhaps, something of a Civil Service Pharisee, and wore on his forehead a broad phylactery, stamped with the mark of Crown property. He thanked God that he was not as those publicans at Somerset House, and took glory in paying tithes of official cumin.'[1] (*Clerks*, 6); the loaves and fishes (*Towers*, 24); and Judith[2] and Holofernes (*House*, 29 and *Chron*, 24).

1. This might well be classified under Echoes rather than Allusions. It is indeed full of echoes, but they are all echoes of phrases in a single passage, and the allusion requires acquaintance with that passage as a whole.
2. The Book of Judith was one of the Apocryphal (Roman Catholics please read 'Deuterocanonical' – though the two terms, incidentally, are not quite identical in reference) books that remained in the Prayer Book Lectionary till 1871, when it disappeared. It disappeared then not because it is Apocryphal (The Wisdom of Solomon, *eg*, remained and remains), but because it is unedifyingly bloodthirsty.

About three-fourths of these are in Trollope's own language and the rest in that of his characters – almost exactly the reverse of the distribution of quotations. Further, of those in Trollope's language, only about a third are used more or less gravely, whereas nearly all those in the language of characters are – and not 'more or less'. Of what I have called echoes, all are Trollope's, and all are jocular. Finally, as we shall see, Trollope quotes the Bible only three times – and never gravely and reverently, though his characters quote it often, and all but always gravely and reverently. It would look as if Trollope felt that for a novelist to quote the Bible gravely was indecorous or even profane (and probably he would have deleted his three jocular quotations if he had thought about it), at least as much as to quote, even without travesty, a sermon.[1] And yet he feels quite free to employ biblical allusions and even brief phraseological echoes secularly, lightly, jocularly, and sometimes irreverently, clearly without feeling it to be 'unbecoming' and without fearing that it would offend his readers.

I must not leave the subject of biblical allusions without sharing with the reader – or reminding him of – a very amusing instance of Trollope's having fun with people who are all for reading the Bible but never get round to it. In Chapter 78 of *Way* – one of Trollope's somberest novels, and one of his greatest – a mother says to her daughter who is engaged to marry a Jew, ' "It seems to me that it can't be possible. It's unnatural . . . I'm sure there's something in the Bible about it. You never would read your Bible, or you wouldn't be going to do this . . . A cursed race; – think of that, Georgiana; – expelled from Paradise!" '

B. *Quotations and Echoes*

According to what I feel sure is a pretty nearly complete record, the forty-one novels (again I exclude *Struggles*) contain at least twenty-seven[2] quotations[3] (now and then immaterially inexact –

1. Cf. *Towers*, 6: 'It would not be becoming were I to travestie [*sic*] a sermon [Mr Slope's impudent one against sung services on his first (and last) appearance in the Barchester Cathedral pulpit], or even to repeat the language of it in the pages of a novel.' (The tongue in the cheek here is barely, if at all, perceptible.)
2. Trollope may have thought, so to speak, that it was about thirty or thirty-one. In *Ray*, 1, Rachel tells her sister that ' "charity begins at home" ', whereupon her sister 'explained, . . . at considerable length, her reading of that text of Scripture.' 'That text' is not in my biblical concordance (an exhaustive one), and I am

an evidence of Trollope's familiarity with the Bible, not the reverse) from the English Bible and echoes of biblical phraseology. What I have called echoes – I have recorded only seven, as distinct from quotations – are all Trollope's own, and all facetious or at least light-hearted, though hardly irreverent. I give them all. (1) '. . . they rejoiced greatly [perhaps another biblical echo itself] that Job's wish had been accomplished, and that their enemy had written a book.' (*Clerks*, 6.) (2) The Bishop of Belgravia 'was, if not as pious, at any rate as wise as St Paul, and had been with such effect all things to all men that though he was great among the dons at Oxford, he had been selected for the most favourite [?] seat on the bench by a Whig Prime Minister.' (*Towers*, 52.) (3) '. . . he did not the less regard the presumed lover to be an iniquitous roaring lion, going about seeking whom he might desire [*sic*].' (*Right*, 41.) (4) 'Oh, deliver us from the poverty of those who, with small means, affect a show of wealth! There is no whitening equal to the sepulchres whited as they are whited!' (*House*, 45.) (5) 'Not in electioneering, Mr Romer, any more than in any other pursuits can a man touch pitch and not be defiled; as thou, innocent as thou art, wilt soon learn to thy terrible cost.' (*Thorne*, 17; an apostrophe to a character.)[1] (6) 'This generation of

---

pretty sure it is a proverb of unknown origin. And it certainly is anything but consistent with the spirit of the New Testament. (The word does not occur in the Old.) Trollope, to be sure, may have been laughing at Rachel's sister. What is probably today, owing to the increasing ignorance of the Bible, an even commoner misattribution is 'God tempers the wind to the shorn lamb', which is from Sterne's *A Sentimental Journey*, and which Trollope quotes (without quotation marks) in *Towers*, 2, though, admittedly, without any clear sign that he thought it biblical. But in *Chron*, 50, Mr Crawley, of all people, is made to say to his wife and children who, with him, face the loss of their scant livelihood, ' "We must bear it with such fortitude as God will give us. We are told that He tempers the wind to the shorn lamb." ' It seems to me that there can be hardly any doubt that Trollope thought he was making Mr Crawley quote Holy Writ. (He is made to repeat the quotation in *Chron*, 61, though this time without such a clear implication that he thinks it biblical.)

3. I do not include the long quoted passages in the account (*Bertrams*, 6) of George Bertram's visit to the Mount of Olives, from the story of David's purchase of the site of the Temple and from the Gospel account of Jesus's survey of the Temple; they are presented for their own sake, and are not examples of Trollope's and his characters' habit of quoting the Bible.

1. This is from Ecclesiasticus, one of the Apocryphal (Roman Catholics please again read 'Deuterocanonical') books still appearing in the Lectionary – in the face of the protests first of Puritans and later of some Evangelicals.

unregenerated vipers was still perverse . . .' (*Towers*, 43; in Trollope's own words, but as if Mrs Proudie had said it.) Incidentally Trollope's echo here involves, in its elaboration of the phrase, a sort of pun. (7) See Chapter V, Section 5 (B).

The quotations are a different matter. Excluding, for the moment, one comically and almost blasphemously distorted quotation from the English Bible, four from the Vulgate, and three sermon texts, there are at least nineteen quotations, of which sixteen are in the speech of characters, and only three in Trollope's own. Further, of the sixteen, all but two are meant seriously and reverently by the speakers (though three of them are from the mouth of a speaker whom Trollope does not like, and thus have a comic effect), whereas all three in his own language are jocular. In short, Trollope felt free to make a jesting use of biblical phraseology (as he did much oftener of biblical allusions), but seldom himself quotes the Bible *in extenso* literally – and then *never* gravely – and *very* seldom makes his characters quote it otherwise. The only two exceptions are in *Towers*, where Bertie Stanhope quotes jocularly Acts i.21: ' "His bishoprick [*sic*] let an other take [*sic*]" ', and in *House*, 58, where Lily Dale quotes to her mother jocularly (though somewhat bitterly) the Decalogue: ' "I have never envied Bernard his man-servant, or his maid-servant, or his ox, or his ass, or anything that is his." '[1]

Of the serious quotations in dialogue, one appears – though never complete – four times. This is Ruth i.16, 17: '. . . Entreat me not to leave thee, or to return from following after thee: for whither thou goest, I will go; and where thou lodgest, I will lodge: thy people shall be my people, and thy God my God: Where thou diest, will I die, and there will I be buried: the Lord do so to me, and more also, if aught but death part thee and me.' Despite the fact that the words were spoken by a young widow to her mother-in-law, Trollope always puts them into the mouth (as most people have done before and since) of a woman speaking to or of her actual or intended husband or a man speaking to or of his actual or intended wife. Considering the prominence of love affairs and matrimony in the novels generally, the frequency is

1. I suspect that Lily remembered the Commandment not so much from private reading as from hearing it at church at least fifty or so times a year in the Ante-Communion. Indeed, it might here almost be counted as a quotation from the Book of Common Prayer rather than from the Bible.

anything but strange. The Lord's Prayer is quoted at least twice: once in *Castle*, 39, and once in *Towers*, 30, where Mr Arabin, endeavouring to dissuade Eleanor Bold from marrying Mr Slope, virtually confesses his own love:

'. . . Mrs Bold, I am beginning to think that I mistook myself when I came hither. A Romish priest now would have escaped all this.[1] Oh, Father of heaven! how good for us it would be, if thou couldst vouchsafe to us a certain rule.'

'And have we not a certain rule, Mr Arabin?'

'Yes – yes, surely; "Lead us not into temptation but deliver us from evil." But what is temptation? what is evil? Is this evil, – is this temptation?'

Three quotations in the mouth of the speaker are used gravely by the speaker, but inappositely or at least unfairly in the view of Trollope, who makes her utter them in order to put her into a ludicrous light. The quoter is Mrs Proudie each time, and each time she is with characteristic presumption instructing a clergyman in his duties. The first appears in *Towers*, 5, where Mrs Proudie, deploring to Mr Harding Sunday – or as she always says, Sabbath-day – amusements and especially travel, quotes from the prohibition of labour in the Decalogue (not, notice, amusements or travel) the words ' " 'Neither thou nor thy son, nor thy daughter, nor thy man servant, nor thy maid servant . . .' " ' (She prudently refrains from continuing with 'nor thy cattle'.) The other two appear in a single speech in *Towers*, 43, where Mrs Proudie is lecturing Dr Gwynne about the importance of 'Sabbath-day schools', and adduces from the Gospels two of our Lord's utterances about children – with the implication that they definitely

1. In his youth, Mr Arabin all but seized that path of escape; see *Towers*, 20. There it is stated that he was dissuaded from doing so by 'the poor curate' – left unnamed – of a small Cornish parish. Four years later, in *Framley*, 14, we are introduced to Mr Crawley, also the poor curate of a small Cornish parish (at £70 a year), visited almost every year by his old college friend, Mr Arabin, who assists him to the limited extent that Mr Crawley's pride will allow. On becoming Dean of Barchester, Mr – now Dr – Arabin becomes rich enough to pay off Mr Crawley's debts (a little over £100); and eighteen months later, the perpetual curacy of Hogglestock (at £130 a year), which is in his gift as Dean, falling vacant, he bestows it on Mr Crawley (see *Framley*, 15). Mr Crawley must almost certainly have been the unnamed Cornish curate of *Towers*, but Trollope never says so, for what reason I cannot think. When writing *Towers*, he probably had no thought of reintroducing the Cornish curate, but that hardly seems a sufficient reason for not making the identification in *Framley*.

and specifically require parsons to maintain such schools. ' " 'Suffer little children, and forbid them not,' " said she. "Are we not to remember that, Dr Gwynne? 'Take heed that ye despise not one of these little ones.' Are we not to remember that, Dr Gwynne?" And at each of these she raised at him her menacing forefinger.'

Once (in *Chron*, 67) Trollope mischievously and rather heartlessly makes Bishop Proudie (in his silent thoughts) bitterly and almost blasphemously distort Scripture: 'Then [on his wife's death] there came the words – into his mind, not into his mouth – "The Lord hath sent the thorn, and the Lord hath taken it away. Blessed be the name of the Lord." ' (If the bishop is also thinking of II Corinthians xii.7, the blasphemy is still worse.)

Trollope gives the texts of three sermons (and these, certainly, he had to look up instead of depending, as often, on his memory). One of them, Mr Arabin's for his first sermon (in *Towers*, 23) as Vicar of St Ewold's – 2 John, 9, 10 – was not chosen by Trollope with any humorous intent, but the other two certainly were. The first, Archdeacon Grantly's for his sermon at Evensong on the same day – 'I beseech thee for my son Onesimus, whom I have begotten in my bonds' – makes the Archdeacon look slightly humourless (as indeed he is): he is hardly old enough to be Mr Arabin's even 'father figure', he himself does not remind us forcibly of St Paul, and certainly he has never been in 'bonds', literal or figurative. The second is funnier – not in itself, but from the preacher's wrenching (much like Mrs Proudie's) of the Scriptures to suit his partisan purposes. The occasion is Bishop Proudie's first appearance on his throne at service in his cathedral (*Towers*, 6); the preacher is (at the Bishop's request) his chaplain, Mr Slope; and Mr Slope's text is 'Study to show thyself approved unto God, a workman that needeth not to be ashamed, rightly dividing the word of truth.' The sermon turns out to be for most of its length an attack on singing the service (where singing it, and singing it well, has long been the pride and boast of the chapter and the choir and the delight of the people). Says Trollope:

Having . . . , according to his own opinion, explained how a clergyman should show himself approved unto God, he went on to explain how the word of God should be divided; and here he took a rather narrow view of the question, and fetched his arguments from afar. His object was to express his abomina-

tion of all ceremonious modes of utterance, to cry down any
religious feeling which might be excited, not by the sense, but
by the sounds of words, and in fact to insult cathedral practices.
Had St Paul spoken of rightly pronouncing, instead of rightly
dividing the word of truth, this part of his sermon would have
been more to the purpose; but the preacher's immediate object
was to preach Mr Slope's doctrine, and not St Paul's . . . Here
was a sermon to be preached before Mr Archdeacon Grantly,
Mr Precentor Harding, and the rest of them! before a whole
dean and chapter assembled in their own cathedral! before men
who had grown old in the exercise of their peculiar services,
with a full conviction of their excellence for all intended
purposes!

Trollope quotes the Vulgate four times – always, I am pretty sure,
without knowing that he was doing so. (1) Twice we have *'noli me
tangere'*, from our risen Lord's speech to Mary Magdalene,[1] used
in such a purely secular way that I cannot believe Trollope can
have been aware of the very specially sacred context; if he had
been, he as much as his readers would have thought the quotation
blasphemously tasteless. The two instances are in *Bertrams*, 33
('Her bow was very gracious, and said much; but *"noli me tangere"*
was part of its eloquence') and *Hotspur* ('he . . . [showed] his
pride chiefly by a certain impalpable *"noli me tangere"*.'). The
Vulgate phrase had become proverbial, and remains so; it never
occurred to Trollope, and does not occur to most people, that it is
biblical, and still less that it is the equivalent of the familiar passage
in the English Bible. (2) The chapter heading of *Framley*, 24 is
'Magna est Veritas'; and in the course of the chapter, Martha
Dunstable says, ' *"Magna est veritas* . . . The bishop of Barchester
taught me as much Latin as that, but there was a long word, and I
forget it." ' The 'long word', of course, is *prævalebit* (preceded by
et), in the form that had become and remains proverbial, and that
Bishop Proudie almost certainly quoted it in. It is from an
Apocryphal (*not* Deuterocanonical) book, 1 (or 3) Esdras, iv.41,
and reads, in the King James Bible, 'Great is truth, and mighty
above all things' – sufficiently different, I think, from the Vulgate
(or rather the *Vetus Latina* – which reads, incidentally, *'prævalet'*,

1. St John, xx. 17: 'Jesus saith unto her, Touch me not; for I am not yet ascended to
my father . . .'

not '*prævalebit*') for even the bishop to miss the connexion. The book disappeared from the Prayer Book Lectionary in 1871. (3) A much more inexact quotation from the Vulgate occurs in *Scarb*, 17. 'It was understood in [Mr Grey's] household that though half-past six was the hour named for dinner, half-past seven was a much more probable [*sic*] time. Mr Grey pertinaciously refused to have it changed. "*Stare* [*sic*] *super vias antiquas*," he had shortly said when the proposition had been made to him.' The Vulgate verse here imperfectly quoted is Jeremiah vi.16: '*State super vias, et videte, et interrogate de semitis antiquis, quæ sit bona, et ambulate in ea . . .*'[1] Unlike the quotations from the Vulgate given above, it has never, I think, been proverbial, and where Trollope can have come across it (especially in an inaccurate form) and why he makes Mr Grey (who is not a Roman Catholic) use it I cannot imagine. Possibly it is the motto of some school or college.

Counting only the quotations and echoes of the English Bible (since those from the Latin Trollope almost certainly did not recognize as biblical), more than half – fifteen – occur in *Towers*, which is strikingly exceptional in this way as in many others. No other novel contains more than three, and I have noted none at all in the thirteen written from 1866 to 1876.

4. THE BOOK OF COMMON PRAYER

Trollope, who seems to have gone to church pretty regularly (though I should wager seldom more than once a Sunday), was naturally well acquainted with the Book of Common Prayer, or at least certain parts of it, and reasonably expected most of his readers to be. He quotes or echoes it at least fourteen times – not counting the considerable number of biblical quotations and echoes of the Bible that he and his readers probably knew not so much from private reading as from hearing at church the Lessons at Mattins and Evensong and the Epistles and Gospels of the Communion Service. (On all but from four to fourteen times a year, depending on the parish (I confess I do not know whether this was in practice true of cathedrals, though it should not have been, according to

---

1. Chaucer uses the same passage, and a little more, as the epigraph – practically the 'text' – of the Parson's Tale (which is really a sermon), but I hardly think Trollope ever read the Parson's Tale.

the rubrics), he is likely to have heard only the Ante-Communion, but that is where the Epistles and Gospels are. As a compensation, if that is the word, he heard the Litany every Sunday – unless he went to Evensong instead of Mattins, which I doubt.)

When he did not give Sunday Mattins and its sequels a miss, he seems to have got there on time. Though there is only one echo of the Exhortation – 'Months and months had passed over him since he had allowed himself to be told that the Scriptures moved him in sundry places to acknowledge and confess his sins.' (*Bertrams*, 26) – there are three (*Kellys*, 1 and 30, *Mack* 1; two of them in Trollope's own language) of the following General Confession – all adaptations of 'We have left undone those things which we ought to have done; And we have done those things which we ought not to have done.' A single petition of the Litany is echoed twice – once in the form 'envy, hatred and malice' (*Ayala*, 3), and once in *Framley*, 23, where it is followed, in a conversation, by an echo of the Catechism:

'That arises from envy, malice, and all uncharitableness,' said Harold Smith.

'Yes; and from picking and stealing, evil speaking, lying, and slandering,' said Supplehouse.

Belton, 2 has 'lying, evil speaking, and slandering' (Trollope's memory of the order of the items in the Duty to One's Neighbour was forgivably shaky after some decades, but not his memory of the items themselves). From the same context comes the echo in the Signora Neroni's (hypocritical) assurance to Mr Slope (*Towers*, 27) that she ' "will teach [the 'Sabbath-school' pupils] . . . to submit themselves to their spiritual pastors and masters." '

Long after Trollope had learnt – and inexactly remembered – the Catechism, he must have attended a fair number of christenings (probably more than once as a godfather), as even gentlemen who seldom went to church on Sundays did; it is not surprising, therefore, to find two adaptations (*Kellys*, 2 and *Framley*, 28 – both jocular) of 'renounce the devil and all his works, the vain pomp and glory of the world, with all the covetous desires of the same, and the carnal desires of the flesh.' And he probably attended even more weddings, and anyway, matrimony being as prominent in the novels as it is, had at least frequent reason to think of the Marriage Service (and of the form for the publication of the banns,

which he would have heard often in the Ante-Communion).
Accordingly, the chapter heading of *Framley*, 38 is 'Is There Cause
or Just Impediment?' – which appears again, in an incorrect order,
in ' "Do you see any just cause or impediment?" ' in *Dark*, 22. To
pass from banns to wedding, someone in *Senator*, 73 says,
' "Marriage is an honourable state [*sic*]," ' and in the last chapter
of *Towers* '. . . Mr Arabin and Eleanor . . . were married. "Wilt
thou have this woman to thy wedded wife," and "wilt thou have
this man to thy wedded husband, to live according to [*sic*] God's
ordinance?" Mr Arabin and Eleanor each answered, "I will." We
have no doubt that they will keep their promises; the more
especially as the Signora Neroni had left Barchester[1] before the
ceremony was performed.'

I have observed only one other echo of the Prayer Book. This
is in *Love* 5, where a character is said to think of 'the changes and
chances to which his career must be subject . . .' 'Changes and
chances' here is a phrase from the first of the six collects printed
at the end of the Communion Service, 'to be said after the
Offertory, when there is no Communion, every such day one or
more; and the same may be said also, as often as occasion shall
serve, after the Collects either of Morning or Evening Prayer,
Communion, or Litany, by the discretion of the Minister.' I
suspect that, just because this collect *was* (and is) the first of the
six, it got said oftener than any of the rest, and hence was most
familiar to church-goers.

Of the fourteen Prayer Book echoes, nine are Trollope's own,

---

1. This is, I am afraid, a snigger, unworthy of Trollope. And uncharacteristic; I can
think of only two other examples. One is in *Kellys*, 37: '[The Church of Ireland
clergyman] was the father of all the Protestant children to be found [in the
parish] – without the slightest slur upon his reputation be it said.' The other is in
Warden, 7: '[Archdeacon Grantly] walked across [his study] and locked the door,
took from the secret drawer beneath his table a volume of Rabelais, and began to
amuse himself with the witty mischief of Panurge . . .' This is a blot not only on
Trollope's taste but on his (then immature) art; as Sadleir says in his introduction
to his edition of the novel (Boston and New York: Houghton Mifflin Company,
1931; the projected edition of all the novels was unhappily never finished), 'Dr
Grantly, with all his faults, was surely beyond this very ordinary surreptiousness?
He was a mature and successful man, to whom (if he were indeed an amateur of
the curious) Rabelais would be very small beer and (if he were a student of French
literature) the most permissible of reading. Admittedly Trollope at this stage had
not "thought out" the Archdeacon all the way; but he had realized a large part of
him, and it is surprising to find an author, whose most perfect quality is his sense
of values in characterization, introducing a clumsy improbability of this kind and –
into the bargain – introducing it with a perceptible snigger.'

and five his characters'. Though not more than two or three can be called solemn, none can be called exactly profane or even, at least markedly, irreverent. Nine of the fourteen appear in the nine novels written before 1861; and in the eleven from 1866 to 1874 there are none at all.

5. CLASSICAL ALLUSIONS

Classical allusions, unlike classical quotations and echoes, (1) are heavily concentrated in *Towers*, (2) are almost always in humorous contexts and given a humorous application, and (3) come much oftener from the Iliad than from any other single source.

Much the most detailed and elaborate – tiresomely so – is in *Framley*, 20, where Harold Smith's entry into the 'Gods' ' (*ie*, the Whigs') Cabinet (which has replaced the 'Giants' ', *ie*, the Tories') as 'Lord Petty Bag'[1] moves Trollope to the following reflection:

It must be a proud day for any man when he first walks into a Cabinet. But when a humble-minded man thinks of such a phase of life, his mind becomes lost in wondering what a Cabinet is. Do they sit on chairs, or hang about on clouds? When they speak, is the music of the spheres audible in their Olympian mansion, making heaven drowsy with its harmony? . . . Are all the voices of all the deities free and equal? Is plodding Themis from the Home Department, or Ceres from the Colonies, heard with such rapt attention as powerful Pallas of the Foreign Office . . . ? Does our Whitehall Mars make eyes there at bright young Venus of the Privy Seal, disgusting that quaint tinkering Vulcan . . . ? Old Saturn of the Woolsack sits there mute . . . Is our Mercury of the Post Office ever ready to fly nimbly from globe to globe . . . while Neptune, unaccustomed to the waves, offers needful assistance to the Apollo of the India Board? How Juno sits apart, glum and huffy, uncared for, Council President though she be . . . – does she not cling retiring near the doors . . . ? But Jove, great Jove – old Jove, the king of Olympus . . .

1. Until 1873 there was a Petty Bag Office, headed by a Clerk, which dealt with the limited common-law business of the Court of Chancery, but there was certainly never a 'Lord Petty Bag'. The title is doubtless a parody of *Lord Privy Seal*.

There is more, but I will spare my readers, as Trollope did not his. And laboured as the thing is, he evidently fancied it; he returns to it, though less elaborately, more than once later in the novel. The Olympian names,[1] of course, come from no single specific source. Trollope does the best he can to assign more or less plausible portfolios to the several Gods, but sometimes fails, as anyone would, and is so taken with the conceit that he cannot bear to leave anyone out.

References to Medea are a favourite with Trollope, and occur at least three or four times. A heavily ironic one associates her with Constance as a devoted mother (*Towers*, 25; cf. Section 2 above). Another, in *Towers*, 33, compares Mrs Proudie to Medea (*not* ironically, but with humorous exaggeration), after she has fallen out with Mr Slope: 'Medea, when she describes the customs of her native country . . . assures her astonished auditor that in her land captives, when taken, are eaten. "You pardon them?" says Medea. "We do indeed," says the mild Grecian. "We eat them!" says she of Colchis . . . Mrs Proudie was the Medea of Barchester; she had no idea of not eating Mr Slope.'[2]

Plutarch may be the earliest source of two allusions (though the first has long been a commonplace, used by thousands who have never read Plutarch) and, though perhaps more dubiously, of a third. (1) In *Towers*, 38, at Miss Thorne's *fête champêtre*, Madeline Neroni chides Mr Arabin for not being so ambitious as Mr Slope, saying that ' "speculative men of talent . . . sit all rapt as you now are, cutting imaginary silken cords with their fine edges, while those [like Mr Slope] not so highly tempered sever the Gordian knots of the world's struggle, and win wealth and renown." ' (2) In *Forgive*, 26, a lady is made to say of a reluctant potential bride, ' "I rather think that when he plays Bacchus she plays Ariadne, with the full intention . . . of flying from him in earnest." ' (Here the source may rather be Ovid, *Metamorphoses* viii.) (3) In *Towers*, 25, when Mrs Quiverful is roused to fury by Mr Slope's (temporary) destruction of her husband's hopes to become Warden of Hiram's Hospital, Trollope observes that Mr

1. At least once Trollope calls on his readers to identify an Olympian goddess by a mere (double) reference to the principal locale of her cult: 'Would you worship the Paphian goddess,' he says in *Warden*, 14, 'the groves of Cyprus are not more taciturn than those of the Temple' (where Tom Towers lives; it is earlier in the chapter appropriately called 'the most favoured abode of Themis').
2. Trollope says, 'I am quoting from Robson's edition.' I *think* this is a joke.

Slope was lucky not to have come in her way. 'There is nothing so
odius to a man as a virago. Though Theseus loved an Amazon,
he showed his love but roughly; but from the time of Theseus
downward, no man ever wished to have his wife remarkable rather
for forward prowess than retiring gentleness.' Here the immediate
source may be Plutarch, but perhaps Statius – or even Chaucer or
Shakespeare.

Of specifically Homeric allusions (*ie*, other than some above
that only *may* be at least chiefly Homeric), there are at least eight –
five in *Towers*, two in *Warden*, and one in *Fay*. Only one is from the
Odyssey: in *Towers*, 37 Eleanor Bold is pictured as between the
Scylla of Bertie Stanhope and the Charybdis of Mr Slope. As for
the Iliad, (1) in *Towers*, 5, Dr Proudie, who has, through a change
of ministry from Tory to Whig fortuitously coinciding with old
Bishop Grantly's death, snatched the episcopal crosier of Barchester from the outstretched hands of Archdeacon Grantly, 'was
playing Venus to his Juno, and [the Archdeacon] was prepared to
wage an internecine war against the owner of the wished for
apple . . .' (2) A protracted mock-heroic allusion to the closely
related story of Aphrodite's rewarding Paris for his judgement
with Helen occurs in *Fay*, 61, where a lower-middle-class lover is
called 'another Paris who had torn a Helen from her Menelaus, –
only in this case an honest Paris, with a correct Helen, and from a
Menelaus who had not yet made good his claim. But the subject
was worthy of another Iliad, to be followed by another Æneid.
By his bow and spear he had torn her from the arms of a usurping
lover, and now made her all his own. Another man would have
fainted and abandoned the contest, when rejected as he had been.
But he had continued the fight, even when lying low on the dust
of the arena.' (3) In *Towers*, 2, *The Jupiter* (*ie*, *The Times*) puts
forward a proposal for the proper employment of John Hiram's
legacy; 'but Cassandra was not believed, and even the wisdom of
the Jupiter sometimes falls on deaf ears . . .' (4) *Warden*, 5,
entitled 'Iphigeneia', recounts Eleanor Harding's resolution to
save her father's wardenship – 'Was not so good an Agamemnon
worthy of an Iphigeneia?' – by appealing to John Bold, the man
she loves, and the instigator of the dispute, to drop the case – a
resolution taken with the knowledge that Bold will then make a
proposal of marriage – which she will be obliged to refuse. But
she happily wins everything: she appeals to Bold, he promises to

do what he can to bring the matter to an end, and then he proposes – and she accepts. 'And so,' the chapter ends, 'the altar on the shore of the modern Aulis reeked with no sacrifice.' (5) When Mr Arabin arrives in Barchester to assist Archdeacon Grantly in his conflict with Mr Slope, 'The frogs and mice,' says Trollope, 'would be nothing to [the future warfare of Arabin and Slope], nor the angers of Agamemnon and Achilles.' (6) In *Towers*, 26, Mrs Proudie, having lost, in Mr Slope's presence, a skirmish with her husband over Mr Quiverful's appointment as Warden of Hiram's Hospital, 'would not despair'; she looked forward to the curtain lecture. 'As Achilles warmed at the sight of his armour . . . so did Mrs Proudie look forward to fresh laurels, as her eye fell on her husband's pillow.' (7) Finally, at an earlier stage of the contention over what to do about the wardenship and about Mr Harding, it is proposed (*Warden*, 19) that the philoprogenitive Mr Quiverful, incumbent of Puddingdale at £400 a year (the wardenship yielded £800), should exchange livings[1] with Mr Harding, and (*Warden*, 20), the next morning Archdeacon Grantly 'drove over to Puddingdale, and obtained the full consent of the wretched clerical Priam, who was endeavouring to feed his poor Hecuba and a dozen of Hectors on the small proceeds of his ecclesiastical kingdom.' The parallel will not bear any very searching scrutiny. (For that matter, no more will the second Homeric allusion in this paragraph.)

6. CLASSICAL (AND A FEW OTHER LATIN) QUOTATIONS AND ECHOES

Of the several features of Trollope's style that may be called ornaments – some good, some bad – one of the few that (a) are not of much more frequent occurrence in *Towers* than in any other novel, and (b) do not tend to appear less frequently in the later novels than in the earlier ones, is quotations (a few times in translation) from the Latin classics. I have recorded eighty-one – just about all there are, I am sure. They occur in his first novel, *Macd*, in his last,

1. This is not quite accurate. Though the wardenship was a living in the strict sense, the term was (and is), in everyday use, most of the time restricted to parochial livings (much the commonest kind); and that the term was so used in this instance is clear from Mr Cummings, the archdeacon's attorney's, saying not, 'Let [Mr Harding] exchange livings,' but ' "Let him exchange . . . for *a* living." '

Land, and in twenty-six of the remaining forty – *ie,* in precisely two out of three. They are most numerous from 1856 to 1861, again from 1866 to 1868, and finally from 1873 to 1882, but there is never a complete lapse for more than two years. Plainly Trollope never came to regard them, as he pretty clearly did several other ornaments – *eg,* classical *allusions* and gratuitous French words and phrases (see Introduction and Chapter V) – as laboured, affected, or in bad taste; he never seems to regard them, or to think that his readers will regard them, as pedantic or ostentatious, and a good many more than half of them are employed seriously and in serious contexts. He never gives the impression of having said to himself, 'It's about time for another bit of Horace': the bits of Horace seem to have sprung irresistibly to his mind.[1]

I mention Horace specifically here because he was clearly the classical writer whom Trollope knew – and presumably loved – best: there are forty quotations from Horace – all but half the whole number.[2] Vergil is a poor second, with eighteen from the

1. Trollope's skill at Latin, and love of it, are chiefly attributable not to his schooling but to his own voluntary efforts in later years. He says in the first chapter of his *Autobiography* that throughout his twelve years of schooling 'no attempt had been made to teach me anything but Latin and Greek, and very little attempt to teach me those languages. When I think of how little I knew of Latin and Greek on leaving Harrow at nineteen, I am astonished at the possibility of such waste of time. I am now [1875] a fair Latin scholar, – that is to say, I read and enjoy the Latin classics, and could probably make myself understood in Latin prose. But the knowledge which I have, I have acquired since I left school, no doubt aided', he adds perhaps a little grudgingly, 'by that groundwork of the language which will in the process of years make its way, even through the skin.' What gave him a start towards becoming 'a fair Latin scholar', he tells us in Chapter 6, his reading of the first two volumes (published 1850) of Merivale's *History of the Romans under the Empire,* the stimulus it gave to the interest he already had in Julius Caesar, 'probably the greatest man who ever lived', his re-reading of Caesar's *Commentaries* and of much else in Latin – and 'a taste generally for Latin literature, which has been one of the chief delights of my later life.' That this was indeed so is evident from the intimate acquaintance with that literature (or at least with Horace and the Aeneid) shown throughout his novels. A belated and much less important consequence was his abridged translation of the *Commentaries,* written and published in 1870, which, to his chagrin, was – most unjustly, he thought (*Autobiography,* Chapter 17) – received with contempt where it was not received with silence.

2. Speaking of his early G.P.O. days in London in his *Autobiography,* Chapter 3, Trollope says, 'In those days I read a little, and did learn to read French and Latin. I made myself familiar with Horace . . .' These two sentences taken together may seem a little at odds with the quotation from Chapter 6, in n. 1 above, but it is possible to reconcile the two passages. The one in Chapter 3 suggests that his intimate acquaintance with Horace, the only classical writer there mentioned, dated from the 1830s (and clearly continued throughout his life).

Aeneid (including three quoted twice and two others three times), and two from *Georgics* i (the same phrase both times – '. . . *labor omnia vincit* [only Vergil wrote *vicit*]/*Improbus* . . .'; the altered form, in which people always quote the line (for a good practical reason), suggests that Trollope did not know the poem well, and that he was quoting the phrase as a familiar proverb, the source of which he could very possibly not have identified). Of the remaining twenty-three quotations, nineteen are divided among seven writers: Juvenal, six (including two quoted twice); Ovid, five (including one quoted twice); Terence, three (the same phrase all three times); Livy, two (the same phrase both times); and Caesar, Martial, and Tacitus one each. Two I have not been able to trace, even with the assistance of the learned.[1]

The quotations, in short, do not demonstrate that Trollope's memory was full of passages from a broad range of classical Latin literature; they demonstrate that it *was* full of Horace and, very secondarily, of the Aeneid – all the quotations from which are, incidentally, from the first six books, which may well be all that he ever read more than once. Most readers, I think, would agree with his apparent opinion that Vergil's Odyssey is more entertaining than his Iliad.

Of Horace's *Odes*, the novels contain quotations from Book I, Odes ii, iii, and iv; Book II, Ode iii (the same passage twice); Book III, Odes i (the same passage twice), ii, iii, viii, xi, xix, and xxvi (the same passage twice); from Book IV, Odes i and xii. Of the *Epodes*, only iii and iv are quoted (the latter said to be 'from an ode' [*sic*]). The only one of the *Satires* quoted is the seventh of Book II – the same half-line all three times, '*teres atque rotundus*'. The most apt of the three instances is in *Finn*, 18: 'There was no sore spot about him, and probably his first thoughts on waking every morning told him that he . . . was *teres atque rotundus*.' The *Epistles*, and more of them, are quoted much oftener: I.i.9, 14, 27, 61 (four times – '*Nil conscire sibi, nullâ pallescere culpâ*'; '*Hic*,' says

---

and partly explains the predominance of Horace in his Latin quotations; the one in Chapter 6, dating his interest in Latin literature *generally* from the 1850s, is not really contradictory.

1. These are (1) '*Omnes omnia bona dicere*' (heading of *Framley*, 1); and (2) '*Non olet*', which an East End parson would say (*Right*, 29) when he got a generous cheque from a manure maker in his parish. The second is probably *based on* a passage in Suetonius's life of Vespasian.

Horace, '*murus æneus esto.*'). The most apt quotation (but of the first half only, and adapted) is in *Land*, 16. Florian Jones, a ten-year-old boy, has been lying, but refuses to confess it. ' "*Nil con-scire tibi* [*sic*]," said [his] father, who had taught his son so much Latin as that.', and 73; vi, xi, xiv, xviii, and II.i, ii, and iii (the *Ars Poetica*). Of the five quotations from this, four are from among Horace's literary precepts. The slightest of these is the mere phrase '*In medias res*', which forms the (appropriate) heading of *Children*, 9. The second, Trollope applies seriously to his own writing. In *Way*, 76, having told us that the brutal Augustus Melmotte beats his own grown daughter, Trollope quotes part of Horace's warn-ing that scenes of violence should not be presented on the stage: ' "*Nec pueros coram populo Medea trucidet.*" ' Then, after supplying a translation, as he very seldom does, he goes on, 'Nor will I attempt to harrow my readers by a close description of the scene which follows.' The two other Horatian literary precepts are in a comic setting, and are used jocularly; they appear in *Clerks*, 19, when Charley Tudor (who is in a considerable degree a portrait of the youthful Trollope) outlines to his much better-educated friend Harry Norman the absurd blood-and-thunder romance that he has written according to the prescription of the editor who he hopes will publish it. A part of Charley's plan is to insert into his narrative of a romantic love affair of high life, his real subject, ' "a succinct little account of the Conquest, which will be beneficial to the lower classes." ' ' "*Omne tulit punctum*," ' Norman comments dryly and with comic appositeness. He presumably expects (or pretends to expect) Charley to supply the following '*qui miscuit utile dulci*', but Charley, whether he could supply it or not, says merely, ' "Yes, I dare say," ' and rushes on with his synopsis. Earlier in the same conversation, Charley quotes his editor as insisting on an abrupt and startling beginning, followed by ' "a chapter of horrors," ' but permitting, ' "about the end of the first volume," ' the recital of ' "everything about everybody's father and mother for just as many pages as you want to fill." ' ' "*Meleager ab ovo* may be introduced with safety when you get as far as that," suggested Norman. "Yes, you may bring him in too," said Charley, who was somewhat oblivious of his classicalities.' Here Trollope's very familiarity with the *Ars Poetica* seduces him into a (harmlessly) inaccurate and conflated quotation; what Horace wrote was '*Nec reditum Diomedis ab interitu Meleagri,/Nec gemino bellum Trojanum orditur ab ovo.*'[1]

We have seen one example of Trollope's quoting Latin and then adding a translation. Now and then he gives the English only; *eg, Orley*, 10 has ' "The equal mind, – as mortal Delius was bidden to remember – . . . should be as sedulously maintained when things run well, as when they run badly.' (Horace, *Odes* II.iii.) In *Land*, 40, we have it in Latin – and, as the context shows, facetiously and not very aptly applied: '. . . a man, when he undertakes to advise another, should not be down in the mouth himself. *Equam [sic] memento rebus in arduis servare mentem . . .*' Another is in *Chron*, 6, where Trollope says of Miss Annabella Prettyman, a schoolmistress, who had a great reputation in Silverbridge for wisdom, virtue, and charity, but who hardly ever left her house, that 'She was . . . perhaps taken to be magnificent partly because she was unknown.' The Latin original – *'Omne ignotum pro magnifico'*, from the *Agricola* of Tacitus, who is nowhere else quoted in the novels – has long been so proverbial that probably most people would recognize it more easily than they would such an English paraphrase, or rather adaptation, and that they – including, I think, Trollope – could not identify the source.

One at least equally hackneyed quotation Trollope gives never in Latin, but at least twice in English – and in different forms. *Claver*, 2 has ' "I see a better path, and know how good it is, but I follow the worse," ' whereas in *Ayala*, 38 we get ' " 'The better course I see and know; – /The worser one is where I go.' " ' The source is probably known to a good many more people than that of the quotation from Tacitus above, and was almost certainly known to Trollope; it is Ovid's *Metamorphoses* vii.20, 21, where Medea says to herself, *'Video meliora proboque;/Deteriora sequor.'*

Once in a while a conversation starts in Latin and ends in English. Thus in *Children*, 25, the (younger) Duke of Omnium says to his son Gerald, who, as often, is in disgrace with his father, ' "You know your Horace, I hope. *'Scandunt eodem quo dominus . . .'* "

---

1. In the last chapter of *Clerks*, Norman once more displays his knowledge of what the classical poets had to say about the craft of writing. Charley has by this time become a well-known novelist, and his mother-in-law (and Norman's) reads aloud at a family gathering what she pretends, for a joke, is a review, from *The Daily Delight*, of his third published novel, *The World's Last Wonder*. The 'review' is very long, chiefly because it includes an extract from the novel of no less than three columns. Says Charley, ' ". . . that's an easy way of making an article – eh, Harry?" ' ' " *Aliter non fit, amice, liber,*" said the classical Norman.' The source is Martial (*Epigrams* I.xvi) – his only appearance in the novels.

"I recollect that," said Gerald. "Black care sits behind the horse-man." ' The source is Horace, *Odes* III.i. Gerald was doubtless glad to please his father by recognizing the source, but didn't trust himself to cap the line with the following one, or the one follow-ing that except in English. In *Children*, 65, Gerald is in trouble again; he confesses to his father that he has lost £3,400 at cards. ' "*Facilis descensus Averni!*"[1] said the Duke . . . "*Noctes atque dies patet atri janua Ditis.*" ' No doubt, he thought, that as his son was at Oxford, admonitions in Latin would serve him better than his native tongue.'

The familiarity with the classics expected, and with justified confidence, of and among educated men is nicely illustrated by a speech of the Duke of St Bungay in *Prime*, 76. He is urging upon another politician that a third, an aging one of long and distin-guished service, should not be obliged to undertake yet another arduous post in the Ministry. ' "The old horse should be left to graze out his last days. *Ne peccet ad extremum ridendus.*" ' What Horace wrote in *Epistles* I.i is ' "*Solve senescentem mature sanus equum, ne/Peccet ad extremum ridendus et ilia ducat.*" ' The Duke, that is, not only expects his collocutor to understand the quoted phrase, but to know its source and to recognize – very possibly to have already recognized – the preceding English sentence as a para-phrastic translation of the preceding Latin line – the last word of which he necessarily includes in his quotation.

When Trollope quotes the classics for comic effect, he most often does so by ludicrously comparing small things to great; *eg*, in *Right*, 47, '. . . he thought that he never in his life had seen anything so unshapely as that huge wen [an oversized chignon affected by a young lady naturally attractive] at the back of her head. "*Monstrum horrendum, informe, ingens!*" He could not help quoting the words to himself.' (I hope a fair number of readers will still recognize the description of Polyphemus in *Aeneid* iii.) A similar example occurs in *Scarb*, 28. Mr Harkaway, an M.F.H., is angry with his opposite number in another hunt, which has collided with and disrupted his. (Trollope loved to write hunting scenes even when he was no longer able to hunt; *Scarb* was written in the year before his death.) 'Then he would urge on his

1. A variant reading, *Averno*, is nowadays favoured. *Averni* is reflected in the heading of the chapter, ' "Easy Is the Slope of Hell" ', and Trollope writes '*Averni*' in the other place where he quotes the line (*Caldig*, 20).

old horse, and gnash his teeth; and then, again, he would be ashamed. *"Tantæne animis cœlestibus iræ!"* ' (Readers who have not got as far as the third book of the Aeneid, but have struggled through even the first few lines of the first, will recognize Vergil's shocked comment on Juno's relentless enmity towards the Trojans.)

But Trollope much oftener applies his classical quotations a good deal more, when not altogether, seriously. He does so always with a favourite one, from the description of Venus in *Aeneid* i. 'But perhaps the most wonderful grace about her was her walk. *"Vera incessu patuit Dea."* ' (*Bertrams,* 9); '. . . Blanch had a bright complexion, and a fine neck, and a noble bust [this in 1860!], *et vera incessu patuit Dea* – a true goddess, that is, as far as the eye went.' (*Framley,* 10); 'She was a tall, handsome woman, with a sublime gait – *"Vera incessu patuit Dea."* ' (*Fay,* 5.)

By far the most extensive, skilfully introduced, apt, and moving of Trollope's introduction of quotations from the classics occurs in *Love*, written in 1882 – the last novel he lived to finish. Mr Whittlestaff, the 'old man' of the title, a country gentleman who has kept up his Latin, had a favourite spot in a glade in the wood on his grounds where he 'was wont to sit and read his Horace, and think of the affairs of the world as Horace depicted them. Many a morsel of wisdom he had here made his own, and had then endeavoured to think whether the wisdom had in truth been taken home by the poet to his own bosom, or had only been a glitter of the intellect, never appropriated for any useful purpose. " '*Gemmas, marmor, ebur,*' " he had said. " '*Sunt qui non habeant; est qui non curat habere.*' I suppose he did care for jewels, marble, and ivory, as much as anyone. '*Me lentus Glyceræ torret amor meæ.*' I don't suppose he ever loved her really, or any other girl." ' (Mr Whittlestaff was evidently accustomed to carrying a complete Horace, and to ranging in it freely: '*Gemmas*', etc., and '*Sunt qui*', etc., are from an Epistle (II.ii), and '*Me lentus*', etc., from an Ode (III.xix). But this account of his habits is given merely to prepare us for a specific visit to his retreat, where he goes to debate with himself whether to release his foster-daughter, half his age, from her promise to marry him, as he knows she wishes he would do.[1] He 'walked off to the wooded path with his Horace. He did not read it very long.

---

1. One is ineluctably reminded of Mr Jarndyce and Esther Summerson. Mr Jarndyce was wiser than he knew. Or perhaps only luckier.

The bits which he usually read never amounted to much at a time. He would take a few lines and then digest them thoroughly, wailing over them or rejoicing, as the case might be. He was not at the present much given to joy. "*Intermissa, Venus, diu rursus bella moves? Parce, precor, precor.*" This was the passage to which he turned at the present moment; and very little was the consolation which he found in it. What was so crafty, he said to himself, or so vain as that an old man should hark back to the pleasures of a time of life which was past and gone! "*Non sum qualis eram,*" he said . . .' (The quotations are the opening two lines and most of the third of *Odes* IV.i.) This is not mawkish, but genuinely pathetic; and I cannot help thinking that it is in part 'auto-psychographical'.[1]

After that, anything is anticlimactic, but there are a few odds and ends worth adding. (1) The (adapted) quotation from the Georgics mentioned above I have said that Trollope probably knew as a familiar proverb, rather than from a recollection of Vergil's poem. The same is even more probably true of three other passages (two of them mere phrases). (a) ' "*Amantium iræ amoris redintegratio est.*" ' This is the chapter heading of *Framley*, 5, and the first two words of it, the chapter heading of *Finn*, 73; and in *Chron*, 53 we have, in English, an adaptation so radical that it might better be called an echo: ' ". . . the quarrels of lovers, when they are of so

---

1. I mean with quite specific reference to his relations with and, I feel sure, fantasies about Kate Field. I agree with Sadleir, who, having said (p. 219), 'He never made love to her; he was not that kind of man. But in love with her he certainly was,' adds (p. 220), '. . . it may be suspected he had [her] and himself in mind when in old age he wrote that short . . . tale *An Old Man's Love*, which tells of the fondness – half protective and half passionate – of a man of fifty for a girl some thirty years his junior.' (See further Sadleir's index for many other references to Kate and her importance to Trollope.) Pope-Hennessy, on the other hand, who gives her even more space (see his index), and who quite agrees that Trollope was in some sense 'in love with' Kate, says (p. 220), 'The tale has *clearly* [italics mine] nothing to do with Anthony's feeling for Kate Field' – apparently for what seems to me the quite irrelevant reason that he finds the temperamental dissimilarity (which, furthermore, he exaggerates, and exaggerates misleadingly) between Mr Whittlestaff and Trollope too great. Trollope never names her in his *Autobiography*, but says poignantly (Chapter 17) that 'not to allude to [this woman] in these pages would amount almost to a falsehood. I could not write truly of myself without saying that such a friend has been vouchsafed to me.' He refrains from naming her even though he deliberately deferred publication of the book till after he should die; but everyone in his circle knew of the relation, including especially his wife, who not merely condoned it (so far as it could be said to need condonation) but encouraged it. Rose Trollope was a wise woman. (Escott over-delicately nowhere mentions or even alludes to Kate.)

very serious a nature, are a bad basis for the renewal of love." '
The source is the *Andria* of Terence, iii.555 – which in modern
editions has the prosodically better[1] reading '*Amantium iræ amoris
integratiost*', but which is almost always quoted as above. Trollope
is less likely, I think, to have recalled it from Terence than to have
known it, if not as a mere isolated proverb, then from its use as
the title of the familiar poem by Richard Edwards (1524–1566)
beginning 'In going to my naked bed as one that would have
slept,' each stanza of which ends with 'The falling out of faithful
friends renewing is of love.' (b) *Bertrams*, 25 has 'What does a man
and a grocer want? *Panem et circenses . . .*' The source is Juvenal's
tenth *Satire*, but I think Trollope very probably knew it as a
common catch-phrase, as most people do. (c) The same is probably
true of another tag from Juvenal (*Satire*, 6) – '*Rara avis in terra*',
the chapter heading of *Finn*, 58; and in *Towers*, 3 we have an echo:
'Some few years since . . . liberal [clergymen] were "*raræ
aves*". . .'

(2) Three familiar Latin proverbs of post-classical (and variously
assigned) origin appear: (a) '*Ruat coelum, fiat justitia*' (*Chron*, 56;
oftener found in the form '*Fiat justitia et ruat coelum*'); (b) ' "*Quos
Deus vult perdere, prius dementat.*" Whom God will confound, them
he first maddens.' (*Bertrams*, 33; again in Chapter 36, without the
translation.) This is commonly found with almost every possible
variation: *Quem* for *Quos*, *Juppiter* for *Deus*, and *dementat prius* for
prius dementat. (c) 'Let Mr Slope do the *fortiter in re*, he himself
[Bishop Proudie] would pour in the *suaviter in modo*.' (*Towers*, 11.)
This very familiar apophthegm, its two parts usually quoted in
the reverse order, is commonly associated with the Jesuits, and
perhaps unjustly, though Burton Stevenson's *Home Book of
Proverbs*, etc. (New York: The Macmillan Company, 1948) sug-
gests that it has its roots in '*Fortes in fine consequendo, et suave* [*sic*] *in
modo*', which occurs in a casuists' manual by a Jesuit General,
Claudio Aquaviva, published in 1606.

(3a) '*Requiescat in pace*' is the chapter heading of *Chron*, 66, and
the closing words of the next chapter. It is the inscription chosen
by Bishop Proudie for his wife's monument, and, as such, it is
ironically equivocal. It originates in the Mass for the Dead and the
form for the committal of the corpse to the grave in the Latin rite.

1. Professor Donald Swanson, of the Department of Classics in the University of
Minnesota, confirms my condignly shaky opinion on this point.

It is not even in substance preserved in the Book of Common Prayer, but it lingered in the English popular mind after the Reformation, probably not so much as a recollection of the old rite as from its frequent preservation on pre-Reformation tombstones.

(3b) In *Macd*, 12, an Irish Roman Catholic priest, about to solemnize a marriage, says to the best man, ' ". . . when I come to *salute nostrâ* – those are the last words – you're to kiss the bride." ' According to the Rev. Philip Weller, of Minneapolis, an eminent authority on the Roman *Rituale*, this phrase must have been in an Irish rite,[1] differing from the Roman, in which it does not appear. The accompanying ceremony, if it may be called that, is equally unknown, according to Father Weller, at least in the United States, and is probably extinct in Ireland. Whether or not it is now, it clearly was not in Trollope's time; plainly he had been present at Roman Catholic weddings during his many years of residence in Ireland, and had given curious and intelligent attention to what went on.

(4) Trollope's most numerous class of readers, I believe, was young unmarried ladies,[2] and yet his novels, as we have seen, are full of quotations from the classics, which he evidently expected his readers not only to understand but to recognize. Now in his day, and for a long time before, an understanding of the Latin language, let alone an intimate familiarity with Latin literature, was very commonly regarded as not only unexpected, but even somehow unfeminine and perhaps especially unladylike, and this view is reflected at least six times in Trollope's novels (*Clerks*, 20 – 1857; *Framley*, 24 – 1860; *Ayala*, 26 and 30 – 1878; and *Love*, 13, twice – 1881). The two best specimens are probably the following: ' "*Carpe diem*," ' he said to [her] laughing. "Do you know what '*carpe diem*' means?" "It is Latin perhaps." "Yes; and therefore you are not suffered to understand it. This is what it means. As an

1. The Council of Trent, in revising the Roman rite and prescribing it for common use, permitted the continued use of a good many local liturgical rites and ceremonies (and some peculiar to particular religious orders) of 'immemorial antiquity' (*ie*, over 200 years old). Many have disappeared, but some persist – or at least did till the recent *Aggiornamento*.

2. At least, when he pauses to address his readers, as he so often does, especially in his earlier novels, if he addresses any single class explicitly, it is most commonly that one. And cf. Pope-Hennessy (p. 305): 'Even when translating and condensing Julius Caesar, he had kept his favourite group of hypothetical readers in mind – English girls in English schoolrooms . . .'

hour for joy has come, do not let any trouble interfere with it." '
(*Ayala*, 26.) In *Love* 13, the Rev. Mr Harbottle, absentee Vicar of
Alresford, has died, and is to be succeeded by his curate, the Rev.
Mr Blake, who will then be enabled to marry his fiancée, Katherine
Forrester. Conventional regret is expressed at the news of Mr
Harbottle's death, whereupon someone says, ' "Miss Forrester
won't wish to have his *resurgam* sung, I warrant you." "I don't
know much about *resurgam*," said the young lady, "but I don't see
why the parish shall [*sic*] not be just as well off in Mr Blake's
hands." ' Trollope, that is, quoted the classics so naturally and so
lovingly that he simply forgot that it was unusual, and perhaps
almost unseemly, for his favourite readers to understand him.

As a sort of comic appendix to this, there is one passage in
Senator, 28 in which an English gentleman assumes – or perhaps
pretends to assume – that an American gentleman (Senator
Gotobed) is a good classical scholar, only to be met with inverted
snobbery. The Senator speaks:

'. . . you never seem to have anything to do.'

'That's not quite so flattering, – and would be killing only
that I feel that your opinion is founded on error. *Mens conscia
recti*,[1] Mr Gotobed.'

'Exactly. I understand English pretty well; better, as far as I
can see, than some of those I meet around me here; but I don't
go beyond that, Mr Green.'

'I merely meant to observe, Mr Gotobed, that as, within my
own breast, I am conscious of my zeal and diligence in her
Majesty's service, your shafts of satire pass me by without
hurting me.'

1. '*Conscia mens recti famæ mendacia risit*,' Ovid, *Fasti* iv.

CHAPTER VII

Character Versus Plot

𑀕𑀕𑀕𑀕𑀕𑀕

I T will be appropriate and illuminating to begin this chapter with four quotations from Trollope.

> *Doctor Thorne* has, I believe, been the most popular book that I have written . . . The plot . . . is good,[1] and I am led there-fore to suppose that a good plot, – which, to my feeling, is the most insignificant part of a tale, – is that which will most raise it or condemn it in the public judgment . . . A novel should give a picture of common life enlivened by humour and sweetened by pathos. To make that picture worthy of attention, the canvas should be crowded with real portraits, not of individuals known to the world or to the author, but of created personages with traits of character which are known. To my thinking, the plot is but the vehicle for all this; and when you have a vehicle without the passengers, a story of mystery in which the agents never spring to life, you have but a wooden show.' (*Autobiography*, Chapter 7.)

> I think the highest merit which a novel can have consists in perfect delineation of character, rather than in plot, or humour, or pathos. (*Autobiography*, Chapter 9.)[2]

> The plot of *Orley Farm* is probably the best I have ever made;

---

1. 'I had finished *The Three Clerks* just before I left England, and when in Florence [September 1857] was cudgelling my brain for a new plot. Being then with my brother [Thomas Adolphus, 1810–1892, himself a novelist – and a man of parts], I asked him to sketch me a plot, and he drew out that of the next novel . . . *Doctor Thorne*. I mention this particularly, because it was the only occasion in which I have had recourse to some other source than my own brains for the thread of a story.' (*Autobiography*, Chapter 6).
2. Trollope would seem to have changed his mind between Chapter 7 and Chapter 9 about the importance of humour and pathos, perhaps because it occurred to him that in some of his later novels, particularly, one or the other of these elements is slight.

but it has the fault of declaring itself and thus coming to an end too early in the book . . . Independently, however, of this the novel is good. Sir Peregrine Orme, his grandson, Madeline Stavely, Mr Furnival, Mr Chaffanbrass, and the commercial gentlemen, are all good . . . Mr Moulder carves his turkeys admirably, and Mr Kantwise sells his tables and chairs with spirit. I do not know that there is a dull page in the book. I am fond of *Orley Farm* . . .' (*Autobiography*, Chapter 9.)

And now, O kind-hearted reader, I feel myself constrained, in the telling of this little story, to depart altogether from those principles of story-telling to which you have probably become accustomed, and to put the horse of my romance before the cart. [*sic*] There is a mystery respecting Mr and Mrs Peacocke [i.e., whether they were legally married] which, according to all laws recognized in such matters, ought not to be elucidated till, let us say the last chapter but two, so that our interest should be maintained almost to the end . . . It is my purpose to disclose the mystery at once, and to ask you to look for your interest, – should you choose to go on with my chronicle, – simply in the conduct of my persons, during this disclosure to others . . . It may be that when I shall have once told the mystery there will be no longer any interest in the tale to you. That there are many such readers of novels I know. I doubt whether the greater number be not such . . . Therefore, put the book down if the revelation of some future secret be necessary for your enjoyment. Our mystery is going to be revealed in the next paragraph, – in the next half-dozen words. Mr and Mrs Peacocke were not man and wife. (*Wortle*, 3.)

There can be no doubt that Trollope meant what he said in the foregoing quotations about character's being in his view more important than plot (or humour or pathos). Indeed, even if he had not said it so often, and so emphatically, or even at all, no reader of his novels could help perceiving that that was indeed his view, and that his practice was, at least from *Warden* through his penultimate novel, consistent with that view. To be sure, the novels, being novels, have and must have plots, as Trollope of course knew and acknowledged, and, not being plays, must contain a good deal of straight authorial (or *persona's*) narrative; and even in a novel in which the interest lies almost solely in the plot, at least some dialogue almost must be present, if only for the sake of relief and variety. Theoretically, in such a novel, no dialogue might be present except that which advances the story; and even in novels in which the interest is primarily in the revelation of character, as it is in Trollope's, and much of the dialogue introduced to that end, some will not be so exclusively or chiefly or even at all. This is true of Trollope, who does not make his dramatis personae talk *only* when their speeches have solely or chiefly or even at all the function of revealing their characters. And even when they have, they are not the only means, or sometimes even the most important, that he uses for that function.

The others are portraits, chiefly and often even wholly mental, and analytical expositions of states of mind.

The portraits appear most often, naturally, at the first introduction of the character portrayed, though sometimes they are supplemented and often qualified much later. They are frequently blended with accounts of the characters' antecedent lives. The longest and most elaborate, I think, is that of Mr Arabin in *Towers*, 20, which occupies the first six pages of the chapter, is interrupted by a couple of pages of narrative and dialogue, and then is resumed in the last three. It is much too long to quote. Another shorter but still long – and devastating – one in the same novel (Chapter 4) is that of Mr Slope. That of Bishop Proudie (in Chapter 3) is less interesting and less notable generally, chiefly because Bishop Proudie is not an interesting or notable man. But the portrait immediately following his *is* interesting and notable because it is that of a woman herself possessing those qualities.

Dr Proudie may well be said to have been a fortunate man, for he was not born to wealth, and he is now bishop of Barchester; but nevertheless he has his cares. He has a large family, of whom the three eldest are daughters, now all grown up and fit for a fashionable life; and he has a wife. It is not my intention to breathe a word against the character of Mrs Proudie [!], but I still cannot think that with all her virtues she adds much to her husband's happiness. The truth is that in matters domestic she rules supreme over her titular lord, and rules with a rod of iron. Nor is this all. Things domestic Dr Proudie might have abandoned to her, if not voluntarily, yet willingly. But Mrs

Proudie is not satisfied with such home dominion, and stretches her power over all his movements, and will not even abstain from things spiritual. In fact, the bishop is henpecked . . .

This lady is habitually authoritative to all, but to her poor husband she is despotic. Successful as has been his career in the eyes of the world, it would seem that in the eyes of his wife he is never right. All hope of defending himself has long since passed from him; indeed he rarely even attempts self-justification; and is aware that submission produces the nearest approach to peace which his house can ever attain.

Mrs Proudie has not been able to sit at the boards and committees to which her husband has been called by the state; nor, as he often reflects, can she make her voice heard in the House of Lords. It may be that she will refuse to him permission to attend to this branch of a bishop's duties; it may be that she will insist on his close attendance to his own closet. He has never whispered a word on the subject, but he has already made his fixed resolve. Should such an attempt be made he will rebel. Dogs have turned against their masters, and even Neapolitans against their rulers, when oppression has been too severe. And Dr Proudie feels within himself that if the cord be drawn too tight, he also can muster courage and resist.

Ten years after writing this, near the beginning of that chapter (66) of *Chron* at the end of which Mrs Proudie's death is recounted, Trollope retouched and softened the portrait; I think her character grew rounder and deeper and in a way almost admirable in her creator's mind, and made him feel compelled to give her her due – though not a jot more.

[She] was a woman not without a conscience, and by no means indifferent to the real service which her husband, as bishop of the diocese, was bound to render to the affairs of the Church around her. Of her own struggles after personal dominion she was herself unconscious; and no doubt they gave her, when recognized and acknowledged by herself, many stabs to her inner self, of which no single being in the world knew anything . . . It cannot be said that she was a bad woman, though she had in her time done an indescribable amount of evil. She had endeavoured to do good, failing partly by ignorance and partly from the effects of an unbridled, ambitious temper.

Trollope does much the same thing, and far less if at all grudgingly, for Archdeacon Grantly. In the last chapter of *Warden*, Trollope says, 'On the whole, the Archdeacon of Barchester is a man doing more good than harm, – a man to be furthered and supported, though perhaps also to be comforted; and it is a matter of regret to us that the course of our narrative has required that we should see more of his weakness than his strength.' And this is reinforced in *Towers*, 1. Old Bishop Grantly's death has for weeks been expected to occur at any moment, but he clings to life, and only five days remain before the Conservative Prime Minister, who would appoint the archdeacon his father's successor, will give way to a Liberal one, who would not. The archdeacon, sitting by the deathbed, 'thought long and sadly, in deep silence, and then gazed at that still living face, and then at last dared to ask himself whether he really longed for his father's death.

'The effort was a salutary one, and the question answered in a moment. The proud, wishful, worldly man sank on his knees by the bedside, and taking the bishop's hand within his own, prayed eagerly that his sins might be forgiven him.'

Once, at least (*Orley*, 79), Trollope says in so many words that one of his characters has risen in his own estimation as he has proceeded with his story:

And now we will say farewell to [Lady Mason, the leading character], and as we do so the chief interest of our tale will end. I may, perhaps, be thought to owe an apology to my readers in that I have asked their sympathy for a woman who had so sinned as to have placed her beyond the general sympathy of the world at large. If so, I tender my apology, and perhaps feel that I should confess a fault. But as I have told her story that sympathy has grown upon myself till I have learned to forgive her, and to feel that I too could have regarded her as a friend.

Sometimes, on the other hand, Trollope conceives and presents a character as despicable at the very beginning, and never relents. This is true of the consistently detestable Lizzy Eustace, as described, briefly but savagely, in *Eustace*, 9:

[Lord Fawn] didn't see why this woman he was about to marry [for her money] should not be a good wife to him! And yet he knew nothing about her, and had not taken the slightest trouble to make inquiry. That she was pretty he could see; that she lived in Mount Street was a fact; that she was the undoubted mistress of a large income was beyond dispute. But, for aught he knew, she might be afflicted with every vice to which a woman can be subject. In truth, she was afflicted by so many, that the addition of all the others could hardly have made her worse than she was. She had never sacrificed her beauty to a lover – she had never sacrificed anything to anybody – nor did she drink. It would be difficult, perhaps, to say anything else in her favour; and yet Lord Fawn was quite content to marry her, not having seen any reason why she should not make a good wife! Nor had Sir Florian [her first husband] seen any reason; but she had broken Sir Florian's heart.

Trollope's characters are extremely seldom even tentatively identifiable with real people, but do indeed appear to be 'created personages with traits of character . . . known' 'to the world or to the author'.[1] There are, however, three notable and amusing exceptions, though of a highly special and unusual kind, to put it mildly. These are the satirical representations, in *Warden*, 6, under the guise of Archdeacon Grantly's three growing boys, of three eminent bishops of the time: Charles James Blomfield, 1786–1857

---

1. Doubt has often been expressed of the complete accuracy of this. Escott says flatly (p. 264), that Mr Daubeny (in *Finn* and *Redux*) is Disraeli, and is inclined to think that Phineas Finn is Sir John Pope-Hennessy. (James) Pope-Hennessy (Sir John's grandson) quotes (p. 280) T. P. O'Connor in support of this latter identification, and mentions a few others that have from time to time been suggested. He also says, however (*loc. cit.*), that Trollope, on being charged in a newspaper with 'drawing pen portraits of living politicians such as Disraeli', *et al.*, 'pugnaciously replied that none of his political characters was in any way related or intended to be related to any statesman of the day.' But there is no doubt whatever about the identities of two characters in *Clerks*, and one of them, certainly, qualified (though later) as a 'statesman'. The first is Mr (later Sir Gregory) Hardlines, Chief Clerk of the Office of Weights and Measures, a severe examiner of aspirants to posts in the Civil Service, who, Trollope says in his *Autobiography*, Chapter 6, 'was intended for Sir Charles Trevelyan, – as anyone at the time [1857] would know who had taken an interest in the Civil Service. "We always called him Sir Gregory," Lady Trevelyan said to me afterwards, when I came to know her and her husband. I never learned to love competitive examinations; but I became, and am, very fond of Sir Charles Trevelyan.' The second is Sir Warwick Westend, a Devonshire baronet. Says Trollope (*loc. cit.*), 'Sir Stafford Northcote, who is now [1876] Chancellor of the Exchequer, . . . appears in *The Three Clerks* under the feebly facetious name of Sir Warwick West End [*sic*].' In 1885 he became first Earl of Iddesleigh and Viscount St Cyres.

(Charles James Grantly); Henry Phillpotts, 1778–1869 (Henry Grantly); and Samuel Wilberforce, 1805–1873 (Samuel Grantly). Trollope started by wanting to portray three bishops. The exigencies of his plot, and a sense of propriety, and even of caution, would not permit of his introducing them as grown men and bishops. With bold impudence he proceeded to portray them – and portray them elaborately – as the archdeacon's half-grown sons, who share their Christian names with the bishops, and who, quite unlike the subjects of all Trollope's other portraits, play no part whatever in the action of the novel. (The implication that the child is father to the man is a bonus.)

Though all three portraits are amusing, the last – that of Samuel Wilberforce under the guise of Samuel Grantly – is decidedly most so. All Trollope's other hostile descriptions of clergymen are hostile because the clergymen are Evangelicals, whom Trollope loathed. This description is not. Wilberforce at least passed for an (increasingly moderate) High Churchman; and Trollope loathed him not for his Churchmanship, but for what he regarded (as many others did – witness the popular name 'Soapy Sam') as slyness, pliability, hypocrisy, insincere affability, an excessive appetite for popularity, and even timeserving. Trollope's portrait of Bishop Wilberforce is too deliciously wicked to leave unquoted.

. . . perhaps Samuel was the general favourite; and dear little Soapy, as he was familiarly called, was as engaging a child as ever fond mother petted. He was soft and gentle in his manners, and attractive in his speech; the tone of his voice was melody, and every action was a grace; unlike his brothers, he was courteous to all, he was affable to the lowly, and meek even to the very scullery maid. He was a boy of great promise, minding his books and delighting the hearts of his masters. His brothers, however, were not particularly fond of him; they would complain to their mother that Soapy's civility all meant something; they thought that his voice was too often listened to at Plumstead Episcopi, and evidently feared that, as he grew up, he would have more weight in the house than either of them; there was, therefore, a sort of agreement among them to put young Soapy down. This, however, was not so easy to be done; Samuel, though young, was sharp; he could not assume the stiff decorum of Charles James, nor could he fight like Henry;

but he was a perfect master of his own weapons, and contrived, in the teeth of both of them, to hold the place which he had assumed. Henry declared that he was a false, cunning creature; and Charles James, though he always spoke of him as his dear brother Samuel, was not slow to say a word against him when opportunity offered. To speak the truth, Samuel was a cunning boy, and those even who loved him best could not but own that for one so young, he was too adroit in choosing his words, and too skilled in modulating his voice.

Later in the same chapter Trollope adds, 'For half an hour or so I certainly did like Sammy's gentle speeches; but one gets tired of honey, and I found that he preferred the more admiring listeners whom he met in the kitchen-garden and back precincts of the establishment; besides, I think I once caught Sammy fibbing.'[1]

And he cannot let Sammy alone, as witness his address (Chapter 9) to John Bold and its sequel:

'Oh, Mr Bold, . . . papa, I'm sure, will be glad to see you. I suppose you want to see papa. Shall I hold your horse for you? Oh what a very pretty horse!' and he turned his head and winked funnily at his brothers; 'papa has heard such good news about the old hospital to-day. We know you'll be glad to hear it, because you're such a friend of grandpapa Harding, and so much in love with aunt Nelly!' . . . Samuel stayed till the servant came, chatting and patting the horse; but as soon as Bold had disappeared through the front door, he stuck a switch under the animal's tail to make him kick, if possible.

It is pretty certainly no accident that, though Charles James is much later mentioned (in *Chron*) as a rising clergyman, and Henry

1. The pretence exemplified here that Trollope's characters are real people, and that he knows them, now and then appears in some of the earlier novels. Later there is a modification: the characters are still real people, but the author doesn't know them – and yet he gets news of them from (unnamed) common acquaintances, who are of course also necessarily represented as real people. Both these varieties are inconsistent with the omniscient point of view, which becomes increasingly the one Trollope writes from; and both they and it are inconsistent with his (decreasingly) frequent reference to the novels as fiction, and still more so, if possible, with his (also decreasingly frequent) disclaimer of being himself certain about how the story is going to come out. In his early and middle periods two or more of these logically immiscible *loci standi* are sometimes assumed in different parts of the same novel.

appears there prominently as 'Major Grantly', Trollope kills Samuel off in his later youth.

Detailed portraits such as these appear with comparative infrequency after about 1860. One later one is exceptional in coming not at the first introduction of the character, and not only later, but in a different novel. This is the portrait of 'Planty Pall' in *Forgive*, 24 (1864). He first appears in *House* (1863), where he plays a part, and no very creditable one, in a secondary plot; but he becomes a leading character, and an estimable one, in *Forgive* and the remaining five novels of the Parliamentary series – the protagonist, indeed, in the last two. I feel sure that, in *House*, Trollope had no intention of later making him that (or probably of reintroducing him at all); when he decided to do so, he refurbished him, so to speak, for new purposes.

The second method of giving his readers insights into his characters that Trollope uses besides dialogue is the frequent passages, often long, of analytical exposition of the characters' states of mind. Such passages sometimes precede or follow conversations, and perhaps as often interrupt them, and very commonly contribute more – sometimes much more – to our conceptions of the characters than the conversations do. Indeed, I suspect that many readers, reading, as is natural, with little attention to how much both of their developing and of their final impressions of the characters is owing to speeches and how much to the author's psychological analyses, unconsciously blend in their memories the contributions of the two kinds of discourse to the whole picture and give a good deal of credit to the former that belongs to the latter: they quite honestly come to think that *characters* have *said* things that as a matter of fact *Trollope* has *told* us they *thought*.

Such passages appear throughout Trollope's career. He was very good at them, he knew it, and he enjoyed writing them. One of the best portrays the agony of indecision in the mind of a man, contemplating an evil action, who tries to persuade himself that he does not believe in punishment after death. The passage occurs in *Henry*, 20. Henry Jones has inherited his uncle's estate under the last discoverable will; though the uncle was known to have almost certainly written a later one, making his niece his heir, it cannot be found, and he is supposed to have destroyed it. But Henry has later discovered it. Cupidity keeps him from revealing his discovery, but timidity keeps him from destroying the will, and thus committing a felony – and a sin. He increasingly feels, however, that he can overcome the timidity.

During the whole Tuesday he was thinking of [destroying the will]. Could he bring himself to believe that all the story of a soul tormented for its wickedness in an everlasting fire was but an old woman's tale? If he could but bring himself to believe that! If he could do that, then could he master his qualms. And why not? Religious thoughts had hitherto but little troubled his life. The Church and her services had been nothing to him. He had lived neither with the fear nor with the love of God at his heart . . . Why, then, should qualms afflict him?

That prayer [the Lord's Prayer, especially 'lead us not into temptation'] which he was accustomed to repeat to himself as he went to rest was but a trick of his youth. It had come down to him from his old, innocent days; and though it was seldom omitted without a shiver, nevertheless it was repeated with contempt. In broad daylight, or when boon companions had been with him round the candles, blasphemy had never frightened him. But now, – now in his troubles, he remembered that there was a hell. He could not shake from himself the idea. For unrepented sin there was an eternity of torment which would last forever! Such sin as this which he premeditated must remain unrepented, and there would be torment for him for ever. Nevertheless, he must do it. And, after all, did not many of the wise ones of the earth justify him in thinking that that threat was but an old woman's tale?

. . . The moment had come for the destruction of the document.

. . . Could it be that so great a result could come from so short an act? The damning of his own soul! Would it in truth be the giving up of his own soul to eternal punishment? God would know that he had not meant to steal the property! God would know that he did not wish to steal it now! God would know that he was doing this as the only means of escape from misery which others were plotting for him! God would know how cruelly he had been used. God would know the injustice with which the old man had treated him! Then came moments in which he almost taught himself to believe that in destroying the will he would be doing nothing more than an act of rough justice, and that God would certainly condemn no one to eternal punishment for a just act. But still, whenever he would turn round to the candle, his hand would refuse to raise the paper to the flame. When done, it could not be undone! And whether those eternal flames should or should not get possession of him, there would be before him a life agonized by the dread of them . . .

The Wednesday would at any rate do as well. Why rob himself of the comfort of one day during which his soul would not be irretrievably condemned? Now he might sleep. For this night, at any rate, he might sleep. He doubted whether he would ever sleep again after the doing of the deed . . . He thought it would be well to have another day of life in which he had not done the deed. He therefore put the will back into the book and went to his bed.

Perhaps equally impressive is a passage from *Way*, 82, which describes the thoughts of Augustus Melmotte, the protagonist of the novel, a criminal financial manipulator, who faces exposure and ruin. Unfortunately it must be omitted for reasons of space.

No novel of Trollope's, I think, has more of such passages, at least about a single character, than *House*, which again and again gives long spaces to the examination of the perfidious Adolphus Crosbie's inner consciousness; and I should say that it is Adolphus Crosbie, and such passages about him, and not Lily Dale (and certainly not Johnny Eames!), that make *House* the great novel that it is. A good specimen is from Chapter 12, where Crosbie tries to tell Lily that they cannot marry at once. Unlike the preceding example, it is inserted within a dialogue; but note how little space the dialogue occupies, and how little it does except its simple and workaday job of advancing the story a step.

'You know,' said [Adolphus], 'how anxious I have been that our marriage should not be delayed . . . Of course I must be very anxious, but I find it not so easy as I expected.'

'You know what I said, Adolphus. I said that I thought we had better wait. I'm sure mamma thinks so. And if we can only see you now and then – '

'That will be a matter of course. But, as I was saying – Let me see. Yes, – all that waiting will be intolerable to me. It is such a bore for a man when he has made up his mind on such a matter as marriage, not to make the change at once, especially when he is going to take to himself such a little angel as you are, . . . but – ' and then he stopped. He wanted to make her understand that this change of intention on his part was caused by the unexpected misconduct of her uncle. He desired that she should know exactly how the matter stood; that he had been led to suppose that her uncle would give her some small fortune; that he had been disappointed, and had a right to feel the disappointment keenly; and that in consequence of this blow to his expectations, he must put off his marriage. But he wished her also to understand at the same time that that did not in the least mar his love for her; that he did not join her at all in her uncle's fault. All this he was anxious to convey to her, but he did not know how to get it said in a manner that would not be offensive to her personally, and that should not appear to accuse himself of sordid motives. He had begun by declaring that he would tell her all; but sometimes it is not easy, that task of telling a person everything. There are things which will not get themselves told.

'You mean, dearest,' said she, 'that you cannot afford to marry at once.'

'Yes; that is it. I had expected that I should be able, but – '

Did any man in love ever yet find himself able to tell the lady whom he loved that he was very much disappointed on discovering that she had got no money? . . . Crosbie found himself unable to do it, and thought himself cruelly used because of the difficulty. The delay to which he intended to subject her was occasioned, as he felt, by the squire, and not by himself. He was ready to do his part, if only the squire had been willing to do the part which properly belonged to him. The squire would not; but when he came to the telling of it, he found that the story would not form itself properly. He must let the thing go, and bear the injustice, consoling himself as best he might by the reflection that he at least was behaving well in the matter.

Another much longer and even more notable example of a dialogue illumined and vivified by interspersed paragraphs of psychological analysis – and of both the interlocutors, in turn – is to be found in *Finn*, 39, where Phineas comes to Lady Laura

Kennedy (*née* Standish) to ask her help in his suit for Violet Effingham. His situation is delicate for two reasons: (1) he has previously loved Lady Laura (and she, though now married, still loves him), and (2) she is anxious that her brother Oswald should marry Violet. Unfortunately, the passage is too long to quote; but anyone who has not read it should, and anyone who has read it should re-read it.

Trollope's dialogue has commonly been admired for the light it throws on his characters, and justly so, though, as I have said, I think it has been overestimated at the expense of his portraits, and much more at that of his passages of psychological analysis, which he writes more of, and writes more expertly, in my opinion, than any of his contemporaries. Most of the dialogues are short, and do little but advance the story; most of the long ones do illustrate character, but these are commonly interrupted by the author's accounts of the states of mind of the speakers (which we are likely to blend with the dialogue in our memories). Two very notable exceptions – uniquely notable, I should say – are in *Bertrams*, 35 and 36. Caroline Waddington has broken off with the man whom she loves and who loves her, her cousin George Bertram, jr, because he insists on her marrying him before he can support her luxuriously. She marries Sir Henry Harcourt, who can so support her, but warns him that she can never love him. Against her will, Harcourt invites Bertram to their house, in the hope of ingratiating himself with his wife's rich grandfather, Bertram's uncle. In Chapter 33, Caroline, having submitted to her husband's command to acquiesce in the invitation, sits alone after he has gone to bed. 'For the next hour, Lady Harcourt sat there looking at the smouldering fire. *"Quos Deus vult perdere, prius dementat."* Not in such language, but with some such thought, did she pass judgement on the wretched folly of her husband.' The next day, Bertram, having arrived, calls on her, and there follows a very long and revealing dialogue, which Trollope for once interrupts with almost no comments, and even with very few 'he saids' and the like. I think he meant to experiment with departing in this way from his habits, or perhaps, on reading over the passage, perceived that he had done so. At any rate, in the next chapter (36), he tries harder and does it again, and this time almost entirely; it is the only dialogue of anything like such length in all the novels that could be put into a play with scarcely any omission.

Virtually all of what little else there is amounts to (brief) stage directions, indicated below by marks of ellipsis.

Sir Henry has come home, learns of Bertram's visit from the servant, and summons his wife.

'George Bertram has been here to-day? . . . And would you object to telling me what passed between you?' . . .

'Would I object to telling you what passed between us? The question is a very singular one;' and then she paused a moment. 'Yes, Sir [!] Henry, I should object.'

'I thought as much,' said he . . .

'May I go now?' she asked, after a while.

'No; not quite yet. Sit down, Caroline; sit down. I wish to speak to you. George Bertram has been here, and there has been that between you of which you are ashamed to speak!'

'I never said so, Sir Henry – nor will I allow you to say so. There has been that between us to-day which I would rather bury in silence. But if you command me, I will tell you.'

'Command! you are always talking of commands.'

'I have to do so very often. In such a marriage as ours they must be spoken of – must be thought of. If you command me, I will tell you. If you do not, I will be silent.' . . .

'Sit down, Caroline.' She then sat down just opposite to him. 'I should have thought that you would have felt that, circumstanced as he, and you, and I are, the intercourse between you and him should have been of the most restrained kind – should have had in it nothing of the old familiarity.'

'Who brought us together again?'

'I did so; trusting to your judgement and good taste.'

'I did not wish to see him.'

'Nonsense. Why should you have been so afraid to meet him?'

'Because I love him.'

As she said this, she still looked into his face fearlessly – we may almost say boldly; so much so that Sir Henry's eyes almost quailed before hers. On this she at any rate resolved that she would never quail before him . . .

'And he has been here to-day in order that you might tell him?'

'He has been here to-day, and I did tell him,' said Caroline, looking still up into her husband's eyes. 'What brought him here I cannot say.'

'And you tell me this to my face.'

'Well, would you have me tell a lie? Did I not tell you the same when you first asked me to marry you? Did I not repeat it again but a week before we were married? Do you think that a few months could make the difference? Do you think that such months as these could have effaced his memory?'

'And you mean, then, to entertain him as your lover?'

'I mean to entertain him not at all. I mean that he shall never again enter any house in which I may be doomed to live. You brought him here; and I – though I knew that the trial would be hard, I thought that I could bear it. I find that I cannot. My memory is too clear; my thoughts of other days too vivid; my remorse – '

'Go on, madam; pray go on.'

'No, I shall not go on. I have said enough.'

'Ah! you said more than that to him when he was here.'

'Not half so much.'

'Was he not kneeling at your feet?'

'Yes, sir, he did kneel at my feet;' . . .

'Well, and what then? Since you are so little ashamed of the truth, tell it all.'

'I am not at all ashamed of the truth. He came to tell me that he was going – and I bade him go.'

'And you allowed him to embrace you – to hold you in his arms – to kiss you?'

'Ah, me, yes – for the last time. He did kiss me. I feel his lips now upon my brow. And then I told him that I loved him; loved none but him; could love none other. Then I bade him begone; and he went. Now, sir, I think you know it all . . .'

'Such audacious effrontery I never witnessed in my life – never heard of before.'

'What, sir, did you think that I should lie to you?'

'I thought there was some sense of shame left in you.'

'Too high a sense of shame for that. I wish you could know it all. I wish I could tell you the tone of his voice, and the look of his eye. I wish I could tell you how my heart drooped, and all but fainted, as I felt that he must leave me for ever. I am a married woman, and it was needful that he should go . . .

Now, Sir Henry, I think you know it all. Now may I go?' . . .

'Brazen-faced harlot!' he exclaimed . . . : 'unmitigated harlot!'

'Yes, sir,' she answered, in a low tone, coming up to him as she spoke, laying her hand upon his arm, and looking still full into his face – looking into it with such a gaze that even he cowered before her. 'Yes, sir, I was the thing you say. When I came to you, and sold my woman's purity for a name, a house, a place before the world – when I gave you my hand, but could not give you my heart, I was – what you have said.'

'And were doubly so when he stood here slobbering you on your neck.'

'No, Sir Henry, no. False to him I have been; false to my own sex; false, very false to my own inner self; but never false to you.'

'Madam, you have forgotten my honour.'

'I have at any rate been able to remember my own.' . . .

'You have forgotten yourself, Caroline – '

'Stop a moment, Sir Henry, and let me finish, since you will not allow me to remain silent. I have never been false to you, I say; and, by God's help, I never will be – '

'Well, well.'

'Stop, sir, and let me speak. I have told you often that I did not love you. I tell you so now again. I have never loved you – shall never love you. You have called me now by a base name; and in that I have lived with you and have not loved you, I dare not say that you have called me falsely. But I will sin no more.'

'What is it you mean?'

'I will not deserve the name again – even from you.'

'Nonsense; I do not understand you. You do not know what you are saying.'

'Yes, Sir Henry, I do know well what I am saying. It may be that I have done you some injury; if so, I regret it. God knows that you have done me much. We can neither of us now add to each other's comfort, and it will be well that we should part.'

'Do you mean me to understand that you intend to leave me?'

'That is what I intend you to understand.'

'Nonsense; you will do no such thing.'

'What! would you have us remain together, hating each

other, vilifying each other, calling each other base names as you just called me? And do you think that we could still be man and wife? No, Sir Henry; I have made one great mistake – committed one wretched, fatal error. I have so placed myself that I must hear myself so called and bear it quietly; but I will not continue to be so used. Do you think he would have called me so?'

'Damn him!'

'That will not hurt him. Your words are impotent against him, though they may make me shudder.'

'Do not speak of him, then.'

'No, I will not. I will only think of him.'

'By heavens! Caroline, your only wish is to make me angry.'

'I may go now, I suppose?'

'Go – yes, you may go; I will speak to you to-morrow, when you will be more cool.'

'To-morrow, Sir Henry, I will not speak to you; nor the day afterwards, nor the day after that. What you may wish to say now I will hear; but remember this; after what has passed to-day, no consideration on earth shall induce me to live with you again. In any other respect I will obey your orders – if I find it possible.'

She stayed yet a little while longer, . . . waiting to hear whether or no he would answer her; but as he sat silent, looking before him, but not at her, . . . she without further words withdrew, and quietly closed the door after her.

The only almost pure dialogue I remember that approaches this in length is that between Madeline Neroni and Mr Slope in *Towers*, 27; and it is a comic fencing match (a very great one) – farcical, not tragic, and not nearly so genuinely dramatic. I think Trollope found it alien to his genius to write dramatically at any length, at least in serious scenes, and to resist the temptation to interrupt with sage commentary; if so, it may go some distance towards explaining the failure of both the two plays he wrote to be performed.[1] There is, indeed, one other almost purely dramatic dialogue, and a very great one, but uniquely interesting for the

1. These are *The Noble Jilt*, written in 1850, which remained unpublished till 1923, and a dramatization of *Chron* under the title *Did He Steal It?*, written in 1869, and privately printed (according to Sadleir, but he does not say when). This constituted an unproducible play made from a successful novel; from the earlier equally unproducible play Trollope made, after fourteen years, a successful novel,

simplicity and ingenuity of the single device it employs to make us hear the very voices, and divine the inmost feelings, of the two interlocutors – a mere contrast in the length (and tone) of their speeches. In appears in *Chron*, 66. The speakers are the Proudies. Mrs Proudie, by her meddling, has indirectly caused Mr Crawley to resign his parish, and thus put her husband into the cruel dilemma of having either to ignore the resignation, continue Mr Crawley's suspension, send the Rev. Mr Thumble to Hogglestock as *locum tenens*, and continue the commission of inquiry – which will almost certainly vindicate Mr Crawley, and show the bishop to have been unjustified in appointing it – or to discharge the commission, thus himself confessing by implication that he ought not to have appointed it. If he does the former, he will be in trouble with everyone but his wife; if he does the latter, he will be in trouble with her – and still look a fool. His spirit is completely broken.

Mrs Proudie confronts her husband in his study; and in the ensuing conversation, her sixteen speeches average about thirty words, his fifteen [!] about eight. And a single speech of his of forty-four words exaggerates the average length; without it, the average is hardly six, the next longest being twelve.

The great scene between the bishop, his wife, and Mr Crawley in *Chron*, 18 – ' "Peace, woman," Mr Crawley said, addressing her at last. The bishop jumped out of his chair at hearing the wife of his bosom called a woman. [Cf. *Pickwick*, Chapter 32.] But he jumped more in admiration than in anger' – is indeed great, but it is not to be compared, nor is any other dialogue – perhaps any other passage of any kind – in all the novels, to the masterly and hilarious five-part dissonant polyphony in *Towers*, 5, when Archdeacon Grantly and Mr Harding first call on the bishop – and find his wife and Mr Slope present. It is far too long to quote, but no Trollopian can forget it, or resist returning to it often. (The immediate sequel, at the beginning of the next chapter – the archdeacon's volcanic eruption to Mr Harding when they have left the

---

Forgive. Six years later still, he had some fun with it. In *Eustace*, 52, he makes Lizzy Eustace and two other ladies (if 'other' is the word) go to the Haymarket Theatre to see 'a new piece, "The Noble Jilt," from the hand of a very eminent author'. Later in the chapter Trollope says, 'The critics . . . were somewhat divided . . . As it was not acted above four or five dozen times, it must be regarded as a failure.'

palace, and Mr Harding's mild and brief interpositions – though
it involves only two speakers, of whom one says very little, is
worthy of what precedes it.)

In the foregoing dialogues, no speaker says anything inconsistent in substance with his character, but few of Trollope's
dramatis personae have what can be called an idiolect. Trollope,
that is, gives no character a mode of speech so distinctive that he
can hardly utter a word without our recognizing him instantly and
infallibly; there are no Mr Micawbers or Sam or Tony Wellers or
Alfred Jingles or Sairey Gamps or Silas Weggs or Mr Pecksniffs
or Uriah Heeps or Mrs Nicklebys in Trollope's novels. His closest
approaches to these are, I should say, Martha Dunstable, the
Duchess of Omnium ('Lady Glen'), and 'La Signora Madeline
Vesey Neroni, *nata* Stanhope' – in that order. And they are not
really very close, in that their manners of speech are much more
like some now and then heard in real life than those of Mr
Micawber *et al.*; Trollope had not Dickens's magical power to
make us believe the incredible. Miss Wallachia Petrie, 'the
American Browning', in *Right*, is Trollope's only attempt at the
Dickensian, and it is not very successful; Trollope lacked the
trick, and I think he knew it. Some readers will wonder why I do
not place Archdeacon Grantly and Mrs Proudie in this class, or
even at the head of it, but I think that a great deal of the impression
we get of the distinctiveness of their speech comes from a simple
and rather mechanical device – the archdeacon's constant 'Good
heavens!' and Mrs Proudie's equally constant 'surely, surely' and
'Sabbath-day'. This is only less true of Mr Crawley, whose
peculiarities are not limited to a phrase or two, but are exhibited
by a pervasive old-fashioned and bookish formality. Mary Thorne,
Lucy Robarts, Miss Mackenzie (too little known), Clara Amedroz,
and Violet Effingham sound a good deal alike (when they do not
sound like most people) because they *are* a good deal alike, at least
in being possessed of what many of Trollope's contemporaries
probably regarded as almost unfeminine and particularly unladylike – sturdy independence and staunchness of spirit, and their outward sign, outspokenness and even sometimes acerbity, when the
plots give them occasion, as they often do, to exercise their
talents. And when no such occasion presents itself, most of them
are given to a certain offhand informality that is often jocose, even
pert, and sometimes slangy, as Lily Dale's, too, often is.

Let us look at examples of the characteristic speech of some of these figures.

Until *Thorne*, 16, we know nothing of Martha Dunstable except that she is the very rich unmarried heiress of an ointment manufacturer, and 'about' thirty years old. (This is the fashionable world's euphemism; Trollope says honestly, in Chapter 38, 'well past forty'.) We are introduced to her – or rather she introduces herself – in the earlier chapter, most of whose ten pages are given over to conversations in which she is the principal speaker. The scene is Courcy Castle, where Lady de Courcy has entrapped her nephew, Frank Gresham, and arranged a house party to which she has invited Miss Dunstable with a view to securing her as a wife for Frank (who is in love with Mary Thorne and is resolved to marry no one but her, but 'was prepared to go through a certain amount of courtship, in obedience to his aunt's behests, and . . . felt a little nervous at being brought up in that way, face to face, with two hundred thousand pounds'). On entering the drawing-room before dinner on the first evening of the party, he finds Miss Dunstable seated between Mrs Proudie and his aunt, who introduces the young people and then speedily leaves, first excusing herself to Mrs Proudie (who, unaware of Lady de Courcy's designs, remains – characteristically). Miss Dunstable has just come down from London, and Frank, seizing on that as a subject on which to make polite noises, 'expressed a hope that Miss Dunstable was not fatigued by her journey.'

'Fatigued!' said she in a voice rather loud, but very good-humoured, and not altogether unpleasing; 'I am not to be fatigued by such a thing as that. Why, in May we came through all the way from Rome to Paris without sleeping – that is, without sleeping in a bed – and we were upset three times out of the sledges coming over the Simplon. It was such fun! Why, I wasn't to say tired even then.'

'All the way from Rome to Paris!' said Mrs Proudie – in a tone of astonishment, meant to flatter the heiress – 'and what made you in such a hurry?'

'Something about money matters,' said Miss Dunstable, speaking rather louder than usual. 'Something to do with the ointment. I was selling the business just then.'

Mrs Proudie bowed, and immediately changed the conversa-

tion.[1] 'Idolatry is, I believe, more rampant than ever in Rome,'
said she; 'and I fear there is no such thing at all as Sabbath
observance.'

'Oh, not the least,' said Miss Dunstable, with rather a joyous
air; 'Sundays and week-days are all the same there.'

'How very frightful!' said Mrs Proudie.

'But it's a delicious place, I must say. And as for the Pope, if
he wasn't quite so fat, he would be the nicest old fellow in the
world. Have you been in Rome, Mrs Proudie?'

Mrs Proudie sighed as she replied in the negative, and
declared her belief that danger was to be apprehended from
such visits.

'Oh! – ah! – the malaria – of course – if you go at the wrong
time; but nobody is such a fool as that now.'

'I was thinking of the soul, Miss Dunstable,' said the lady-
bishop, in her peculiar, grave tone. 'A place where there are no
Sabbath observances – '

'And have you been at Rome, Mr Gresham?' said the young
lady, turning almost abruptly round to Frank, and giving a
somewhat uncivilly cold shoulder to Mrs Proudie's exhortation.

This first, short conversation immediately tells us a number of
Miss Dunstable's salient characteristics – zest, liveliness, unaffected
willingness to speak of her money's having come from trade,
antipathy to sanctimoniousness and quick perception of it,
innocent-sounding mischievous pretence at misunderstanding,
and carelessness of the deference to persons whose station, and
not their worth, conventionally demands it. (I have no doubt that
Mrs Proudie felt personally aggrieved that bishops' wives do not
share their husbands' official precedence. She should have blamed
Queen Elizabeth I.) Most of Miss Dunstable's subsequent speeches,
at least the long ones, display the same qualities. Trollope sums her
up neatly in *Framley*, 24: 'Miss Dunstable was not worldly, though
it was possible that her present style of life might make her so; she
was affectionate, fond of truth, and prone to honesty . . . But she
was fond of ease and humour, sometimes of wit that might almost
be called broad, and she had a thorough love of ridiculing all the
world's humbugs.' The most unusual freedom – and impunity (for

1. She bows in obsequious deference to Miss Dunstable's riches, but changes the
   subject because they have proceeded from trade – and a somehow comic trade, at
   that – and thus has it both ways.

a lady) – with which she uses slang is illustrated above in Chapter
II, Section 1.

Until her marriage to Dr Thorne, she is tormented with suitors
whom she knows perfectly well to be interested only in her
money; and she disclaims with genuine modesty having any other
attractions. This is the subject of more than one of her longer
speeches, of which the best is probably the following from
Framley, 38. Her good friend Mary (Thorne) Gresham says to
her, ' ". . . I think you would be a happier woman and a better
woman, if you were married . . . [But] I would not have you
marry any man that looked to you for your money principally." '
To this, Miss Dunstable makes the following characteristic reply:

'And how is it possible that I should expect any one to look to
me for anything else? You don't see my difficulty, my dear? If
I had only five hundred a year, I might come across some decent
middle-aged personage, like myself, who would like me, myself,
pretty well, and who would like my little income – pretty well
also. He would not tell me any violent lie, and perhaps no lie at
all. I should take to him in the same sort of way, and we might
do very well. But, as it is, how is it possible that any disinterested
person should learn to like me? How could such a man set
about it? If a sheep have two heads, is not the fact of the two
heads the first, and indeed only, thing which the world regards
in that sheep? Must it not be so as a matter of course? I am a
sheep with two heads. All this money which my father put
together, and which has been growing since like grass under
May showers, has turned me into an abortion. I am not the
giantess eight feet high, or the dwarf that stands in the man's
hand – '

'Or the two-headed sheep – '

'But I am the unmarried woman with – half a dozen millions
of money – as I believe some people think. Under such circumstances have I a fair chance of getting my own sweet bit of
grass to nibble, like any ordinary animal with one head? I never
was very beautiful, and I am not more so than I was fifteen
years ago.'

'I am quite sure it is not that which hinders it. You would
not call yourself plain; and even plain women are married every
day, and are loved too, as well as pretty women.'

'Are they? Well, we won't say any more about that; but I don't expect a great many lovers on account of my beauty. If ever you hear of such an one, mind you tell me.'

The Duchess of Omnium ('Lady Glen') retains in middle age all the qualities of character and the manner of speech of her youth: confidence in her judgement; insight into character – especially that of her husband, whom she had married unwillingly, but whom she has the sense to respect and admire; pride in the eminence he has attained – and a little in what she shares of it as his wife; awareness of what she has done to help him attain it, but still more of the abilities she has displayed in doing it – all expressed in short, impetuously rushing sentences, full of plain speaking, racy, colloquial diction, imagery vivid, concrete, homely, and not calculated for rhetorical effect, but springing to her mouth because that is the kind of mind she has. A single specimen will have to do, from *Prime*, 37. She has been entertaining lavishly and indiscriminately, against her husband's inclination, and, for that matter, contrarily to her own tastes, because she thinks she ought to do so in order to maintain his popularity. Her friend Mrs Flynn expresses the opinion that she is overdoing it. The Duchess does not agree:

'What's the use of money if you don't spend it? The Duke would go on collecting it and buying more property, – which always means more trouble, – not because he is avaricious, but because for the time that comes easier than spending. As it is, my property is more even than his own. If we can do any good by spending the money, why should n't [*sic*] it be spent?'

'If you can do any good!'

'It all comes round to that. It is n't [*sic*] because I like always to live in a windmill! I have come to hate it. At this moment I would give worlds to be down at Matching with no one but the children, and to go about in a straw hat and a muslin gown. I have a fancy that I could sit under a tree and read a sermon, and think it the sweetest recreation. But I've made the attempt to do all this, and it is so mean to fail!'

'But what is to be the end of it?'

'There shall be no end as long as he is Prime Minister. He is the first man in England. Some people would say the first in

Europe, – or in the world. A prince should entertain like a prince.'

'He need not always be entertaining.'

'Hospitality should run from a man with his wealth and his position, like water from a fountain. As his hand is known to be full, so it should be known to be open. When the delight of his friends is in question he should know nothing of cost. Pearls should drop from him as from a fairy. But I don't think you understand me.'

'Not when the pearls are to be picked up by Captain Gunners, Lady Glen.'

'I can't make the men any better, – nor yet the women. They are poor mean creatures. The world is made up of such. I don't know that Captain Gunner is worse than Sir Orlando Drought or Sir Timothy Beeswax. People seen by the mind are exactly different to people seen by the eye. They grow smaller and smaller as you come nearer down to them, whereas things become bigger. I remember when I used to think that members of the Cabinet were almost gods, and now they seem to be no bigger than the shoeblacks, – only less picturesque. He told me the other day of the time when he gave up going into power for the sake of taking me abroad. Ah me! how much was happening then, – and how much has happened since that! We didn't know you then.'

'He has been a good husband to you.'

'And I have been a good wife to him! I have never had him for an hour out of my heart since that, or ever for a moment forgotten his interest. I can't live with him because he shuts himself up reading blue books, and is always at his office or in the House; – but I would if I could. Am I not doing it all for him? You don't think that the Captain Gunners are particularly pleasant to me! Think of your life and of mine. You have had lovers.'

'One in my life, – when I was quite entitled to have one.'

'Well; I am Duchess of Omnium, and I am the wife of the Prime Minister, and I had a larger property of my own than any other young woman that ever was born; and I am myself, too, – Lady Glencora M'Cluskie that was, and I've made for myself a character that I'm not ashamed of. But I'd be the curate's wife to-morrow, and make puddings, if I could only have my own husband and my own children with me. What's the use of it all? I like you better than anybody else, but you do nothing but scold me.'

Let us pass on to Archdeacon Grantly, beginning with his speech to his wife in *Warden*, 2.

'Why not!' almost screamed the archdeacon . . . ; 'why not! – that pestilent upstart, John Bold – the most vulgar young person I ever met!' [Bold is not vulgar at all, as the archdeacon would acknowledge in a calmer moment, but they disagree, and that is enough for the archdeacon.] 'Do you know that he is meddling with your father's affairs in a most uncalled for – most – ' And being at a loss for an epithet sufficiently injurious, he finished his expression of horror by muttering, 'Good heavens!' in a manner that had been found most efficacious in clerical meetings of the diocese.

'Good heavens!' is the archdeacon's trademark, and many of his speeches might but for its presence be made by almost anyone sharing his opinions. And sometimes Trollope merely says that the archdeacon said it; *eg*, in *Warden*, 21, Trollope summarizes a long dialogue between the archdeacon and his father the bishop as follows.

It was in vain that the archdeacon argued and lectured, and even threatened; in vain he my-lorded his poor father in his sternest words; in vain his 'good heavens!' were ejaculated in a tone that might have moved a whole synod, let alone one weak and aged bishop. Nothing could induce his father to fill up the vacancy caused by Mr Harding's retirement.

But Trollope does not always depend entirely for his effect on making the archdeacon say 'good heavens!' or on merely saying that he said it. In *Chron*, 50, Mr Harding has just told his son-in-law that Eleanor is to marry Mr Arabin, and in the account of the ensuing conversation the archdeacon says nothing (except for a 'well, well') but 'good heavens!' – and says it no fewer than five times:

'Good heavens!' said the archdeacon, walking up and down Eleanor's drawing-room. 'Good heavens! Good heavens!' Now these exclamations certainly betokened faith. Mr Harding gathered from it [*sic*] that, at last, Dr Grantly did believe the fact. The first utterance clearly evinced a certain amount of distaste at the information he had received; the second, simply indicated surprise; in the tone of the third, Mr Harding fancied that he could catch a certain gleam of satisfaction . . . 'Well, well,' said [the archdeacon]. 'Good heavens! good heavens!' and the tone of the first expression made Mr Harding fully aware that content was reigning in the archdeacon's bosom.

The speech of Miss Wallachia Petrie, 'the American Browning', who appears in *Right*, is, as I have said, Trollope's only attempt (with the possible exception of Mr Crawley) at a Dickensian idiolect. Her longest utterance is an oration (briefly interrupted here and there) in Chapter 77 on living under a monarchy, an oration that Trollope calls 'American buncom of a high order of eloquence':

'I cannot adapt my body to the sweet savours and soft luxuries of the outer world with any comfort to my inner self, while the circumstances of the society around me are oppressive to my spirit. When our war[1] was raging all around me I was light-spirited as the lark that mounts through the morning sky.'

'I should have thought it was very dreadful,' said Lady Rowley.

'Full of dread, of awe, of horror, were those fiery days of indiscriminate slaughter; but they were not days of desolation, because hope was always there by our side. There was a hope in which the soul could trust, and the trusting soul is ever light and buoyant.'

'I dare say it is,' said Lady Rowley.

'But apathy, and serfhood, and kinghood, and dominion, drain the fountain of its living springs, and the soul becomes like a plummet of lead, whose only tendency is to hide itself in subaqueous mud and unsavoury slush.'

This is fairly – but *only* fairly – close to the speeches given by Dickens to 'the mother of the modern Gracchi'. It is interesting that Trollope himself uses an Americanism in describing it.

Mr Crawley, long estranged by his poverty from good society, speaks a formal, bookish, archaic, and even stilted English: ' "I

1. The American Civil War, 1861–65; *Right* was written in 1868.

regret to say, sir, that I cannot assist you by supplying another steed." ' ' "When I have found a shelter for my wife and children I shall leave [Hogglestock]; nay, peradventure, I must do so before any such shelter can be found." ' ' ". . . in that house the wife wears that garment which is supposed to denote virile command . . ." ' ' "I will not ask you into my poor house, . . . for that my wife is ill." ' ' "I hope it be not so with the bishop." ' ' "It seemeth to me that you are a messenger of glad tidings . . ." ' ' ". . . I postponed the elaborated result of my own memory to [the Dean's] word." ' ' ". . . unwittingly false, indeed, nathless very false . . ." ' ' ". . . it seemeth to me that it may . . . be in your power to nominate me again . . ." ' ' ". . . our utterances thereanent would receive more attention." ' ' "Surely the price of the cloth wanted to perfect the comeliness of the garment cannot be much." ' ' "It hath the old bishop's manuscript notes, which I will study carefully." ' And Mr Crawley is a stickler for accuracy of expression. In *Chron*, 18, Bishop Proudie says to him, ' "You are in the position of a man amenable to the criminal laws of the land." ' To which Mr Crawley replies with precise correctness, ' "There are no criminal laws,[1] my lord, . . . but to such laws as there are we are all amenable, – your lordship and I alike." '

The common qualities of the speech of Trollope's favourite kind of character – the spirited young lady – can be sufficiently illustrated by the quotation of parts of three dialogues. The first is in *Framley*, 21. Lucy Robarts has refused Lord Lufton's offer of marriage, though she loves him, because his mother disapproves. Lucy's sister-in-law Fanny, on a drive in her pony carriage, speaks to Lucy, who is driving.

'Do you know, I have an idea . . . that Lord Lufton will marry Griselda Grantly.' Lucy could not refrain from giving a little check at the reins which she was holding, and she felt that the blood rushed quickly to her heart. But she did not betray herself. 'Perhaps he may,' she said, and then gave the pony a little touch with her whip.

'Oh, Lucy, I won't have Puck beaten. He was going very nicely.'

1. In *Chron*, 63, Trollope forgot this nicety: he makes Mr Crawley speak of himself as ' "subject to the criminal laws of my country." ' Incidentally, Mr Crawley would not have objected, nor would anyone, to '*criminal law*', meaning a *branch* of (the practice of) the law.

'I beg Puck's pardon. But you see when one is trusted with a whip one feels a longing to use it.'

'Oh, but you should keep it still. I feel almost certain that Lady Lufton would like such a match.'

'I dare say she might. Miss Grantly will have a large fortune, I believe.'

'It is not that altogether: but she is the sort of young lady that Lady Lufton likes. She is ladylike and very beautiful – '

'Come, Fanny!'

'I really think she is; not what I should call lovely, you know, but very beautiful. And then she is quiet and reserved; she does not require excitement, and I am sure is conscientious in the performance of her duties.'

'Very conscientious, I have no doubt,' said Lucy, with something like a sneer in her tone. 'But the question, I suppose, is whether Lord Lufton likes her.'

'I think he does, – in a sort of way. He did not talk to her so much as he did to you – '

'Ah! that was all Lady Lufton's fault, because she didn't have him properly labelled.'

'There does not seem to have been much harm done?'

'Oh! by God's mercy, very little. As for me, I shall get over it in three or four years I don't doubt – that's if I can get ass's milk and a change of air.'

'We'll take you to Barchester for that. But as I was saying, I really do think Lord Lufton likes Griselda Grantly.'

'Then I really do think that he has uncommon bad taste,' said Lucy, with a reality in her voice differing much from the tone of banter she had hitherto used.

'What, Lucy!' said her sister-in-law, looking at her. 'Then I fear we shall really want the ass's milk.'

'Perhaps, considering my position, I ought to know nothing of Lord Lufton, for you say that it is very dangerous for young ladies to know young gentlemen. But I do know enough of him to understand that he ought not to like such a girl as Griselda Grantly. He ought to know that she is a mere automaton, cold, lifeless, spiritless, and even vapid. There is, I believe, nothing in her mentally, whatever may be her moral excellences. To me she is more absolutely like a statue than any other human being I ever saw. To sit still and be admired is all that she desires; and if she cannot get that, to sit still and not be admired would almost suffice for her. I do not worship Lady Lufton as you do; but I think quite well enough of her to wonder that she should choose such a girl as that for her son's wife. That she does wish it I do not doubt. But I shall indeed be surprised if he wishes it also.' And then as she finished her speech, Lucy again flogged the pony. This she did in vexation, because she felt that the tell-tale blood had suffused her face.

'Why, Lucy, if he were your brother you could not be more eager about it.'

'No, I could not. He is the only man friend with whom I was ever intimate, and I cannot bear to think that he should throw himself away. It's horribly improper to care about such a thing, I have no doubt.'

'I think we might acknowledge that if he and his mother are both satisfied, we may be satisfied also.'

'I shall not be satisfied. It's no use your looking at me, Fanny. You will make me talk of it, and I won't tell a lie on the subject. I do like Lord Lufton very much and I do dislike Griselda Grantly almost as much. Therefore I shall not be satisfied if they become man and wife. However, I do not suppose that either of them will ask my consent; nor is it probable that Lady Lufton will do so.' And then they went on for perhaps a quarter of a mile without speaking.

'Poor Puck!' at last Lucy said. 'He shan't be whipped any more, shall he, because Miss Grantly looks like a statue? And, Fanny, don't tell Mark [Fanny's husband and Lucy's brother] to put me into a lunatic asylum. I also know a hawk from a heron, and that's why I don't like to see such a very unfitting marriage.'

The 'energy' of Mary Thorne's style is well represented in her conversation in *Thorne*, 4 with Beatrice Gresham after Lady Alexandrina De Courcy has left the discussion of Augusta Gresham's wedding in dudgeon at Mary's easy familiarity with the Gresham girls.

'There,' said Mary, . . . 'I have made an enemy for ever, perhaps two.'

'And why have you done it, Mary? When I am fighting your battles behind your back, why do you come and upset it all by making the whole family of the De Courcys dislike you? In such a matter as that, they'll all go together.'

'I am sure they will,' said Mary; 'whether they would be equally unanimous in a case of love and charity, that, indeed, is a different question.'

'But why should you try to make my cousin angry; you that ought to have so much sense? Don't you remember what you were saying yourself the other day, of the absurdity of combating pretences which the world sanctions?'

'I do, Trichy, I do; don't scold me now. It is so much easier to preach than to practise. I do so wish I was a clergyman.'

'But you have done so much harm, Mary.'

'Have I?' said Mary, kneeling down . . . at her friend's feet. 'If I humble myself very low; if I kneel through the whole evening in a corner; if I put my neck down and let all your cousins trample on it, and then your aunt, would not that make atonement? I would not object to wearing sackcloth, either; and I'd eat a little ashes – or, at any rate, I'd try.'

'I know you're very clever, Mary; but still I think you're a fool. I do, indeed.'

'I am a fool, Trichy, I do confess it; and am not a bit clever: but don't scold me; you see how humble I am; not only humble but umble, which I look upon to be the comparative, or, indeed, the superlative degree. Or perhaps there are four degrees; humble, umble, stumble, tumble; and then, when one is absolutely in the dirt at their feet, perhaps these big people won't wish one to stoop any further.'

Finally, a light-hearted and good-humoured example, from *Finn*, 55. Violet Effingham has just announced her engagement to Lord Chiltern, whom her aunt does not approve of.

'My dear Violet,' said her aunt . . . , 'I do not know what to say to you.'

'Say "how d'you do?" aunt,' said Violet.

'How can I say nothing about it? How can I be silent? Or how am I to congratulate you?'

'The least said perhaps, the soonest mended,' and Violet smiled as she spoke.

'That is all very well, and if I had no duty to perform, I would be silent. But, Violet, you have been left in my charge.

If I see you shipwrecked in life, I shall ever tell myself that the fault has been partly mine.'

'Nay, aunt, that will be quite unnecessary. I will always admit that you did everything in your power to – to – to make me run straight, as the sporting men say.'

'Sporting men! Oh, Violet!'

'And you know, aunt, I still hope I shall be found to have kept on the right side of the posts. You will find that poor Lord Chiltern is not so black as he is painted.'

'But why take anybody that is black at all?'

'I like a little shade in the picture, aunt.'

Each of the three principal speakers in the foregoing dialogues might well say what either of the others says, and say it as they say it, if placed in the same circumstances; Lucy and Mary and Violet speak not so much idiolects as a 'typolect'. But it is a charming typolect, and Trollope delighted in making his spirited young ladies speak it.

CHAPTER VIII

Trollope the Preacher

𝕊𝕊𝕊𝕊𝕊𝕊

I N Chapter 8 of his *Autobiography*, Trollope quotes Hawthorne's praise of his novels for their general truth to life:

'. . . the novels of Anthony Trollope . . . [are] just as real as if some giant had hewn a great lump out of the earth and put it under a glass case, with all its inhabitants going about their daily business, and not suspecting that they were being made a show of.' . . . the criticism . . . describes with wonderful accuracy the purport that I have ever had in view in my writing. I have always desired to 'hew out some lump of the earth,' and to make men and women walk upon it just as they do walk among us – with not more of excellence, nor with exaggerated baseness, – so that my readers might recognize human beings like themselves, and not feel themselves to be carried away among gods or demons.

In the words between dashes, Trollope at least comes close to reading into Hawthorne's praise something a little more specific than was intended; but beginning with the next sentence, he beyond question reads in something very much more specific indeed.

If I could do this, then I thought I might succeed in impregnating the mind of the novel-reader with a feeling that honesty is the best policy; that truth prevails while falsehood fails; that a girl will be loved as she is pure, and sweet, and unselfish; that a man will be honoured as he is true, and honest, and brave of heart; that things meanly done are ugly and odious, and things nobly done beautiful and gracious. I do not say that lessons such as these may not be more grandly taught by higher flights than mine. Such lessons come to us from our greatest poets. But there are so many who will read and understand novels, who either do not read the works of our great poets, or reading them miss the lesson! And even in prose fiction the character whom the fervid imagination of the writer has lifted into the clouds, will hardly give so plain an example to the hasty normal reader as the humbler personage whom that reader unconsciously feels to resemble himself or herself. I do think that a girl would more probably dress her own mind after Lucy Robarts than after Flora Macdonald.

There are many who would laugh at the idea of a novelist teaching either virtue or nobility . . . They look upon the teller of stories as among the tribe of those who pander to the wicked pleasures of a wicked world. I have regarded my art from so different a point of view that *I have ever thought of myself as a preacher of sermons* [italics mine], and my pulpit as one which I could make both salutary and agreeable to my audience. I do believe that no girl has risen from the reading of my pages less modest than she was before, and that some may have learned from them that modesty is a charm well worth preserving. I think that no youth has been taught that in falseness and flashiness is to be found the way to manliness; but some may perhaps have learned from me that it is to be found in truth and a high but gentle spirit. Such are the lessons I have striven to teach; and I have thought it might best be done by representing to my readers characters like themselves, – or to which they might liken themselves.

Trollope goes in these two paragraphs from the simple and general excellence for which Hawthorne actually praised him – realism – to the superiority of ordinary characters to extraordinary, and from that to the reason for that superiority, *viz.*, that ordinary characters are more effective in teaching ordinary readers morality – which in his view is the novelist's proper and principal business, though ulterior to telling an entertaining story. And he did not wait till 1875 to express these opinions; he expressed them, in digressive essays in his novels, several times, and at length. The two best examples, I think, are in *Ralph*, 56 (1869) and *Eustace*, 35 (1870). In the former, he devotes some three pages to a defence of his choice of an unheroic 'hero' as more effective than an heroic one in teaching the average reader what temptations he is himself likely to fall into and how to escape them – a defence interrupted by an assertion that it is the main duty of novelists to teach morality.

> It is the test of a novel-writer's art that he conceals his snake-in-the-grass; but the reader may be sure that it is always there. No man or woman with a conscience, – no man or woman with intellect sufficient to produce amusement, can go from year to year spinning stories without the desire of teaching; with no ambition of influencing readers for their good. Gentle readers, the physic is always beneath the sugar, hidden or unhidden. In writing novels we novelists preach to you from our pulpits, and are keenly anxious that our sermons shall not be inefficacious. Inefficacious they are not, unless they be too badly preached to obtain attention. Injurious they will be unless the lessons taught be good lessons.

Eustace, 35 contains another three-page essay, this time on the imperfections of human nature in real life, ending with the following paragraph:

> The persons whom you cannot care for in a novel because they are so bad, are the very same that you so dearly love in your life because they are so good. To make them and ourselves somewhat better, not by one spring heavenward to perfection, because we cannot so use our legs, but by slow climbing, is, I presume, the object of all teachers, leaders, legislators, spiritual pastors, and masters. He who writes tales such as this probably also has, very humbly, some such object distantly before him. A picture of surpassing godlike nobleness, a picture of a King Arthur among men, may perhaps do much. But such pictures cannot do all. When such a picture is painted, as intended to show what a man should be, it is true. If painted to show what men are, it is false. The true picture of life as it is, if it could be adequately painted, would show men what they are and how they might rise, not indeed to perfection, but one step first, and then another, on the ladder.

In all the preceding quotations, when Trollope says that the novelist's duty is to preach, and to preach morality, the preaching he is talking about is preaching indirectly and implicitly through the representation of the actions and speeches and thoughts of characters, not through direct and explicit allocution to the reader.

He was very much aware that his novels were full of the first kind of preaching; but I think he had little notion of how much space he devotes to the latter.[1] These sermons express his opinions on a large number of social questions. They are always suggested by some incident in the narrative, but they interrupt it, sometimes for only a short paragraph, but often for several pages, and, however interesting they often are in themselves, to the detriment of the progress of the story. The commonest subject by far is matrimony, concerning which Trollope expresses views at variance with those conventional in his day. The subject seems to have obsessed him from 1858 to 1870: he expounds his views of it in eleven of the twenty novels written in those years, but seldom, if at all, before or after. (Perhaps someone told him he was overdoing it.) He felt strongly (1) that it is natural and proper, and salutary, both for them and for society, for young women to want to marry – and to do so.

> I believe that a desire to get married is the natural state of a woman at the age of – say twenty-five to thirty-five, and I think also that it is good for the world in general that it should be so . . . There is, I know, a feeling abroad among women that this desire is one of which it is expedient that they should be ashamed; that it will be well for them to alter their natures in this respect, and learn to take delight in the single state . . . But I confess to an opinion that human nature will be found too strong for them. Their school of philosophy may be graced by a few zealous students . . . but it will not be successful in the outer world. The truth in the matter is too clear. A woman's life is not perfect or whole till she has added herself to a husband. (*Mack*, 11.)

(2) A young woman should, furthermore, *admit*, both to herself and to the world, that she wants to marry, without feeling shame or suffering censure.

---

1. This belief seems supported by a passage (quoted by Sadleir, p. 285) in a letter of literary advice written on 28 May 1868 to his beloved Kate Field, who had sent him the manuscript of part of a novel she was engaged in writing. 'You should avoid the "I" . . . Your reader should not be made to think that *you* are trying to teach, or to preach, or to convince . . . We are very jealous of preachers. We admit them at certain hours and places for certain reasons. We take up a story for recreation, and the mind, desirous of recreation, revolts from being entertained with a sermon.' Trollope's advice here is almost comically at variance with his practice.

Nature prompts the desire, the world acknowledges its ubiquity, circumstances show that it is reasonable, the whole theory of creation requires it; but it is required that the person most concerned should repudiate it, in order that a mock modesty may be maintained, in which no human being can believe! Such is the theory of the censors who deal heavily with the Englishwomen of the present day. Our daughters should be educated to be wives but, forsooth, they should never wish to be wooed! The very idea is but a remnant of the tawdry sentimentality of an age in which the mawkish insipidity of the women was the reaction from the vice of that preceding it. That our girls are in quest of husbands, and know well in what way their lines of life should be laid, is a fact which none can dispute. (*Vicar*, 37.)

(3) A young woman should admit, at least to herself, as freely as a young man, that she has fallen in love, and not pretend to the world, and still less to herself, to fall in love, or admit it, only when she has been proposed to by a young man who reciprocates her passion, when she is expected to fall in love on the spot – *unless* the parents of either oppose the match. This is well illustrated in *Thorne*, 23, where Mary Thorne, in love with Frank Gresham, who is in love with her, refuses because his parents oppose the marriage.

If it was so that Frank's folly had been listened to with a certain amount of pleasure, Mary did not even admit so much to herself. But why should it have been otherwise? Why should she have been less prone to love than he was? Had he not everything which girls do love? which girls should love? which God created noble, beautiful, all but godlike, in order that women, all but goddesslike, might love? To love thoroughly, truly, heartily, with her whole body, soul, heart and strength; should not that be counted for merit in a woman? And yet we are wont to make a disgrace of it. We do so most unnaturally, most unreasonably; for we expect our daughters to get themselves married off our hands. When the period of that step comes, then love is proper enough; but up to that – before that – as regards all those preliminary passages which must, we suppose, be necessary – in all those it becomes a young lady to be icy-hearted as a river-god in winter.

(4) Both men and women who marry in haste probably have occasion to repent no oftener – and even less often – than those who marry at leisure. Trollope preaches this doctrine in four novels, *Orley*, 33, *Right*, 33, *Forgive*, 11, and *Ralph*, 56, of which the last furnishes the best example.

Whether marriage should be made in heaven or on earth, must be a matter of doubt to observers; – whether, that is, men and women are best married by chance, which I take to be the real fashion of heaven-made marriages; or should be brought into that close link and loving bondage to each other by thought, selection, and decision. That the heavenly mode prevails the oftenest there can be hardly a doubt. It takes years to make a friendship; but a marriage may be settled in a week, – in an hour. If you desire to go into partnership with a man in business, it is an essential necessity that you should know your partner; that he is honest, – or dishonest, if such be your own tendency, – industrious, instructed in the skill required, and of habits of life fit for the work to be done. But into partnerships for life, of a kind much closer than any business partnership, – men rush without any preliminary inquiries. Some investigation and anxiety as to means there may be, though in this respect the ordinary parlance of the world endows men with more caution, or accuses them of more greed than they really possess. But in other respects everything is taken for granted. Let the woman, if possible, be pretty; – or if not pretty, let her have style. Let the man, if possible, not be a fool; or, if a fool, let him not show his folly too plainly. As for knowledge of character, none is possessed, and none is wanted. The young people meet each other in their holiday dresses, on holiday occasions, amidst holiday pleasures, – and the thing is arranged. Such matches may be said to be heaven-made.

It is a fair question whether they do not answer better than those which have less of chance, – or less of heaven, – in their manufacture. If it be needful that a man and woman take five years to learn whether they will suit each other as husband and wife, and that then, at the end of the five years, they find that they will not suit, the freshness of the flower would be gone before it could be worn in the button-hole. There are some leaps which you must take in the dark if you are to jump at all.

We can all understand well that a wise man should stand back on the brink and hesitate; but we can understand also that a very wise man should declare to himself that with no possible amount of hesitation could certainty be achieved. Let him take the jump or not take it, – but let him not presume to think that he can so jump as to land himself in perfect bliss. It is clearly God's intention that men and women should live together, and therefore let the leap in the dark be made.

(5) Widows should not prolong their mourning because they think they should, or the appearance of it because society thinks they should.

There will, of course, be some to say that a young widow should not be happy and comfortable – that she should be weeping her lost lord, and subject to the desolation of bereavement. But as the world goes now, there is, perhaps, a growing tendency in society to claim from them year by year still less of any misery that may be avoidable. Suttee propensities of all sorts, from burning alive down to bombazine and hideous forms of clothing, are becoming less and less popular among the nations, and women are beginning to learn that, let what misfortunes will come upon them, it is well for them to be as happy as their natures will allow them to be. A woman may thoroughly respect her husband, and mourn him truly, with her whole heart, and yet enjoy thoroughly the good things which he has left behind him for her use. (*Eustace*, 21.)

(6) A man who has fallen out of love, or whose first love has rejected him, should feel guilty neither about falling in love with another woman and marrying her – *nor* about forever recalling his first love with tenderness, though without any diminution in his love of his wife, or regret that he has married her, or the least thought of infidelity.

When I declare that as yet [Harry Clavering] had not come to any firm resolution [as to which of two women he should keep his promise to marry], I fear that he will be held as being too weak for the rôle of hero even in such pages as these. Perhaps no terms have been so injurious to the profession of the novelist as those two words, hero and heroine. In spite of the latitude which is allowed to the writer in putting his own interpretation upon those words, something heroic is still expected; whereas, if he attempt to paint from nature, how little that is heroic should he describe! How many young men, subjected to the temptations which had befallen Harry Clavering, – how many young men whom you, delicate reader, number among your friends, – would have come out from them unscathed? A man, you say, delicate reader, a true man can love but one woman, – one at a time. So you say, and are so convinced, but no conviction was ever more false. When a true man has loved with all his heart and all his soul, – does he cease to love, – does he cleanse his heart of that passion when circumstances run against him, and he is forced to return elsewhere for his life's companion? Or is he untrue as a lover in that he does not waste his life in desolation, because he has been disappointed? Or does his old love perish, and die away, because another has crept into his heart? No; the first love, if that was true, is ever there; and should she and he meet after many years, though their heads be grey and their cheeks wrinkled, there will still be a touch of the old passions as their hands meet for a moment. Methinks that love never dies, unless it be murdered by downright ill-usage. It may be so murdered, but even ill-usage will more often fail than succeed in that enterprise. (*Claver*, 28.)

Trollope would have said, I am sure, that the same principle applies to women.

Next to matrimony, politics is the commonest theme of Trollope's harangues to his readers. Examples, especially the first, from the novels may be illuminatingly preceded by a summary of Trollope's political opinions set forth in Chapter 16 of his *Autobiography*, as a preface to his account of his standing (unsuccessfully) for Parliament for the Yorkshire borough of Beverley in 1868.

'Writing now [1875] at an age beyond sixty, I can say that my political feelings and convictions have never undergone any change . . . I consider myself to be an advanced, but still a Conservative-Liberal, which I regard not only as a possible but as a rational and consistent phase of political existence. I can, I believe, in a very few words, make known my political theory . . .' He then proceeds to do so (though in rather more than 'a very few words'). His points are (1) that human inequality in wealth is ordained of God; (2) that the rich, Liberals as well as Conservatives, recognize that fact, but believe that God's ordinance must be wise; (3) that the fact is none the less painful to the (sensitive and benevolent) rich Conservative as well as to the sensitive and benevolent rich Liberal; (4) that Conservatives and Liberals differ in that the former believe that the ordinance is designed to be permanent, and that it is their duty to preserve the inequality undiminished, whereas the latter believe that God has also ordained that it should be diminished, and that it is their duty to diminish it; (5) extreme Liberals wish to diminish it precipitately, without regard to the continuing stability of society; (6) 'Conservative-Liberals' wish to diminish it gradually, so as to preserve that stability.

Trollope, *ie*, was a humane meliorist, but his motto was *festina lente*, and he had and pretended no liking for sweaty nightcaps and stinking breath. (See *Children*, 55.) Further, as witness the following quotation from *Thorne*, 1, he had an emotional attachment to the old landed 'aristocracy' (including the lesser landed gentry). Here he interrupts a description of Greshamsbury House, being led off the track by mention of the display, in the stonework, of the Gresham crest (he *means* 'crest'; he does not share the vulgar error that the word means 'arms' or 'achievement') and motto.

'. . . the old symbols remained, and may such symbols long remain among us; they are still lovely and fit to be loved. They tell us of the true and manly feelings of other times; and to him who can read aright, they explain more fully, more truly than any written history can do, how Englishmen have become what they are. England is not yet a commercial country in the sense in which that epithet is used for her; and let us hope that she will not soon become so. She might surely as well be called feudal England, or chivalrous England. If in western civilized Europe there does exist a nation among whom there are high signors, and with whom the owners of the land are the true aristocracy, the aristocracy that is trusted as best and fittest to rule, that nation is the English. Choose out the ten leading men of each great European people . . . and then select the ten in England whose names are best known as those of leading statesmen; the result will show in which country there still exists the closest attachment to, the sincerest trust in, the old feudal and now so-called landed interests.

How strangely – and sadly – these words read only a little more than a century later!

This passage, written in 1858, if it does not exactly prove that Trollope's 'political feelings and convictions [had] never undergone any change' by 1875, does demonstrate that he thought a good deal about politics before 1868. So does another passage in the same novel (Chapter 22), where, taking off from Mr Moffat's petition against Sir Roger Scatcherd for corrupting voters, Trollope preaches a page-and-a-half sermon on the hypocrisy of much of the fuss made about political bribery. His 'text' is as follows:

It is a bad thing, certainly, that a rich man should buy votes; bad also that a poor man should sell them. By all means let us repudiate such a system with heartfelt disgust.

With heartfelt disgust, if we can do so, by all means; but not with disgust pretended only and not felt in the heart at all. The laws against bribery at elections are now so stringent that an unfortunate candidate may easily become guilty, even though actuated by the purest intentions.

Such was Trollope's life-long interest in politics that in an even earlier novel, *Clerks* (1857) he finds himself talking about it without its being immediately suggested to him by an incident in the story, as his sermons almost always are. In Chapter 29, the account of the peculations of Alaric Tudor, the trustee of an estate, leads, naturally enough, to a sermon on the dishonesty, in money matters, of rich men; but this in turn leads, *not* very naturally, to a sermon on the dishonesty, in political matters, of politicians, and this to a third on Sir Robert Peel as an example; and finally, because the case is not very strong, Trollope soon passes from Peel's dishonesty, such as it was, to his tergiversation. The whole succession of linked sermons takes over three pages, of which two are devoted to Peel. As is hardly surprising, the return to Alaric Tudor's peculations is not very deftly made.

Twice Trollope prolongs his political sermons unmercifully, once in an early novel, *Castle* (1860), and again in a very late one – his last, indeed – *Land* (1882), left unfinished at his death, and published posthumously. At the beginning of *Castle*, 17, he spends six pages in commenting on the potato famine of 1846–47 (the years in which the action of the novel takes place). The essay combines dubious theology with dubious economics. Midway he says, 'But seeing that this book of mine is a novel, I have perhaps already written more on a dry subject than many will read' – and then immediately reverts to it for another three pages. Then, after a brief reference to the impact of the famine on the inhabitants of the locale of the story, he returns to the general subject yet again, and continues for three pages more. In one way or another, well over half the chapter of sixteen pages is devoted to the famine, to its causes, to its alleviation, and to subsequent reforms. (In a way, to be sure, though this is a deviation from the plot proper, it is not altogether a deviation from a string of scenes and incidents that can almost be called a subplot; Trollope himself says in the last chapter, perhaps a little shamefacedly, 'Were it not that I eschew the fashion of double names for a book, . . . I might have called this "A Tale of the Famine Year in Ireland".')

But this is nothing to *Land*. This novel deals with historical events contemporary with the writing: the movement for Irish land reform from 1879 to 1882. In the latter year, while writing what there is of the book, he went twice to Ireland to make observations and gather information. He carries on his plots (one of which deals with the sufferings of a landlord who is boycotted by the Land-leaguers, and the two others of which are love stories – Trollope's least entertaining – involving respectively the landlord's son and his daughter) for forty chapters.[1] Then suddenly, with Chapter 41, he suspends the plots, drops the rôle of novelist, and assumes that of pamphleteer. The chapter opens as follows:

It will be well that they who are interested only in the sensational incidents of our story to [*sic*] skip this chapter and go on to other parts of our tale which may be more in accordance with their tastes. It is necessary that this one chapter shall be written in which the accidents that occurred in the lives of our . . .

1. The characters are generally shallower and fainter than in any other novel (always excepting *Struggles*) chiefly because of the almost total absence of Trollope's *forte* – analytical exposition of their thoughts – but antecedently because he is for once not really interested in the characters or in making their actions and thoughts morally instructive.

heroines shall be made subordinate to the political circumstances of the day [and he *means* 'the day']. This chapter should have been introductory and initiative;[1] but the facts as stated will suit better to the telling of my story if they be told here.[2]

Trollope then proceeds to fill ten large pages in small print with an attack on the Land Law of 1881 as (a) productive of intolerable disorder and violence, (b) monstrously injurious to the landlords, (c) not so contrived as to be permanently beneficial to the tenants, and (d) the fault of Gladstone (who is called that, not 'the Prime Minister').

Such [the chapter concludes – at long last –] have been the results of the Land Law passed in 1881. And under the curse so engendered the country is now labouring. It cannot be denied that the promoters of the Land Laws are weak, and that the disciples of the Land-league are strong. In order that the truth of this may be seen and made apparent, the present story is told.

'The present story' then resumes – and was never finished. One regrets the reason, but one cannot regret the fact.

All in all, I cannot help wondering whether Trollope might not have described his politics a little more accurately if he had called them 'Liberal-Conservative'.

Matrimony and politics are not the only subjects on which Trollope could not resist the opportunity of preaching. Of the others, the most closely related to politics is social distinctions. He recognizes them as unavoidable and even desirable in the world as it is (or was), but he is quick to poke fun – usually good-natured fun – at exaggerations of their importance, or rather at a rigid adherence to some that he regarded as outmoded, if not indeed irrational from their beginning. A good example is from *Vicar*, 9.

Miss Marrable was . . . a lady of very good family, the late Sir Gregory Marrable having been her uncle; but her only sister had married a Captain Lowther, whose mother had been first cousin to the Earl of Periwinkle; and therefore . . . Miss Marrable thought a good deal about blood. She was one of

1. This is an understatement; it should have been the whole book.
2. This is simply not true; the fact is that Trollope had merely lost patience with trying to blend his polemics with his story.

those ladies, – now few in number, – who within their heart of hearts conceive that money gives no title to social distinction, let the amount of money be ever so great, and its source ever so stainless. Rank was to her a thing quite assured and quite ascertained, and she had no more doubt as to her own right to pass out of a room before the wife of a millionaire than she had of the right of the millionaire to spend his own guineas. She always addressed an attorney by letter as Mister, raising up her eyebrows when appealed to on the matter, and explaining that an attorney is not an esquire. She had an idea that the son of a gentleman, if he intended to maintain his rank as a gentleman, should earn his income as a clergyman, or as a barrister, or as a soldier, or as a sailor. Those were the professions intended for gentlemen. She would not absolutely say that a physician was not a gentleman, or even a surgeon; but she would never allow to physic the absolute privileges which, in her eyes, belonged to law and the church. There might also possibly be a doubt about the Civil Service and Civil Engineering; but she had no doubt whatever that when a man touched trade or commerce in any way he was doing that which was not the work of a gentleman. He might be very respectable, and it might be very necessary that he should do it; but brewers, and bankers, and merchants, were not gentlemen, and the world, according to Miss Marrable's theory, was going astray, because people were forgetting their landmarks.

Another passage (in *Right*, 7) on the same subject is a little more broadly funny because it deals with social distinctions not in the world at large, but in provincial towns, where the whole system, because – rather than though – it is small, and narrow in range, is likely to involve finer and more rigid, or perhaps rather merely more arbitrary, distinctions.

It is to be hoped that no reader of these pages will be so un-English as to be unable to appreciate the difference between county society and town society, – the society, that is, of a provincial town, or so ignorant as not to know that there may be persons so privileged, that although they live distinctly within a provincial town, there is accorded to them, as though by brevet rank, all the merit of living in the county. In reference to persons so privileged, it is considered that they have been made free from the contamination of contiguous bricks and mortar by certain inner gifts, probably of birth, occasionally of profession, possibly of merit. It is very rarely, indeed, that money alone will bestow this acknowledged rank . . . Good blood . . . is rarely rejected. Clergymen are allowed within the pale, – though by no means as certainly as used to be the case; and, indeed, in these days of literates, clergymen have to pass harder examinations than those ever imposed upon them by bishops' chaplains, before they are admitted ad eundem among the chosen ones of the city . . .'

Whatever the occasional hesitation to admit all clergymen in provincial towns automatically to 'brevet rank' in county society, they were, of course, technically gentlemen, as Trollope would have acknowledged, but he demanded something more before he would bestow the title otherwise than *pro forma*. The clerical 'literates' mentioned above are non-graduates admitted to Holy Orders. They could always be ordained and given curacies and even benefices, but for a long time before Trollope's day they were not very numerous. Early in the nineteenth century, however, they began to become so. Most of them were Evangelicals, and many were not of gentle birth or even breeding. As one might expect, Trollope's Low Church clergymen – even those that are graduates – are almost never of gentle birth or breeding. (The very few whom he will suffer to be gentlemen are of the Church of Ireland, whom he apparently excused (though silently) because of their understandable, however unamiable, desire to be as different from Roman Catholics as possible.) His twin convictions that a clergyman should be a gentleman, and that Low Church clergymen were very seldom gentlemen, should have led him to the conclusion that almost all clergymen should be of the High Church. In fact, it probably did, though the closest he ever comes to saying so is in a sermon on the importance of a clergyman's being a gentleman that grows out of a portrait of an Evangelical clergyman in *Ray*, 6.

Mr Prong was a devout, good man; not self-indulgent; perhaps not more self-ambitious than it becomes a man to be; sincere, hard-working, sufficiently intelligent, true in most things to the instincts of his calling, – but deficient in one vital qualification for a clergyman of the Church of England; he was not a gentleman. May I not call it a necessary qualification for a clergyman of any church? He was not a gentleman. I do not mean to say that he was a thief or a liar; nor do I mean hereby to complain that he picked his teeth with a fork and misplaced his 'h's.' I am by no means prepared to define what I do mean, – thinking, however, that most men and most women will understand me. Nor do I speak of this deficiency in his clerical aptitudes as being injurious to him simply, – or even chiefly, – among folk who are themselves gentle; but that his efficiency for clerical purposes was marred altogether, among high and low, by his misfortune in this respect. It is not the owner of a good coat that sees and admires its beauty. It is not even they who have good coats who recognize the article on the back of another. They who have not good coats themselves have the keenest eyes for the coats of their better-clad neighbours. As it is with coats, so it is with that which we call gentility. It is caught at a word, it is seen at a glance, it is appreciated unconsciously at a touch by those who have none of it themselves. It is the greatest of all aids to the doctor, the lawyer, the member of Parliament, – though in that position a man may perhaps prosper without it, – and to the statesman; but to be a clergyman it is a vital necessity. Now Mr Prong was not a gentleman.

But even a clergyman who did not satisfy Trollope's definition of a gentleman should, in his view, be prosperous enough to bear the outward port of one – and still more one who *did* satisfy the definition. Mr Crawley decidedly did;[1] and Trollope seizes upon his introduction in *Framley*, 14 as perpetual curate of Hogglestock at £130 a year to write a two-page diatribe on the frequent disparity between a clergyman's work and his pay.

Most of Trollope's ecclesiastical disquisitions, like this one, deal with clergymen; but one, at least (in *Towers*, 20), shows a somewhat surprising but unmistakably genuine interest in the Church herself and in her doctrines – and specifically some considerable sympathy with the Oxford Movement.

1. He satisfied Archdeacon Grantly's, too: ' "We stand," said [the archdeacon to Mr Crawley], "on the only perfect level on which such men can meet each other. We are both gentlemen." ' (*Chron*, 83.)

We are much too apt to look at schism[1] in our church as an un-mitigated evil. Moderate schism, if there be such a thing, at any rate calls attention to the subject, draws in supporters who would otherwise have been inattentive to the matter, and teaches men to think upon religion. How great an amount of good of this description has followed that movement in the Church of England which commenced with the publication of Froude's Remains![2]

I feel sure that Trollope did not count the Evangelical reaction to 'that movement' as composing much if any part of the 'great amount of good'.

Some of Trollope's sermons reflect (1) his own special private interests, (2) sometimes a recent experience, and (3) sometimes – perhaps without his being fully aware of the fact – debates with himself.

(1) As everyone knows, Trollope passionately loved hunting, and delighted in describing hunts; the novels must contain almost a dozen hunting scenes. They are certainly lively and vivid, but not very different from each other, and likely to give a non-hunter a very moderate pleasure at best – especially after the first two or three. But Trollope not only describes hunts; he several times sermonizes on the sport. In *Castle*, 23, *eg*, in recounting the beginning of a hunt, he pauses for almost a page to write a mock-encomium of fox-hunting as the most important of human concerns. As we might expect, the mockery is not quite whole-hearted. And in the preceding chapter of the same novel, the introduction of a gentleman in full hunting rig leads to a page-and-a-half sermon on the ugliness of men's ordinary clothing. He loved the huntsman's clothes, and all the other 'trimmings' of the sport, but in *Fay*, 13 he deplores, at great length, what he regards as a corruption of it, in the form of a shift in emphasis from hunting itself to its trimmings. This shift has taken place, he complains, in most sports – shooting, fishing, rowing, cricket, polo, tennis.

(2) At least one sermon – on drunkenness, and the only one on that subject – though it is made to spring from a specific fictional incident (resumed after the sermon), is so perfervid in tone and so

---

1. Trollope misuses the word; he means the development of parties, as he half-confesses in the next sentence.
2. On the early influence of Newman and F. W. Faber on Trollope, see Escott, p. 84.

protracted that I cannot help feeling that some recent occurrence in Trollope's experience prompted him to write it. It appears in *Orley, 57.*

Graham . . . was shocked at the unmistakable evidence which the man's appearance and voice betrayed. How dreadful to the sight are those watery eyes; that red, uneven, pimpled nose; those fallen cheeks; and that hanging, slobbered mouth! Look at that uncombed hair, the beard half shorn, the weak, impotent gait of the man, and the tattered raiment, all eloquent of gin! You would fain hold your nose when he comes nigh you, he carries with him so foul an evidence of his only and his hourly indulgence. You would do so, had you not still a respect for his feelings, which he has himself entirely forgotten to maintain. How terrible is that loss of all personal dignity which the drunkard is obliged to undergo! And then his voice! Every tone has been formed by gin, and tells of the havoc which the compound has made within his throat. I do not know whether such a man as this is not the vilest thing which grovels on God's earth. There are women whom we affect to scorn with the full power of our contempt; but I doubt whether any woman sinks to a depth so low as that. She also may be a drunkard, and as such may more nearly move our pity and affect our hearts, but I do not think she ever becomes so nauseous a thing as the man that has abandoned all the hopes of life for gin. You can still touch her; – ay, and if the task be in one's way, can touch her gently, striving to bring her back to decency. But the other! Well, one should be willing to touch him too, to make that attempt of bringing back upon him also. I can only say that the task is both nauseous and unpromising. Look at him as he stands there before the foul, reeking, sloppy bar, with the glass in his hand, which he has just emptied. See the grimace with which he puts it down, as though the dram had been almost too unpalatable. It is that last touch of hypocrisy with which he attempts to cover the offence: – as though he were to say, 'I do it for my stomach's sake; but you must know how I abhor it.' Then he skulks sullenly away, speaking a word to no one, – shuffling with his feet, shaking himself in his foul rags, pressing himself into a heap – as though striving to drive the warmth of the spirit into his extremities! And there he stands lounging at the corner of the street, till his short patience is exhausted, and he returns with his last penny for the other glass. When that has been swallowed the policeman is his guardian.

Reader, such as you and I have come to that, when abandoned by the respect which a man owes to himself. May God in his mercy watch over us and protect us both!

(3) *Orley* also contains two fragments of a debate with himself that Trollope was apparently carrying on while writing the novel. The subject of the debate is what is the happiest period of human life. (He was forty-five or forty-six at the time.) In Chapter 49, his vote is for early manhood.

'I wonder whether you ever think of the old days when we used to be so happy in Keppel Street?' [Repetition of a sentence in a letter from an aggrieved wife to her husband.] Ah me, how often in after life, in those successful days when the battle has been fought and won, when all seems outwardly to go well, – how often is this reference made to the happy days of Keppel Street![1] It is not the prize that can make us happy; it is not even the winning of the prize, though for the one short half-hour of triumph that is pleasant enough. The struggle, the long hot hour of the honest fight, the grinding work – when the teeth are set, and the skin moist with sweat and rough with dust, when all is doubtful and sometimes desperate, when a man must trust to his own manhood knowing that those around him trust to it not at all, – that is the happy time of life. There is no human bliss equal to twelve hours of work with six hours in which to do it. And when the expected pay for that work is worse than doubtful, the inner satisfaction is so much the greater. Oh, those happy days in Keppel Street, or it may be in dirty lodgings in the Borough, or somewhere near the Marylebone work-house; – anywhere for a moderate weekly stipend. Those were to us, and now are to others, and always will be to many, the happy days of life. How bright was love, and how full of poetry! Flashes of wit glanced here and there, and how they came home and warmed the cockles of the heart. And the un-frequent bottle! Methinks that wine has utterly lost its flavour

1. Trollope's parents took up residence on their marriage, on 23 May 1809, at 6 Keppel Street, Bloomsbury, where the first five of their seven children were born, the fifth being Anthony, born on 24 April 1815.

since those days. There is nothing like it; long work, grinding weary work, work without pay, hopeless work; but work in which the worker trusts himself, believing it to be good. Let him, like Mahomet, have one other to believe in him, and surely nothing else is needed. 'Ah me! I wonder whether you ever think of the old days in Keppel Street?'

And then, at the end of a paragraph, lighter in tone, on the staleness of pleasures, in later (successful) life: 'Success is the necessary misfortune of life, but it is only to the very unfortunate that it comes early.'

But in Chapter 59 he has changed his mind in favour of a later period.

There is great doubt as to what may be the most enviable time of life with a man. I am inclined to think that it is at that period when his children have all been born but have not yet begun to go astray or to vex him with disappointment; when his own pecuniary prospects are settled, and he knows pretty well what his tether will allow him; when the appetite is still good and the digestive organs are at their full power; when he has ceased to care as to the length of his girdle, and before the doctor warns him against solid breakfasts and port wine after dinner; when his affectations are over and his infirmities have not yet come upon him; while he can sill walk this ten miles, and feel some little pride in being able to do so; while he has still nerve to ride his horse to hounds, and can look with some scorn on the ignorance of younger men who have hardly yet learned that noble art.

Trollope's discursive disquisitions, in short, were not always persuasive in object or polemic in tone; they were sometimes reflections on human life and happiness – or unhappiness – and (rather touchingly) on his own specifically, though not explicitly.